William Bush

To Quell the Terror

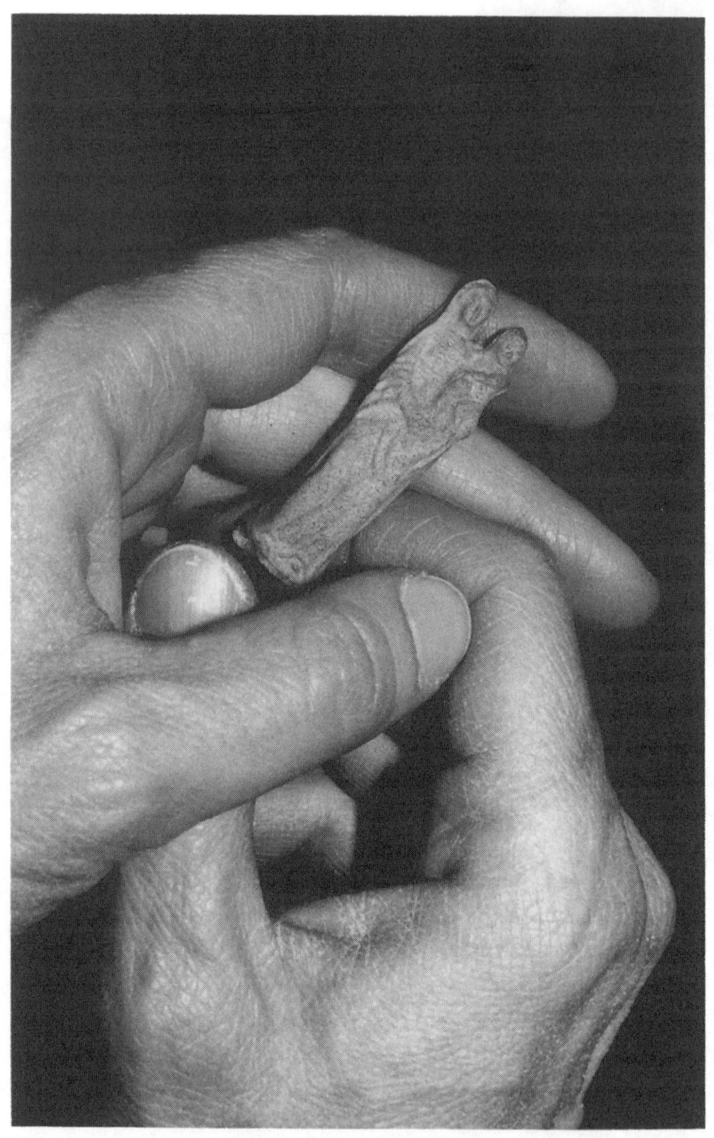

Before mounting the scaffold, the Carmelite martyrs renewed their vows and kissed this tiny terracotta statuette of Madonna and Child held by the prioress (Teresa of St. Augustine).

William Bush

To Quell the Terror

The Mystery of the Vocation
of the Sixteen Carmelites of Compiègne
Guillotined July 17, 1794

ICS Publications
Institute of Carmelite Studies
Washington, D.C.
1999

Cover design by Nancy Gurganus of Grey Coat Graphics

Cover Photo: Winnie Klotz/Metropolitan Opera
from the New York Metropolitan Opera Production of *Dialogues of the Carmelites*

ICS Publications
2131 Lincoln Road NE
Washington, DC 20002–1199
800-832-8489

Typeset and produced in the U.S.A.

Library of Congress Cataloging-in-Publication Data

Bush, William, 1929–
To quell the terror: the mystery of the vocation of the sixteen Carmelites of Compiègne guillotined July 17, 1794 / William Bush.
p. cm.
Includes bibliographical references and index.
ISBN: 0–935216–67–7
1. Discalced Carmelite Nuns—France—Compiègne—History—18th century. 2. Compiègne (France)—Church History—18th century. I. Title.
BX4323.F8B87 1999
272'.9'094435—dc21 98–33217
CIP

For Sylviane Bernanos

† 16 November 1998

"Mater Dolorosa," pastel by Mother Teresa of St. Augustine or Mother Henriette of Jesus (Photo, Hutin)

Table of Contents

Opening scene from the New York Metropolitan Opera production of Poulenc's *Dialogues of the Carmelites*
Photo: Winnie Klotz/Metropolitan Opera

Author's Foreword

I FIRST HEARD OF THE CARMELITES OF COMPIÈGNE through Georges Bernanos's incomparable "last testament," *Dialogues of the Carmelites*, in 1952. I was a graduate student, 23 years of age, completely caught up by Bernanos, foremost Catholic novelist of his time. How could I not be moved by the fact that he, in the last months before his death in 1948 at age 60, had written those dialogues for a film scenario about 16 nuns who, like him, were consciously preparing to appear before God?

The master's thesis I was preparing in 1952 led me to Paris four years later as a Fulbright scholar, pursuing a doctoral thesis at the Sorbonne. I had had the unbelievable good fortune of gaining the support of Bernanos's literary executor, the great Swiss critic, Albert Béguin, my mentor even before meeting him. Indeed, Béguin's preoccupations with Bernanos were precisely my own: to analyze his texts and manuscripts so as to understand all that that visionary Christian prophet was trying to say.

I was thus in the audience in Paris in 1957 both when Francis Poulenc's newly-created *Dialogues des Carmélites* was given at the Opéra de Paris and when a theatrical version of Bernanos's text was produced at the Théâtre Hébertot. I was far from imagining, however, the rendezvous awaiting me a quarter century later with Bernanos's Carmelites.

When, in 1981, they burst upon my staid life as a university professor, I, several books beyond my Sorbonne thesis, was still working on Bernanos manuscripts. Madame Sylviane Bernanos, widow of Bernanos's second son, Michel, through whom I had first met Béguin, had approached me concerning a new Parisian production of *Dialogues of the Carmelites,* directed by Raymond Gerome. Sponsored by the office of the Mayor of Paris, Monsieur Jacques Chirac, a fervent admirer of Bernanos, it would aim at total fidelity to Bernanos's text, not allow for any of the usual cuts, and prove "the great theatrical event marking the end of the century," Madame Bernanos assured me.

As promised, I delivered to Raymond Gerome by the end of 1982 the authentic text left by Bernanos in his copy books when he took to his deathbed in 1948. As for the alterations Béguin had effected in his edition published in 1949, I dismissed them, knowing he was trying desperately to generate income for Bernanos's destitute widow and six children. The following year, 1983, I learned that our "great theatrical event marking the end of the century" had foundered because of Bernanos family politics and mounting production costs.

I found this news singularly unmoving, however. I was already caught up by the actual history of the 16 martyrs of Compiègne, just as I had been, more than 30 years before, by Bernanos himself.

I discovered the historical martyrs through my work on Bernanos's manuscripts. The names assigned many of the nuns by Bernanos had in fact been altered by Béguin in preparing his published volume of *Dialogues of the Carmelites.* Wishing to check the names of the historical martyrs, I dusted off my 25-year-old copy of Father Bruno de Jésus Marie's authoritative compendium, *Le Sang du Carmel,* fruit of 20 years of research on the Compiègne martyrs by France's foremost twentieth-century Carmelite scholar.

History, I found, had nothing to do with the differences in names I had discovered, and true historical parallels existed for four characters only: the two prioresses (Madame de Croissy and Madame Lidoine); the young novice, Sister Constance; and Sister Marie de l'Incarnation. The actions and dialogues of these four characters, however, were largely fictional.

Dialogues of the Carmelites is centred on an imaginary heroine, Blanche de la Force, created by Gertrud von Le Fort as protagonist for her novella *Die Letzte am Schafott* [The Last One at the Scaffold], translated into English as *Song at the Scaffold.* On that novella was based the film scenario for which Bernanos had supplied his dialogues. The actual historical martyrdom was therefore a mere backdrop for Blanche's fictional story. I thus found it imperative to fix my mind firmly on the facts of the actual martyrdom if I were to avoid schizophrenia and deprivation in being denied von Le Fort's too-beautiful heroine.

Thinking of Poulenc's many admirers in English-speaking countries, I suddenly wanted very much to correct, through a modest little volume in English, all the misinformation sown by all the derivatives of Gertrud von Le Fort's novella. For the French material I thought Father Bruno's compendium should suffice, though I did resolve to go consult the English sources at Stanbrook Abbey in England, known to Fr. Bruno only through copies. Seventeen sisters from that contemplative Benedictine community had been imprisoned in Compiègne with the martyrs in 1794 and a written account of the Carmelites' imprisonment and departure for execution in Paris had been piously preserved. In many ways Stanbrook might even be called a major guardian of their cult, for it had served as headquarters for their beatification by Rome in 1906.

Having checked the Stanbrook connection in late 1983, I ardently desired to draw closer to the historical martyrs, indeed to venerate something they had all touched. With this intention I was received in 1984 at the restored Carmel of Compiègne, which held, Father Bruno's volume informed me, the tiny terracotta statuette of the Virgin and Child that the prioress, Madame Lidoine, had cradled in the palm of her hand as she stood at the foot of the scaffold, extending it for each nun to kiss before she climbed the steps of the scaffold.

Compiègne's prioress graciously welcomed my aspiration, as an Orthodox Christian, to present her Sisters' martyrdom in a way that would be as recognizable to Eastern Christians as to Western ones. She presented me to the Sister Archivist who arrived bearing a rather large bureau drawer, heavy with seventeenth-century documents. Among them were the unpublished manuscripts of the martyrs' historian, Marie of the Incarnation. As Fr. Bruno's random quotes from these four manuscripts had caused me considerable confusion, with obvious contradictions between one manuscript and another, I realized that in the contents of that bureau drawer lay an opportunity to understand the martyrdom a bit better. Invited to return for a two-week study-stay, I found myself in 1985 being asked by the prioress if I would consent to prepare a critical edition of Marie de l'Incarnation's manuscripts for them.

This long and detailed four-year project, begun in 1985, was completed in 1988, sustained and nurtured at every step by the attentive, ever-alert regard of Compiègne's archivist who had become an invaluable collaborator, critic, and trusted friend. The finished manuscript lay untouched for four years in the files of the Paris publisher, awaiting the dawn of the 1994 bicentenary and burgeoning sales for books on the Compiègne martyrs that would follow a much-touted bicentenary canonization. Wishing to promote the bicentenary year in advance, the publisher opportunely reissued Father

Bruno's *Le Sang du Carmel*[1] at the end of 1992, followed immediately by the launching of my critical edition of Marie de l'Incarnation's unpublished manuscripts.[2] Thus, a full year in advance, on January 18, 1993, the Bishop of Beauvais presided over this gala event at Cerf publishers in Paris, declaring it the official inauguration for the French Church of the bicentenary of the martyrdom of the Carmelites of Compiègne. Ironically, the publisher's gamble failed: canonization did not materialize in 1994.

I, however, had long since eagerly returned to my "little volume in English" once my critical edition was in the publisher's hands in 1988. But my whole project had suddenly become far more complex than anything I had ever imagined. For a decade I had tried to grasp how the "good" French Revolution with its "rights of man" could have guillotined 16 perfectly innocent women. The answer remained elusive until I resolutely cast aside everything I had ever been taught about the French Revolution and started accepting the plain, hard facts before me.

No longer could I regard Marie Antoinette as "that immoral woman," so falsely accused of uttering the heartless "Let them eat cake!" It was she who had provided, out of her own privy purse, the Carmelite dowry for the prioress of the martyrdom, the Blessed Mother Teresa of Saint Augustine, and had enjoyed quite close ties with her husband's royal Carmelite aunt, Madame Louise de France. As for that royal Carmelite, favourite daughter of Louis XV, she not only became a Carmelite to save her king-father's soul, but had

---

[1] Bruno de Jésus-Marie, *Le Sang du Carmel ou la véritable passion des seize carmélites de Compiègne* (Paris: Éditions du Cerf, 1992). This volume was orginally published by Plon (Paris) in 1954.

[2] Soeur Marie de l'Incarnation, *La relation du martyre des seize Carmélites de Compiègne. Les documents originaux inédits publiés par William Bush.* Préface de Mgr Guy Gaucher (Paris: Cerf, 1993).

directly influenced the vocation of more than one of the Compiègne martyrs.

The great discovery, however, was that Bernanos was totally wrong in regard to Christianity and the French Revolution. There had never been a "good" Revolution in 1789 which, Bernanos maintained, had turned "bad" only in 1793. The destruction of Christianity was blatantly present from the very beginning, as is incontrovertibly proven by the simple fact that on October 29, 1789, no more than three and a half months after the fall of the Bastille, the taking of all religious vows was forbidden in France. Sister Constance in the monastery at Compiègne, for example, could never make her profession as a Carmelite before going to the guillotine five years later. Further proof existed in the fact that just four days after this October 29 decree, on November 2, the totality of Church property throughout all of France was confiscated and declared property of the state, completely stripping religious communities of their means of income.

Thus, from its very beginning, the total eradication of religious orders in France was a clearly stated purpose of the Revolution, as was also the humiliation of the once proud Church of France, brought to her knees before her sanguinary enemies by the decree of November 2, 1789. Her confiscated goods would finance the Revolution for ten years. As Harvard University's Professor Simon Shama pithily observes in his remarkable best-selling reassessment of the French Revolution: "The Terror was merely 1789 with a higher body count."[3]

---

[3] Simon Shama, *A Chronicle of the French Revolution* (New York: Vintage Books, 1989), p. 447. This national bestseller, published for the bicentenary, will hopefully serve to demythologize the highly simplistic views most of us raised in the United States hold both on the French Revolution and on France's ill-fated royal family.

The present volume is neither heavy with footnotes, nor laced with erudite references, being intended for the general reader to whom I hope to convey, before all else, some small aspect of the ineffable spiritual mystery lying behind the vocation of the martyrs. The simple, straightforward chronological narrative I had dreamed of proved too constraining for the constant references to the past, present, and future each chapter demanded. For example, a prophecy from the previous century had determined the prioress's course in proposing that her nuns consecrate themselves as victims of holocaust. Why, how, and when had this come about? Influences such as those of Madame Louise de France on the vocation of at least three of the martyrs determined their destiny as victims, some rather reluctantly so. Curious anecdotes about the Polish queen of Louis XV and one of Compiègne's past prioresses provide priceless insights into that lost world where the martyrs had lived and were formed for their sacrificial death. Above all, I hoped to present, in as graceful a manner as possible, each of the 16 martyrs as a bit more than just a name climbing the scaffold in the last chapter. Each women lived, breathed, and struggled before saying "yes" to being offered up to God as a willing victim of holocaust. Trying to cram the powerful emotions of 16 such vocations into a single opening chapter proved impossible.

Whence the format of ten chapters, with a summary at the beginning of each. Hopefully this will facilitate the reader's grasp of the mystery of that "eternal present" in which every consenting martyr attempts to live, and where prophecies and signs are fulfilled. Easy movement between past, present, and future is, in fact, always vital for holy souls who keep the "eternal present" of God's time clearly in view.

As did Fr. Bruno himself, I have occasionally allowed myself to dwell on Mother Teresa of Saint Augustine's interior reactions in certain key situations. A great grace seemed given me in this regard in 1985, as it were a totally unmerited gift from Mother Teresa herself. In the archives of the Carmel of Sens I discovered, among Marie de l'Incarnation's papers, a previously unknown Christmas carol written by the great prioress as she was already daily offering herself as a victim of holocaust, and specifically relating her strong Christo-centric spirituality to death on the guillotine. How, then, could I not feel compelled, even as Fr. Bruno had been, to reflect on how such a great Christian soul must have thought as she stood on the scaffold, the 15 headless bodies of her sisters swimming in blood in a red-painted cart beside the scaffold?

Father Bruno's own love for Mother Teresa of Saint Augustine indeed sustained me throughout, as did also a hope he expressed almost half a century ago in *Le Sang du Carmel.* He hoped, he said, that someday someone would attempt a literary presentation of the Carmelites' martyrdom that respected the facts of history.

Within the divine economy, Sylviane Bernanos's life ended as this volume passed into proofs. Already in 1983 I had dedicated to her my "little volume in English" as compensation for that "great theatrical event" that had foundered in Paris. She herself had remarked long ago that that failed event had served admirably in launching me into serving the true Carmelite martyrs, rather than the fictitious ones. May these pages on the actual martyrs stand as a memorial to her faith, her friendship, and her patronage.

My abiding gratitude to all the Carmelites of Compiègne for their support over 15 years, and in particular to Soeur Alix-Anne, archivist, incomparable collaborator and friend, and to Mère Christiane, who from our first encounter received me so graciously. The Sister Archivists of the Carmels of Sens, Clamart, and Pontoise in France unfailingly proved helpful and encouraging, as did Monseigneur Guy Gaucher, O.C.D., Auxiliary Bishop of Bayeux and Lisieux, a my very old Bernanosian friend who opened the doors of the Compiègne Carmel for me. The Carmelites of Erie, Pennsylvania (especially the prioress, Mother Emmanuel) and Mother Pauline, former prioress of the Carmel in St. Agatha, Ontario, have faithfully sustained me with their ongoing prayers rooted in the great love we share for their martyred sisters. Thanks are also due to Volker Schachenmayr and Jude Langsam, O.C.D.S., who carefully proofread the text, and to Sr. Susannah, O.C.D., of the Port Tobacco Carmel, who prepared the index.

Father Steven Payne, Director of ICS Publications, has proven a very thoughtful collaborator in dealing so patiently and thoroughly with all those seemingly endless problems arising as a manuscript is prepared for publication. I trust he will forgive my recalling at this point the delightful coincidence involving this volume's first coming into his hands. On a particular morning at the beginning of April, 1994, year of the bicentenary, I had finally decided to mail some samples of these pages to ICS Publications. I addressed the package for posting and stuffed it into my bulging briefcase on my way to work. En route to the post office, I checked my mailbox. Great was my astonishment in discovering a fax, signed by a totally unheard-of "Fr. Steven Payne, O.C.D.," of ICS Publications, asking if I might perhaps have something in English on the Carmelites of Compiègne for the bicentenary of their martyrdom.

Finally, a word of well-deserved recognition and gratitude is due my self-effacing English wife of 40 years. Completely against her non-violent nature, she patiently bore with her American-born husband's two decades of preoccupations with the violence and butchery of the French Revolution, repeatedly consenting, with inerrant graciousness, to proofread every page of this volume in version after version. Even in one's imagination, one could hardly hope to find so rare, so faithful, and so cherished a companion.

WILLIAM BUSH

The Discalced Carmelite Community of Compiègne by Age, July 17, 1794

Age	Family Name	Religious Name and Situation in Community
78	PIEDCOURT	Sr. Jesus Crucified, *choir sister*
78	THOURET	Sr. Charlotte of the Resurrection, *choir sister*
58	BRARD	Sr. Euphrasia of the Immaculate Conception, *choir sister*
52	CRETIEN DE NEUVILLE	Sr. Julie Louise of Jesus, *choir sister*
52	HANISSET	Sr. Teresa of the Heart of Mary, *choir sister*
52	DUFOUR	Sr. Saint Martha, *lay sister*
52	SOIRON	Sr. Catherine, *extern*
51	ROUSSEL	Sr. Marie of the Holy Spirit, *lay sister*
51	TREZEL	Sr. Teresa of Saint-Ignatius, *choir sister*
49	DE CROISSY	Mother Henriette of Jesus, past prioress and novice mistress, *choir sister*
46	SOIRON	Sr. Teresa, *extern*
42	BRIDEAU	Sr. Saint Louis, subprioress, *choir sister*
41	**LIDOINE**	**Mother Teresa of Saint-Augustine, PRIORESS, *choir sister***
34	PELRAS	Sr. Marie Henriette of the Divine Providence, *choir sister*
30	VEROLOT	Sr. St. Francis Xavier, *lay sister*
29	MEUNIER	Sr. Constance, *novice choir sister*. New laws in 1789 alone kept her from making her life vows that year.

PROFESSED MEMBERS WHO ESCAPED BEING ARRESTED

59	LEGROS	Sr. Stanislas (absent at arrest, not martyred)
46	JOURDAIN	Sr. Teresa of Jesus (absent at arrest, not martyred)

32 PHILIPPE* Sr. Josephine-Marie of the Incarnation (absent at arrest, not martyred)

---

*Françoise-Geneviève Philippe (1761-1836), the author of an account of her sisters' martyrdom written shortly before her 1836 death (see Soeur Marie de l'Incarnation, *La relation du martyre des seize Carmélites de Compiègne,* ed. William Bush [Paris: Cerf, 1993]). Madame Philippe returned to Compiègne the year following the Terror. She then amassed an important collection of community documents and relics which still survive, divided between the Carmel of Sens, where she ended her days in 1836, and the revived Carmel of Compiègne with whom Sens has shared these treasures.

Ces Dames ont signé avec nous. à Compiegne le
Onze Janvier mil sept cents, quatrevingt onze

Madelaine Claudine, Lidoine en Religion Thérèse de St. Augustin Supérieure
Marie-anne françoise Brideau, en Religion St. Louis
Marie anne piedcourt, en religion, jesus crucifie
anne, marie, madelaine charlotte, Thouret ditte En Relion Sr. de la Resurection
Marie Claude Cyprienne Brard dite en Religion Euphrasie.
Marie Louise Legros dite en Religion Stanislas
Marie Joseph D'angert, en Religion, Marie de Jesus
marie-françoise-gabriel de Croissy ditte en Religion henriette de jesus leconome
Marie Anne hanisset dit en Religion thérèse du Cœur de Marie
Marie gabrielle Trezel. dit en religion therese de st ignace
Marie Elisabeth Jourdain, ditte en religion therese de Jesus.
Rose Cretien, ditte en Religion Julie Louise de Jesus.
anne pelras ditte en religion marie henriette, de la providence
françoise Geneviève Philippe ditte en Religion Sr. Joséphine Marie
De l'incarnation

Signatures of the choir sisters in the Compiègne community in 1791

1

Martyrdom and France, Literature and Revolution

(i) The tradition of Christian martyrdom. (ii) The end in France of 1,296 years of Christian rule. (iii) The new order's calendar and festivals. (iv) Artistic treatments of the Compiègne Carmelites: Gertrud von le Fort; R. L. Bruckberger; Emmet Lavery; Georges Bernanos; Francis Poulenc. (v) The mystery of their historic vocation; what was sung during the decapitations.

BYZANTINE LITURGICAL TEXTS address the martyrs of Christendom as "bearers of God" offered up for the peace of God's church on earth as the "first-fruits" of the universe.

Such "first-fruits" and "bearers of God" have never been lacking in France. From the martyrdom of the little slave-girl Blandine and her companions in the Lyons arena under Marcus Aurelius in the second century, to the voluntary community immolation of the 16 Carmelites of Compiègne at the Place de la Nation in Paris on the evening of July 17, 1794, the French constellation of martyrs has never ceased illumining the friend of God. The Carmelites' sacrifice is therefore but an integral part of a long and very noble Christian tradition by no means peculiar to France, but true of any country where Christianity finds itself in opposition to a non-Christian culture.

The period in which this event took place is, moreover, unusually rich in examples of Christian martyrdom. Never had the constellation of martyrs for Jesus Christ so suddenly expanded in France as during the early years of the Revolution. Thousands of Christians perished, not only by the guillotine, but also by mass deportations, drownings, imprisonments, shootings, mob violence, and sheer butchery.

It would be surprising had it been otherwise. The ancient pact between France's kings and Christianity's triune God had been overthrown. This ancient pact stretched back to the marriage of the Frankish king, Clovis, to the Christian, Clothilde. On Christmas Day in 496 Clovis had accepted baptism and sacramental anointing as a Christian king by St. Rémi, Bishop of Rheims, thereby inaugurating a twelve-hundred-and-ninety-six-year reign in France of "most Christian" kings. It was to prove the most venerable kingdom in western Europe.

The fall of the Christian monarchy on August 10, 1792, thus marked the beginning of a new order. Gone were the basic nonmaterialistic values the ruling Christian dynasty was at least supposed to incarnate. Gone also was the official obligation of France's king, whatever the enormity or scandal of his sins, to acknowledge before men and angels that he was a subject of the Creator of heaven and earth who, as the Word of God, had been incarnate in Jesus Christ (Col 1:16) by the Holy Spirit and the Virgin Mary. Gone all acceptance of what, for almost 1300 years, France's rulers had held concerning this God-Man to whom they paid homage as Lord and God. He, the King of kings, had not only taken on human flesh, but, after bleeding and dying for humanity, had risen from the dead, ascended into heaven, and, they were obliged to believe, would come again in glory to judge the living and the dead. In that last dread day they, as vassals, believed they would personally have to answer to the One who casts down the mighty from their thrones, who lifts up the humble and meek, and who sends the rich away empty.

Innumerable sites in France still preserve something of the extraordinary splendor resulting from the long and harmonious fusion of French culture with the Christian creed. Such notable monuments as the baptistry of St. John the Baptist at Poitiers, the church of Saint Rémi in Rheims, or the incomparable cathedral of Our Lady of Chartres, are but three examples of that vast national treasure of French monuments where the extraordinarily gracious energies of French Christian civilization linger on.

It was not by coincidence, then, that on October 5, 1793, just nine months prior to the Carmelites' martyrdom, the seven-day Jewish week was officially scrapped by the French National Convention. Simultaneously, a new non-Judeo-Christian dating of time was inaugurated. It aimed at rooting out, once and for all, all possibility of clinging to the weekly commemoration of the resurrection of Jesus Christ on Sunday. On October 5, 1793, "Day One, of Year One, of the One, Indivisible French Republic" was proclaimed as having been ushered in (though completely unannounced and unknown to anyone at the time) more than a year before on September 22, 1792, the first equinox occurring after the August 10 fall of the Christian monarchy. The dating for *Le Moniteur* confirms October 5, 1793, as the date when the Christian "year of the Lord," honoring the Jewish God of the Christians, was officially eclipsed by the Republican calendar imposed by the anti-Christian government.

Such an unprecedented upheaval in daily life was motivated by a simple concept: a new era had dawned at the end of that century of human enlightenment. Thanks to the philosophers, France had now attained a more advanced stage of civilization in which Christianity's fanatical insistence on a personal relationship with its resurrected God, Jesus Christ, was to be allowed no quarter.

ii

PRIOR TO THE OCTOBER 5 RETROACTIVE INAUGURATION of the new calendar in 1793, and before abolishing that last Christian "year of the Lord," France's "most Christian" king had been decapitated on January 21. Nine months later, by the time the new calendar had been proclaimed, his maligned and God-fearing widow had been transferred from the Temple to the Conciergerie. There she would await a show trial on trumped-up charges, including the monstrous and sensational accusation of having sexually abused her seven-year-old son in company with her pious and very noble sister-in-law, Madame Elisabeth of France.

In spite of the repeated cry by bloodthirsty propagandists such as Marat and Hébert that the shedding of the queen's Austrian blood would right all wrongs, her execution on October 16, just 11 days following the imposition of the new calendar, in no way lessened France's seething, bloody ferment. Quite the contrary proved true. Still more malevolent forces seemed immediately unleashed. Over the nine succeeding months those dark forces would mount in intensity to peak in the immediate wake of the Festival of the Supreme Being, staged on June 8, 1794. Just two days following that queen of Republican festivals, the passing of the law of 22 Prairial on June 10 unchained the Great Terror. It would last until the fall of Robespierre on July 27, ten days after the Carmelites' immolation on July 17. In the meantime, the anti-Christian government sought to impose its new, non-superstitious order of human enlightenment through its daily public effusions of blood on the guillotine.

In the history of the Revolution it is paradoxical that the more events moved forward, the more an inexplicable, inexorable tide seemed to roll over France. One wave of revolutionary enthusiasts after another was swept forward to perish on the scaffold. Whether the Girondins, Madame Roland, Philippe Egalité, Hébert, or Danton, the Revolution's most ardent partisans seemed involuntarily propelled toward the vortex of its maelstrom. Like an unleashed monster, the Revolution proved as indifferent to revolutionary partisans as to aristocrats, clergy, and the common people, that vast source for the forgotten majority of its victims. All were devoured equally. The Revolution, like some insatiable Chronos or some gluttonous Saturn, unnaturally ingurgitated its own offspring. Meanwhile its partisans, intoxicated with idealism, touted its having at last brought justice, freedom, equality, and brotherhood to the human race.

October 1793 also precipitated other events, unprecedented in France's nearly 13 centuries of Christian history. By the date of the queen's execution on October 16, an intoxicated revolutionary mob was already pillaging and desecrating the Royal Basilica at Saint-Denis. The mortal remains of France's rulers, going back to King Dagobert, were being pried from their sarcophagi and leaden coffins and, with those of their spouses and children, thrown into a common pit to be devoured by quicklime.

In concert with these public outbursts of darker human passions, an event in Rheims that same month underscored France's absolute rupture with her Christian past. Its impact was of particular significance. Since Clovis, Rheims had been the immemorial site for the sacramental anointing of all France's Christian kings with holy chrism passed down from St. Rémi. Joan of Arc's insistence that the dauphin be anointed there on Christmas day to establish his legitimacy against the English usurper is a familiar instance of this age-old Christian tradition. Indeed, the one exception in the 1,296 years of Christian history had been Henri IV, a Protestant turned Catholic to win the people of Paris. Sacramental anointing with holy chrism at Rheims had not been part of his agenda when he quipped, "Paris is well worth a Mass!"

Henri IV notwithstanding, the anointing of the king at Rheims had provided continuity with the kingdom's Christian identity and provoked that unprecedented public event staged in Rheims on October 7, 1793, by a former Protestant pastor from Alsace named Rühl, dispatched from Paris to Rheims as a missionary of the revolution or, as they were termed, "representative of the people." He presided over a ceremony in which he himself publicly smashed, on the pedestal of the statue of the late Louis XV, the sacred vial containing the holy chrism of St. Rémi. He then sent the broken pieces to the National Convention in Paris. This public repudiation of France's most venerated link between her ancient pact and the Christian God graphically reinforced what, just two days before, the inauguration of ten-day weeks had also intended: a willful, premeditated destruction of all ties between the new order and Christianity.

Should it surprise us, then, that in 1794, the year immediately following these events, 16 Carmelite nuns, consecrated to the Virgin Mother of Jesus Christ, and daily offering themselves in holocaust[1] to restore peace to France and to her Christian church, found themselves condemned to death on July 17 as "enemies of the people" for "annihilating public freedom"?

iii

THE CALENDAR INTRODUCED IN 1793 was neither new nor original. It was in fact an ancient pre-Jewish one borrowed from Egypt and still in effect among the Copts in Egypt and Ethiopia, consisting of twelve thirty-day months with five—or in leap years, six—additional astronomical days inevitably accumulating at the end of each year. Just prior to September 22, New Year's day according to the Republican calendar, such accumulated days were designated as holidays for national

[1] In the Old Testament "holocaust" signified a religious sacrifice offered by the Jews wherein the victim was completely consumed by fire. It thus differed from other sacrifices where a portion of the victim's flesh could be eaten. The present widespread custom of using "holocaust" to designate the genocide of twentieth-century Jews under Hitler (the *Shoah*) can only give to that venerable word a significance rather removed from its strictly religious origins.

games. Called "Les Sansculottides," they honored the romanticized working-class who wore trousers rather than the knee-breeches of the upper classes.

The Revolution's contribution to revamping the ancient calendar was to annihilate the Jewish seven-day week by dividing each thirty-day month into three ten-day "weeks" called "décades." Thereby disappeared all traces both of the Jewish Sabbath and of the Christian "Lord's Day" that commemorated the resurrection of Jesus Christ on Sunday. Specifically aimed at by inauguration of the ten-day *décades* was the eradication of a deeply entrenched Jewish concept, shared with Christians and Muslims alike. This was that after creating the world in six days, God rested on the seventh. Was such an outmoded and absurd concept not totally meaningless for the post-Christian Frenchman of the eighteenth-century "enlightenment," freed at last from the "fanaticism" of Christianity? Had that malignant Jewish sect not already held France for far too long in its unenlightened clutches and impeded progress through its superstitions?

Those churches in France still open for public ceremonies and not already converted to secular uses would gradually be rededicated as temples of a modern civic cult honoring contemporary themes such as "reason," "brotherhood," "freedom," or "equality." The last day of each ten-day décade was named "décadi." After the Terror, this décadi holiday would actually be assigned a particular civic theme to be celebrated in the converted churches. As a replacement for the more frequent Sunday holiday, however, décadi offered only thrice-monthly respites from work. Under the calender of the new order, Sanson, Paris's overworked executioner, was obliged to work nine days out of ten, rather than a mere six out of seven. His guaranteed number of free days in a calendar year thus fell from 52 to 36.

On November 10, 1793, Paris's Cathedral of Notre Dame, rechristened "The Temple of Reason," was the site of a much-publicized religious ceremony honoring its new dedication. On a strange mountain-shaped stage erected in the midst of the vast cathedral, "Reason," personified by a shapely actress draped in classic attire, moved with languid gestures, much to the delight of the male spectators. The imposing *papier mâché* mountain, complete with Greek temple surrounded by trees, was a self-conscious tribute to the powerful Jacobin "Mountain" party of the National Convention. While desecrating the noble edifice raised by Parisian Christians to the Virgin Mother of Jesus Christ, this predictable public spectacle also confirmed the poetic poverty of the Republic.

The republican government offered such contrived, self-conscious pantomimes, one after the other, to replace banished Christian ceremonies. As long as these Republican festivals could vie with one another for the prize in pompous banality, the hope remained alive that the Judeo-Christian concept of man's dependence upon a personal God could be uprooted.

The organization of republican festivals was generally entrusted to the fertile imagination of the celebrated artist, Jacques-Louis David, future portraitist and enthusiastic subject of Napoleon Bonaparte. At this time, however, David was a rabid Jacobin propagandist and member of the all-powerful Committee of Public Salvation—or as it is usually mistranslated, "Committee of Public Safety." His intricate *mise en scène* for these festivals of republican propaganda would indeed be crowned by that of the Supreme Being, celebrated on June 8, 1794, 39 days before the execution of the Carmelites of Compiègne.

iv

THOUGH IT IS HARDLY SURPRISING that martyrs for Christianity abounded during such a time, we may still wonder why the 16 Carmelite martyrs of Compiègne should here be singled out once again for particular attention. Have a short novel by Gertrud von le Fort, a film by R. L. Bruckberger, dramas by Emmet Lavery and Georges Bernanos, and an opera by Francis Poulenc, not already sufficiently recounted this event?

Works of the first order in their respective genres, these twentieth-century artistic treatments have already made the literary and musical public aware of this historic martyrdom. Why then should an event so familiar to such a wide public once again be distinguished from the thousands of other Christian martyrdoms—many of them quite remarkable—that took place during the same period?

The answer is simple. The artistic presentations of the martyrdom of the Carmelites of Compiègne are autonomous from what actually happened, because all emanate from the short novel by Gertrud von Le Fort, *The Song at the Scaffold.* The historical truth is therefore blurred for readers who would base their knowledge of the community martyrdom on any one of these artistic productions, or even a combination of them all. While glorifying this dramatic incident of the Great Terror in magnificent art, they prove of little worth in clarifying exactly what happened, to whom it happened, and why it happened.

This could hardly be otherwise. Gertrud von Le Fort, witnessing the rise of Hitler in Germany, purposely created a totally fictitious heroine, Blanche de la Force, into whom she projected her own metaphysical fear. Gertrud von Le Fort's fearful Blanche in turn completely captivated the genial imagination of the dying Georges Bernanos. In the last months of his life, Bernanos, aware of his physical deterioration, reshaped Blanche's terror to create a dazzling reflection of his own lucid, vibrant meditation before death. His dialogues for Raymond Bruckberger's film, destined in the end not for the film but for a volume called *Dialogues of the Carmelites,* were in fact completed even as he took to his bed, mortally ill, to expire four months later on July 5, 1948.

Blanche de la Force therefore enlightens us concerning the creative genius of both Gertrud von le Fort and Georges Bernanos. Through her, each author attempted in turn to exorcise a very personal fear. Yet Blanche de la Force remains a *fictitious* character, born from the creative imagination of Gertrud von le Fort in the early twentieth century. It would be unreasonable to expect a story centered on a fictitious character to be completely reliable regarding what actually happened.

The hapless reader's confusion is also compounded by the fact that Gertrud von le Fort did utilize four historical names in her work: Madame de Croissy, Madame Lidoine, Sister Constance, and Marie of the Incarnation. Baroness von le Fort also respected four historical facts: 1) Madame Lidoine did succeed Madame de Croissy as Prioress; 2) Marie of the Incarnation did escape the guillotine; 3) there did exist a community act whereby the nuns offered themselves in holocaust; 4) the 16 martyrs did sing as they climbed the steps of the scaffold. These four facts, however, as well as the four historical characters, are all totally subservient to the fictitious Blanche's story. The result is that everything else narrated in all the artistic treatments, insofar as these four historical names are concerned, is also pure fiction.

The dying Madame de Croissy's unforgettable dialogue with Blanche—one of the most extraordinary ever written by the great Bernanos—as well as her offering of her anguished death for Blanche, are unfortunately of no help whatsoever if the reader wishes to grasp who the real Madame de Croissy was. Indeed, even the most intimate familiarity with all the various artistic treatments would never reveal that Madame de Croissy was in fact the community's last novice mistress or that she actually died on the guillotine with her "novitiate," a group that included not only the one unprofessed novice, Sister Constance, but also all those in the community who had recently made their profession.

Officially forbidden to pronounce her vows by revolutionary decrees, the youngest member of the community, Sister Constance, did finally make her profession *in extremis* at the foot of the scaffold after six years as a novice in the community. It was her brother, not Blanche's, who tried to persuade her to return home. Nor was Sister Constance the last to die, but the first. Thus, even if Blanche de la Force had existed, that unforgettable and electrifying climax of both play and opera where, upon hearing a voice taking up the martyr's hymn, Constance joyously looks down from the scaffold to see Blanche emerge from the crowd, would have been impossible.

The last one to climb the scaffold steps was in fact the prioress, Madame Lidoine herself who, presiding over the sacrifice to the very end, blessed each of her 15 daughters as they fulfilled the community oblation she herself had proposed. What Madame Lidoine had proposed, however, was never a "vow of martyrdom" as one reads in the fictional versions, but rather an "act of consecration" whereby each member of the community would join with the others in offering herself daily to God, soul and body, in holocaust to restore peace to France and to her church.

This proposal, we now know, was made sometime between the expulsion from their monastery on September 14, 1792, and the November 27 following, on which date we have confirmation that the consecration was already an established part of the community's daily life. Moreover, the community sacrifice was presided over by Madame Lidoine, its one true mother and Compiègne's great prioress, inspiring, animating, and transfiguring all by her mystical insights.

On the other hand, the historical Marie of the Incarnation—one of the most imposing characters in the fictional versions in which, as "Mother" and "Subprioress," she alone is responsible for the "vow of martyrdom"—proves shockingly different. By age and disposition Sister Marie of the Incarnation far more resembled Blanche de la Force than that magnificent and mature fictitious character invented by Gertrud von le Fort, then glorified by Bernanos, whose own personal preoccupations with honor and sanctity he made incarnate in her. Historically, the act of holocaust to which she, along with the others, had been consecrating herself for some 20 months was not what she really wanted. No desire, mystical or otherwise, to be the last one at the scaffold is discernable in that 32-year-old natural daughter of the late Prince of Conti. And certainly not for her any Bernanosian pleading with the chaplain to be allowed to join her condemned sisters out of a feeling of dishonor at not dying with them.

An orphaned illegitimate daughter of a Prince of the Blood, Françoise-Geneviève Philippe had become a Carmelite following a miraculous cure from an hysterical illness at the Carmel of Pontoise on the Feast of Our Lady of Mount Carmel, July 16, 1784. In November of 1793, her first cousin, Philippe Egalité, had been guillotined in spite of vaunting his supposedly republican sympathies. She, because she had royal blood, was mortally terrified of sharing his fate.

When her sisters were arrested and imprisoned in Compiègne on June 22, 1794, this royal Carmelite was in Paris on business regarding a pension left by her princely father. Upon hearing the news of her community's arrest, she wasted no time, but seized a seemingly providential opportunity to flee the capital by accompanying the prioress's 78-year-old mother, long scheduled to leave Paris around June 24, to go settle permanently in Franche Comté with relatives of her late husband.

Sister Marie of the Incarnation was well aware of this long-planned departure. Since arriving in Paris at the end of March, she had frequented the elderly Madame Lidoine and was sympathetic to her needs. She had even agreed, well before the arrest, to assist the lonely old Madame Lidoine in her melancholy farewell to the capital. When news of her community's arrest ruled out any idea of returning to Compiègne, she thus decided to accompany her prioress's elderly mother. Once in Franche Comté she would find herself near Switzerland, where certain members of the Conti family had already taken refuge from the Revolution. Might she too perhaps be able to slip across the border to safety?

After some three decades of wandering, including a stay at Versailles where, in 1808, her name is found among a group of former Carmelites trying to establish a community, Madame Philippe ended her days in 1836 as a paying guest in an apartment at the Carmel of Sens. There, at more than 70 years of age, she was told by that monastery's superior, Abbé Clément Villecourt, future cardinal and member of the Roman Curia, to write up a "Relation" of her former community's martyrdom. A careful reading of the manuscripts she left has illuminated a number of heretofore unknown details. Crossed-out passages, curious corrections, and numerous rewritings all reveal the painful struggle of the elderly ex-Carmelite of Compiègne in trying to make the hard facts of history conform to her conviction that she was responsible before God for leaving posterity an edifying—even sublime—account of the martyrdom.

We can only admire the heroic courage manifested by this royal and aging ex-Carmelite, professed in the immolated monastery of Compiègne, in thus troubling her last days on earth. Indeed, recalling the community oblation appears to have been not only disturbing for her, but in some ways actually traumatic. For almost two years she, Françoise-Geneviève Philippe, had joined in the daily offering of herself in holocaust, apparently without any real zeal for participating in the final act. Escaping it therefore could only have been a source of profound and secret relief.

V

THE JUSTIFICATION FOR TREATING ONCE AGAIN the story of the Carmelites is found therefore in a need to elucidate the simple historical facts about this rather unusual community holocaust, a number of which have only come to light with the French publication of Marie of the Incarnation's manuscripts.[2] What is surprising is that the mystery of the vocation of the Carmelites seems more resonant when we consider it apart from the unifying thread of Blanche de la Force's fictitious drama. While concentrating on two stark historical facts alone—the 16 nuns did offer themselves in holocaust, and they did sing as they climbed the steps of the guillotine—the fictitious versions remain firmly centered on the imaginary drama of Blanche de la Force, not on the mystery of the Christian vocation of the 16 historical martyrs, offering themselves to quell the Terror.

Even a glance at the facts provides readers who know the opera with a difference that strikingly accentuates the profound Christian implications behind this mysterious community sacrifice. For though the Carmelites did sing the *Salve Regina* on the way to the scaffold, Francis Poulenc's choice of this hymn as the climactic one in his opera for the actual execution is totally nonhistorical, whatever may be the composer's theatrical genius in raising it by a half-tone when the blade of the guillotine crashes down. Certainly the dramatic impact of such an operatic ending is beyond dispute. But the *Salve Regina* did not actually accompany the decapitations. Their final song at the scaffold—for there were several—was Psalm 117, *Laudate Dominum omnes gentes,* which proclaims the mystic truth couched at the heart of the

---

[2] Soeur Marie de l'Incarnation, *La relation du martyre des seize Carmélites de Compiègne. Les documents originaux inédits publiés par William Bush.* Préface de Mgr Guy Gaucher (Paris: Cerf, 1993).

Christian experience of salvation: God's mercy is at the center of all things, even of being guillotined.

> O praise the Lord all ye nations!
> Praise him all ye people!
> FOR HIS MERCY IS CONFIRMED UPON US
> And the truth of the Lord remaineth forever!
> Praise the Lord!

Spontaneously bursting from the lips of Sister Constance as she, designated as first to die, started up the scaffold steps, the austere chanting of the psalm was in fact taken up and carried forward by the others until the end. Thus as the implacable blade cut short each nun's voice and her head dropped into the executioner's leather bag with an effusion of blood, the chanting of women's voices insistently proclaimed before men and angels (1 Cor 4:9) that God's mercy was being *confirmed* upon them.

Such was their final statement, their final word, their final witness. No protest was lodged against the new totalitarian terrorist government, no denunciation of its disgusting daily cult of blood sacrifice. No complaint at this ultimate moment came from these defenseless, dispossessed, and unjustly persecuted Christian women that their most basic human rights were being grossly violated even as the new order celebrated its Declaration of the Rights of Man. Naught but their austere chant of high, solemn joy that, after some 20 months of daily consecrating themselves for this hour, God's mercy was *allowing* them to make their act of holocaust to restore peace to France and her church.

Thus, historically, the nuns' vocal witness to God's mercy constituted an integral part of the mystery made incarnate in Paris on the evening of July 17, 1794. As they offered up to the Lord and Giver of Life the one mortal life he had given them, their voices announced that God's mercy to his creatures is great, and that whatever may be the vicissitudes accompanying human destiny in this fallen world, within the mystical Body of Christ all remains subservient to the mystery of that mercy.

To this chanted, collective witness, provided by the sacred words of the psalm, was also added the unique and very personal visual witness of each transfigured face. Those present could behold with their eyes that the nuns were living out the mystery of God's mercy to the end. With their own ears those watching heard them proclaim his goodness. That final chant rising so boldly from the Carmelites' lips indeed proclaimed what the spilling of their life-blood graphically confirmed: the good estate of the church of God in France.

To such Christians was it given to quell the Terror.

Pastel of Our Lady of Mount Carmel, by one of the Carmelite martyrs of Compiègne (Photo, J. P. Gilson)

2

The Legacy of Louise-Marie of France

(i) A Carmelite princess; her premonition of disaster in 1787. (ii) Her ties with MADAME PHILIPPE (Sister Marie of the Incarnation). (iii) Her royal parents and her personal concern for Louis XV. (iv) Her queen mother's ties with Compiègne's Carmel. (v) Why she could not enter the Carmel of Compiègne. (vi) Her ties with MADAME LIDOINE (Mother Teresa of Saint Augustine) and the role of Marie Antoinette in the latter's vocation. (vii) Her ties with MADAME CRETIEN DE NEUVILLE (Sister Julie Louise of Jesus); the latter's parody of *La Marseillaise;* the role of Madame Louise in the martyrdom.

IN 1770, twenty-four years before the martyrdom of the Carmelites of Compiègne, Louise-Marie of France, tenth child of Louis XV, entered the Carmel of Saint-Denis. Thirty-three years of age, of sickly disposition and, because of an early injury, afflicted with a slight hump on one shoulder, Madame Louise thrived in the austerities of Carmel, much to the astonishment of her family and intimates. As Sister Teresa of Saint Augustine, she delighted in stating that neither the seven hours spent in the choir daily nor the other rigors of Carmelite life proved an obstacle to her new vocation.

Favorite daughter of the aging king, Madame Louise inevitably found herself the most famous Carmelite in France. More than one Catholic court of Europe buzzed briefly in 1770 with speculation about what might lurk behind the King of France's formal announcement that his beloved youngest daughter, Louise-Marie, was entering the order of St. Teresa of Avila.

For 17 years Sister Teresa of Saint Augustine, to her dismay, would remain the most famous Carmelite not only in France, but in all of Europe. Repeatedly elected prioress or appointed novice mistress at the Carmel of Saint-Denis, she would die on December 23, 1787, less than two years before the mighty eruption following the storming of the Bastille on July 14, 1789. She thus escaped the bloody flood that swept away France's ancient Christian monarchy, sending to the guillotine not only her pious royal niece, Madame Elisabeth of France, but also her nephew, Louis XVI, and his Austrian queen, Marie Antoinette.

Did a premonition of these disastrous events precipitate the royal Carmelite's early death? We are told that in May of 1787, when she learned that her nephew had named the libertine Archbishop of Toulouse, Loménie de Brienne, as his Minister, she cried, "France is lost!" and took to her bed. There, seven months later, she breathed her last at age 50.

Madame Louise displayed remarkable intuitive powers in foreseeing the gravity of this appointment by Louis XVI. Two years later, in 1789, when this same prelate's name was suggested as Archbishop of Paris, the king would reject it with the quip, "The archbishop of Paris must at least believe in God!" Yet in 1787 he had chosen Loménie de Brienne as chief minister, hoping the archbishop might persuade his brother bishops, among others of his fellow aristocrats, to vote generous subsidies to the financially troubled crown.

What followed proved the king wrong and confirmed Madame Louise's fears. Realizing that their own exaggerated privileges were being threatened, the Assembly of Notables responded by demanding that the king recall parliament and assemble the Estates General, thereby precipitating de Brienne's fall. Thus, what the upper clergy and other "Notables" had required of the king, in a haughty attempt to perpetuate their own privileges, caused the loss of everything. The threatening tide unleashed in forcing the king's hand mercilessly uprooted them in its first great swell. Jealous of their privileges, they had paved the way for the aggressive dechristianization of western Europe's foremost Christian realm.

Whatever Madame Louise's visionary gifts may have been in foreseeing the destruction of Christian France, her early death did curiously fulfill a prophecy made on her twenty-fifth birthday at Versailles by the venerated Bishop of Langres. He had told her on that day that she had lived out exactly half of her life. This fact is recalled by the princess's biographers as well as by our historian of the Carmelite martyrdom, Françoise-Geneviève Philippe (formerly Marie of the Incarnation), who attests in her manuscripts that she heard it directly from the princess's own lips.

ii

THERE ARE INDICATIONS in Madame Louise's biography that she was responsible not only for the vocation of two of the future Compiègne martyrs, but also for a third member of the community. Whatever may be the importance of a Sister Victoire-Louise Clothilde of St. Teresa, "given to the Carmelites of Compiègne by Madame Louise of France" as reported by Abbé Auger,[1] it is also important to recall that princess's ties with our historian, Madame Philippe, who, as we have already observed, died in her bed as a paying guest at the Carmel of Sens in 1836, 42 years after the 1794 martyrdom.

Though her descent from royal blood was illegitimate, Madame Philippe could claim a common ancestor with

---

[1] M. Auger, Chanoine honoraire de Beauvais, curé de Saint-Antoine, *Notice sur les Carmélites de Compiègne. Annales du Monastère de l'Annonciation du Carmélites de Compiègne* (Paris: Chez Méquignon Junion, 1835), p. 27.

Madame Louise in the person of St. Louis to whose son, Robert de Clermont, all Bourbons traced themselves. Her natural father, Louis-François de Bourbon, Prince of Conti (1717–1776), belonged to that select group of males of royal descent recognized as potential heirs to the throne and officially ranked as France's "Princes of the Blood." Madame Philippe's mother, prior to Françoise-Geneviève's birth, had been quietly married to a man named Philippe. The sister of Madame Philippe's royal father, married to the Duke of Orleans, was the mother of that ill-fated revolutionary Duke of Orleans, Philippe Egalité, to whom we have already referred, guillotined in November of 1793 after voting for the death of the king the previous January.

Nor were Françoise-Geneviève Philippe's ties with her late natural father a secret in royalist circles. Details concerning the revolutionary government's administration of the legacy left to the 15-year-old girl at her royal father's death in 1776 had necessitated her presence in Paris at the time of the community's arrest in Compiègne. Her ties with her father's circles are further confirmed by the fact that ten years prior to the Great Terror, during the early summer of 1784, the Duke of Penthièvre, grandson of Louis XIV and father-in-law of Philippe Egalité, had shown grave concern for her well-being while staying at his chateau at Bizy, even dispatching his private physician to her bedside in nearby Vernon, hoping to cure her chronic hysterical illness.

Yet all the art of the private physician of France's richest and probably most pious nobleman proved useless against her mysterious illness. It was only on July 16, feast of Our Lady of Mount Carmel, that Françoise-Geneviève Philippe, after vowing to become a Carmelite if only she could be cured, was so favored. On that day she found a complete and instantaneous restoration to health at the Carmel of Pontoise, before the relics of the venerated foundress of the first Carmel in France, Madame Acarie.

Madame Acarie, a wealthy and pious widow, had humbly ended her days at the Carmel of Pontoise as the white-veiled lay nun, Sister Marie of the Incarnation. At the beginning of the seventeenth century, however, she had been responsible for the historic trip to Spain made by Cardinal de Bérulle, for the express purpose of escorting back to France a group of nuns of the reform of Saint Teresa of Avila. They were headed by Mother Anne of Jesus, spiritual daughter of St. Teresa of Avila, who in 1604 would become prioress of the first monastery of Discalced Carmelites in France.

Madame Acarie herself entered the Carmel of Amiens as a lay sister and was professed there in 1615. Transferred to Pontoise, France's second foundation, she died there in 1617.

At her entry in the Carmel of Compiègne more than a century later on September 23, 1786, Madame Philippe had assumed Madame Acarie's religious name, Marie of the Incarnation, out of gratitude for her miraculous healing. She had been required to wait two full years after that 1784 miraculous cure to be sure she suffered no relapses.

For three years the Carmels of France had been trying to obtain Rome's beatification of Madame Acarie. Hopes were high that Françoise-Geneviève Philippe's case might provide the missing miracle. From Madame Philippe's own recollections at the end of her life, it would appear that during her six months of postulancy, and while awaiting her clothing as a novice, she was actually summoned from Compiègne to the Carmel of Saint-Denis to learn directly from Madame Louise the decision of Rome's Sacred Congregation of Rites. Though the miracle was recognized, the royal prioress reported, Rome had refused to give it the standing of "miracle of the first class."

Madame Philippe apparently had already met Madame Louise at Saint-Denis in 1784, just after her cure. This second meeting in 1786 thus afforded her an opportunity to compliment the princess on her physical appearance. The royal

Mother Teresa of Saint Augustine made light of this, replying that if she were to believe what the Bishop of Langres had told her on her twenty-fifth birthday, she had only a year to live. Curiously, Madame Philippe attests that this 1786 interview took place a year to the day before Madame Louise's death on December 23, 1787.

Curious prophecies and coincidences of dates aside, during her 17 years as a Carmelite Madame Louise of France did exercise considerable influence outside her own cloister. Whatever may have been her impact in pointing Madame Philippe toward the Carmel of Compiègne, or the brief span of the religious vocation of that Sister Victoire Louise Clothilde mentioned by Abbé Auger, her role in deciding the vocation of two of the Carmelite martyrs is beyond dispute and well documented. In itself this would not be remarkable, given the role she played in Carmelite affairs in France at that time. What is remarkable is that this princess of the Christian house of France was so intimately linked to the community holocaust offered for France and her church. Indeed, the prioress responsible for the martyrdom was actually one of her protégés. While we might hesitate to admit that, even mystically speaking, the Carmelites' oblation did in fact renew the pact made by the princess's royal forebears with the Christian God, we must still admit that their sacrifice bore ardent witness to it.

iii

WHATEVER MADAME LOUISE'S NATURAL DISPOSITION for the religious life, circumstances within her immediate family strongly favored her vocation. A sensitive young woman, she could hardly have been unaware of the abyss that, from her earliest memories, separated her promiscuous French father from her pious Polish mother, Marie Leszczynska. Louis XV's weakness for the pleasures of the flesh never ceased to pain his Polish queen and his four unmarried royal daughters.

In 1725, at 22 years of age, Marie Leszczynska had been given by her father, Stanislas, exiled King of Poland, to be the wife of the 15-year-old Dauphin of France. She dutifully bore him 10 children during the first 12 years of marriage. To her sorrow and the king's bitter disappointment, only one male heir was counted among all these offspring. At the birth of Madame Louise, the last of the 10 in 1737, the king is said to have referred to her as "Madame Dernière" ("Madame Last One"), apparently to indicate his renunciation of further attempts at fathering legitimate heirs.

Whatever the 27-year-old monarch meant by this remark, his affections did stray from his 34-year-old wife following Madame Louise's birth in 1737. For the last three decades of her existence, Marie Leszczynska was condemned to brush aside, with Christian resignation, her husband's public manifestations of amorous infidelities. The long and charmed reign at court of a young and beautiful favorite such as the clever Madame de Pompadour could hardly have made Marie Lesczcynska's inner pain any less.

Immediately following the queen's death in 1768, however, the 58-year-old king's behavior briefly filled his four spinster daughters with hope. Was the king, with the approach of old age, ready at last to return to a more Christian form of conduct? The courtiers at Versailles, desperate for direct links to the throne, could not risk this. They pushed forward the humbly born but attractive Madame du Barry, whose charms proved irresistible to the aging king. She was installed in splendor, showered with gifts and income, and given a place of honor at court. This was not easy for Mesdames Adélaïde, Sophie, Victoire, and Louise who, following their mother's death, held by right of birth the place of first ladies at the most brilliant court in Europe. Now the king's choice obliged them to accept their father's favorite.

This particularly wounded the sensitive 33-year-old Madame Louise. She, whose prayers and hopes for her father's reform had recently soared to such heights and whose piety had always shown great vigor and originality, now contemplated drastic measures. Was the salvation of the king's soul not now suspended over the abyss as never before? Action was needed. Given the urgency of her vision, was she herself not being prompted by heaven to do something?

iv

THOUGH MADAME LOUISE was separated from her royal parents from age two to fourteen while being educated with her sisters by the nuns at Fontrevault, her mother's friendship with the Carmel of Compiègne had actually begun in 1738, when Madame Louise was only a year old and the queen's anguish fresh from losing the king's affections. Given Marie Lesczcynska's situation at court thereafter, it is easy to understand the importance she attached to her friendship with one of the Compiègne Carmel's more remarkable prioresses, Madame Descajeuls, who was not only called "friend" by the queen, but who also shaped the souls of martyrs such as Madame de Croissy.

The court's stay of six to eight weeks each year at Compiègne for hunting favored the queen's intimacy with this compassionate and understanding prioress. Because of its convenient location just opposite the royal chateau, the queen preferred the monastery with its calm to the chateau with its intrigues and passions. The august visitor even obtained permission to furnish an apartment within the monastery of her "good friends, the Carmelites." This circumstance provides an amusing anecdote found in the manuscripts of Marie of the Incarnation. It also demonstrates Madame

Descajeuls's gift for coping with the extravagances of Louis XV's Polish queen.

Originally the queen's intention in furnishing an apartment in the monastery seems to have been to provide herself with a place where her midday meal, sent over from the chateau, might be served. This decision was actually a sort of compromise, however. At first the queen had conceived the grandiose scheme of having the meals for the entire religious community prepared by her own personal chef at the chateau, then transported to the monastery. This had been thwarted, however, much to the prioress's relief. A few attempts had sufficed to persuade even the determined piety of the Polish queen that her royal chef's talents could not be bent to the rigid monastic timetable across the road where pleasures of the table were kept in their place.

Thus alerted to the queen's penchant for well-intentioned impracticality, Madame Descajeuls pointedly remarked to her monarch, upon inspecting the newly furnished royal apartment, that she hoped that the bed she saw there was for appearances only. Her Majesty did realize, did she not, that she would need special permission to sleep there? Such permission had once been accorded the widowed mother of the Duke of Penthièvre, the Countess of Toulouse, but only because she was a widow. Reassuring the prioress, the queen insisted that the bed was not for sleeping at night, but merely for resting after her midday meal.

One evening shortly thereafter, well after the queen and her attendant had been seen leaving the monastery for the day, one of the nuns reported a light in the queen's apartment. The prioress went immediately to investigate. Marie Leszczynska's embarrassed lady-in-waiting answered the prioress's knock through a barely cracked door. Pushing her way in, Madame Descajeuls went up to the bed, pulled back the tightly shut curtains, but could discern no human form under the thick covers. Only when she raised the pillows did the head of a chagrined Marie Leszczynska become visible.

"What, Madame!" the dumfounded prioress cried, "It is your Majesty! But how is it possible your Majesty is here after our extern sisters assured me they saw your Majesty leave the monastery?"

The embarrassed, supine queen explained that wishing to hide that she was staying on in the monastery, she had asked one of her ladies resembling her to dress in her clothes and return to the chateau. It was she whom the extern sister had seen leaving, accompanied by one of the queen's ladies. How much the queen longed for a tranquil night's sleep, something she could never have at the chateau! Could the prioress not allow her the grace of a peaceful, uninterrupted night just this once?

Madame Descajeuls sympathized with the queen but reminded her that, since she had honored her with her confidence and had called her "friend," she would perhaps allow her to point out that sleeping in a monastery for Carmelite nuns was hardly a way to ensure the King's affection. Rather, she must return forthwith to the chateau to be near her husband. Thereupon the Queen of France and her lady-in-waiting were dispatched to the chateau by the prioress, under the escort of one of the extern sisters.

No doubt such familiarity between Madame Louise's royal mother and the monastery of Compiègne played a role in disposing the young princess's affections for Carmel. Already at age 14, her education at Fontrevault completed, Madame Louise had frequented the Compiègne Carmel with her mother and sisters and, we are told, had actually already contemplated becoming a Carmelite. It was therefore really not at all out of character that at age 33, when faced with the reality of her father's liaison with Madame du Barry, she is reported to have said, "Carmel for me, God for the king."

V

ONE MIGHT HAVE EXPECTED Madame Louise to choose the Carmel of Compiègne when she entered religion. Her father expressly forbade it, however, in his written royal consent. For, as in marriage, royal consent was necessary before a daughter of France could take such a step. The king, in his pained reply to her request, pointedly stipulated that he left her free to choose any Carmel in his kingdom except that of Compiègne, which he qualified as "impossible."

Louis XV's religious feelings seem to have dictated this word, "impossible." We are told he could not bear to think of the court amusing itself in a chateau opposite the very monastery where Louise-Marie of France consecrated her days and nights to penances to expiate those courtly pleasures. A man of exquisite sensitivity and breeding, Louis XV could hardly fail to grasp that his favorite daughter's oblation was being made expressly to save the soul of France's "most Christian" king. He, like any good father, knew himself unworthy of such a sacrifice.

Louis XV's deep piety was also shown on his deathbed where, though hideously expiring from smallpox, he still retained a great lucidity before the solemnity of the moment, even commanding that his written plea to his people for forgiveness for all his scandalous offenses be read out a second time, in a still louder voice, so that all standing outside the death chamber might hear that he died sorrowing for his past life. Having learned this detail of her father's death, Madame Louise wrote from Saint-Denis that she, knowing this, could not wish him alive again. Her sacrifice for France's "most Christian" king had not been in vain.

The first step toward this sacrifice had been taken very early one morning in 1770 when this youngest of the four unmarried princesses of France quietly stole away from the palace of Versailles, accompanied only by an equerry and her lady-in-waiting. No one had been advised of her departure. Even her two attendants that morning thought she was simply making the trip to Saint-Denis to hear Mass. Certainly the king knew nothing. Yet, as he waited for his letter of royal consent to bear its austere fruit, the prospect of his daughter's approaching oblation of body and soul to the Divine Majesty must have pricked his paternal conscience persistently.

Even in the beginning, as her plan had begun to take shape, Madame Louise, shy before her virginal love of Jesus Christ, had avoided approaching her father directly. She entrusted the Archbishop of Paris with announcing her "cruel" decision to the king. Nor was the king any less shy. After finally writing his letter of consent, he apparently also avoided all exchanges on this painful subject with his last child. Profoundly aware of his daughter's nobility and spiritual greatness in proposing herself as principal character in an awesome divine drama whereby grace is released through expiation, the king found his heart pierced. He was being called to repentance in spite of himself through his daughter's great supernatural love for him. Totally without defense before that great God in whom he sincerely believed despite his personal sins, the king could hardly avoid contemplating the fiery depths of divine charity that made his daughter's mysterious drama possible. He was both alone and naked before God. How dare he even attempt to speak of these things before the virginal purity of "Madame Last One?"

Madame Louise had taken care that her three older sisters, Mesdames Adélaïde, Victoire, and Sophie, be kept ignorant of her plans. They were informed neither of her departure nor even of her intentions, for the great secret of her burning love could not be shared. Their sisterly bereavement upon learning what lay behind their youngest sister's abrupt disappearance from Versailles was compounded by indignant, dumfounded shock that all three had been so rigidly excluded from any part in her extraordinary project. When informed that Madame Louise had left Versailles, her oldest sister, Madame Adélaïde, is reported even to have quipped indignantly, "And with whom?"

Only the chaplain of the Carmel of Saint-Denis had been privy to the princess's plans. Madame Louise took her encounter with this cleric as an act of divine providence. Indeed, she had barely received her father's letter stating that Compiègne was "impossible," when she learned that the Saint-Denis chaplain was in Versailles. Immediately she commanded his presence at the palace, wishing, she told him, to be informed concerning the "regularity" of his monastery, that is, its adherence to the faith of Rome and to Carmelite tradition. Satisfied by all she heard, Madame Louise swept aside his last objection when she revealed that she had in hand the king's written consent to enter Carmel. From what she had learned from him, Saint-Denis's monastery, poor though it might be, seemed the answer to her search. She commanded him, however, to say nothing beforehand to the prioress and community other than that she wished to hear Mass in their church on a certain morning. Only after that Mass was he to inform them of her desire. She would await their answer in the choir. If their response were favorable, she would immediately enter the cloister as a postulant, never again to return to Versailles.

On that morning, memorable in the history of the Carmels of France, all transpired as ordered. The community responded with boundless joy and tears of gratitude. Her Royal Highness's petition could only be viewed by the Saint-Denis nuns as the most glorious of answers to their recent novena begging heaven to spare them from having to close their monastery for lack of funds. Mysteriously, that novena did in fact coincide with the exact period in which the king was pondering his reply to his daughter's letter. Their prosperity would henceforth be assured by royal bounty, visible today to those visiting the remarkable municipal museum of Saint-Denis, installed in the still-handsome buildings of the Carmel of Madame Louise of France.

Admitted immediately, the royal postulant insisted upon undergoing the full rigors of the Rule, along with the other postulant trying her vocation. No exceptions were to be made, she insisted, either because she was Madame Louise of France or because of what, until her entry into Carmel, had been considered her rather delicate state of health. Even as a postulant, however, Madame Louise was honored, being immediately invited to choose a religious name for her fellow postulant. To underscore her total identity with her new family, she bestowed on this new sister in religion the name of her own oldest sister, "Adélaïde."

The scene in the parlor of the Saint-Denis Carmel when Madame Louise, undoubtedly with a touch of royal humor, had the opportunity to present to the formidable Madame Adélaïde that sister-postulant whom Madame Louise familiarly called "my sister Adélaïde," has unfortunately not been described for us. When the storm broke in 1789 Mesdames de France fled in a carriage to Rome where they resided until forced again to flee before Napoleon's armies, this time finding refuge in Trieste. Destined to end their days there, Madame Louise's sisters would never see France again.

vi

WITH THE BEATIFICATION in Rome in 1906 of "Teresa of Saint Augustine and her fifteen companions," the religious name taken by Madame Louise came to figure on the Roman calendar for July 17, subtly reaffirming the ties between her and the prioress of the martyrdom. For Madame Louise had made possible Madame Lidoine's Carmelite vocation and, out of gratitude, the prioress of the martyrdom took the religious name of the daughter of Louis XV as her own.

Only child of an employee of the Paris Observatory and his 41-year-old wife, Marie Madeleine Claudine Lidoine was baptized in her local parish of Saint Sulpice. She received every educational advantage available to young ladies of the time. Both her poetic gifts and her artistic talents were cultivated, as demonstrated by the numerous examples of her creative work still held by the Carmels of Compiègne and Sens. For the daughter of a modest Parisian employee such education was not only rare, but expensive. Therefore when this cherished only child expressed a desire to become a Carmelite, there was the troubling question of where to find a dowry. Surely it would have been hard for her fond parents to contemplate a girl of her education, for lack of a dowry, becoming a lay sister "of the white veil," serving the others!

This deserving case came to the attention of Madame Louise at Saint-Denis, who wished to meet the girl in question. Convinced of the religious vocation of this future mother of the martyrdom, the royal Mother Teresa of Saint Augustine begged the necessary dowry from her nephew's wife, the young Dauphine of France, Marie Antoinette of Austria, already known and loved for her generosity to the poor and needy. Paying this dowry for the protégé of her Carmelite aunt was therefore not at all a unique action for Marie Antoinette. Contrary to the popular legend of her heartlessness, she was often known to give from her privy purse when other funds were lacking.

No less startling is the intimate association of Marie Antoinette with the Carmel of Saint-Denis. From the moment she, as a 15-year-old Austrian archduchess, had been wed in Vienna by proxy to the dauphin of France, Marie Antoinette was aware of the Carmel of Saint-Denis, since Madame Louise's entry there had been announced only shortly before at Maria-Theresa's imperial court. Immediately after setting foot in France, the young archduchess went to pay her Catholic respects to her newly acquired Carmelite aunt at Saint-Denis even before reaching the court at Versailles.

The bonds formed at that time between the 15-year-old dauphine and her husband's aunt were to continue. When Madame Louise was clothed as a nun, Marie Antoinette was the only member of the family from Versailles who could bear to be present at what all the royal family considered an excruciatingly "cruel" ceremony. It was the beautiful young dauphine therefore who was invited by the monastery to place the novice's veil on her aunt's head.

This act was considered "heroic" by Madame Louise's three maiden sisters: Mesdames Adélaïde, Sophie, and Victoire. Their Christian fortitude, like that of the king, flinched at beholding royal status so lightly tossed upon the scales of eternity in public ceremony as Madame Louise found France's richest silks wanting when weighed against the rough serge of Carmel and the great white prophet's mantle of Elijah. That their nephew's beautiful and gracious young wife wished to be present on this painful occasion and provide a representative from the royal family touched them deeply. For a brief spell it even won considerable esteem at the Bourbon court for the ill-fated Austrian outsider. The inevitable intrigues and slanderous moral denigration they would later carry out against her, substantially contributing to her unpopularity as a foreigner, were, for the moment at least, in abeyance.

As a familiar visitor at the Saint-Denis monastery, Marie Antoinette enjoyed the privilege accorded to the descendants of the family of Saint Louis and their household: free entry into the cloister itself. The Saint-Denis Carmel recalls the occasion when the queen, accompanied by her young daughter, was eating in the refectory with the nuns and one of the older sisters commented on the young Madame Royale's fidelity to the Carmelite custom of brushing up and consuming her crumbs. When this older sister remarked that the little princess would make a good Carmelite, the queen is reported to have replied that should her royal daughter wish to become a Carmelite it would not displease her.

The legend of Marie Antoinette's saying "Let them eat cake!" when the poor lacked bread was propaganda of the winning side. We have seen the grotesque and monstrous lengths to which that side was prepared to go in blackening her character by the preposterous accusation that she and her pious virgin sister-in-law, Madame Elisabeth, were guilty of unnatural conduct with the seven-year-old Dauphin. On that occasion Marie Antoinette's noble character triumphed over her personal disgust in contemplating such a monstrous abyss. Utterly helpless and alone against her accusers, she turned in her shocked grief to those in the courtroom saying, "In regard to that, I appeal to all mothers who are here...."

The queen's condemnation can be linked to that of the Carmelites of Compiègne by ties other than those with Madame Louise, however. The courtroom in which all were tried was one where St. Louis himself used to sit, hard by the chapel he had constructed to house that crown of thorns he had brought back from his crusade. The saint-king's own hall thus provided the setting for Madame Lidoine's bold declaration, before the Revolutionary Tribunal, of the love in the hearts of all of them for Louis XVI and "his august family." More important, however, is the fact that the nuns undertook their act of consecration under Madame Lidoine only after the fall of the monarchy and the massacres of September 1792. Nor was this consecration offered for the restoration of the monarchy any more than for the anti-Christian government of France's new order. The peace they sought to restore was the "peace to men of good will" (Lk 2:14) announced at the birth of Jesus Christ.

vii

THE SECOND MARTYR Madame Louise directed toward the Carmel of Compiègne, Rose Crétien de Neuville, would live out the full mystery of the solemnity on which she had made her own religious profession in 1777: September 14, feast of the Exaltation of the Holy Cross. On that same day in 1792, 15 years later, she and her sisters were forced out of their stripped monastery by the revolutionary government.

Fifty-two at the time of her martyrdom, Madame Crétien de Neuville (in religion Sister Julie Louise of Jesus) provides us with an exceptionally poignant example of that perennial drama often played out when a family becomes aware that one of its members is answering the call to martyrdom. At the height of the Terror, her sister's daughter perished in childbirth along with her baby. Sister Julie of Jesus resisted all appeals to go console her sister in this double loss. Her noble mother accurately foresaw a tragic outcome to her Carmelite daughter's situation.

Madame Crétien de Neuville had married a first cousin, pushing aside her deep inner conviction that God was calling her to the religious life. But the young aristocrat had always felt an aversion for cloisters, nuns, and religious habits. The premature loss of her passionately adored husband brought her to a new awareness, however. Totally depressed and disconsolate from her husband's death, she shut herself away in her room in such deep mourning that her family feared for her sanity. Thanks to a kindly and distinguished cleric attached to her family, she finally emerged from this ordeal aware of a strange new dynamism within, born of a reaffirmation of her old conviction about God's will for her. At her request the cleric arranged for her to be received by Madame Louise at Saint-Denis.

The royal Carmelite believed the young widow did have a Carmelite vocation. She was prepared to receive her as a postulant at Saint-Denis until she learned of her sizable dowry. Thereupon Mother Teresa of St. Augustine directed her toward the Carmel of Compiègne, much more in need of funds than her own monastery with its royal patronage. Thus did Madame Louise unwittingly decide her protégé's vocation to martyrdom.

In a text written at the Conciergerie to celebrate their approaching sacrifice, and sung by the 16 martyrs on the eve of the execution, Madame Crétien de Neuville would urge the Compiègne community to climb the scaffold boldly and "give God the victory" by dying "as did Jesus our God / And our believing King."

As admirable and noble as these sentiments are, we know that for Madame Crétien de Neuville they were hers far more by faith than by feeling. Madame Philippe tells us that the natural inclination of this lucid, reluctant widow was no more to die on the guillotine than it had been to become a nun. The mere mention of the word "guillotine," we read, caused her "to shiver all over." Yet such instinctive reactions were heroically conquered as she doggedly clung to what she believed to be her double vocation of nun and martyr. She was convinced that it was for this that she had come into the world.

In the three days between their incarceration in the Conciergerie on the evening of July 13 and the celebration of the feast of Our Lady of Mount Carmel on the evening of July 16, Madame Crétien de Neuville overcame seemingly insuperable difficulties to compose her usual text for the community's patronal festival. Though writing materials were forbidden in the Conciergerie, by some miracle a scrap of paper was found and she managed to obtain from a kindly prisoner-assistant to the jailer, Denis Blot, some bits of charred wood with which to trace on that precious sheet the words of five stanzas exalting their martyrdom. In Madame Crétien de Neuville's last text, set to the martial tune of the bloodthirsty *La Marseillaise*, the nuns sang gaily, and in the purest tradition of Carmel, of abandoning themselves to God on the guillotine.

Let our hearts be giv'n to joyfulness
The day of glory now is here!
Let us banish all of our weakness,
We can see that the cross now is near! (repeat)
Let's prepare ourselves for the victory!
Let us each as a conqueror go forth!
Under the cross, God's great banner,
Let's all run, let's all fly toward glory!
Let our ardor be enflamed!
Let's give our bodies in his Name!
Let's climb, let's climb, the scaffold high!
We'll give God the victory!

Happiness that's ever beckoning
To all the Catholics of France
To take up the path of the martyrs
Where many another's advanced! (repeat)
The martyrs go off to their passion
As did Jesus, followed by our king.
Our faith as Christians let us bring,
God's righteousness let us adore!
So let the priest with zeal,
And all believers seal,
Their faith, their faith, with all their blood,
In a God who like them died.

Great God who seest all my weaknesses
Although I'm eager, still I fear.
Confidently ardor now guides me,
O do thou lend thine aid and be near! (repeat)
I can't hide from thine eyes my poor heart,
Thinking that it's with death I must pay.
Be thou my comfort, be my stay,

And I'll say, come, let's make our start!
Hasten now the sacrifice!
Thou canst change me in a trice!
O Lord, O Lord, with no delay,
To my heart give joy today.

Holy Virgin, our example.
Of martyrs all the august Queen.
Do thou deign to sustain our great ardor
Cleanse our desires, make us all pure and clean! (repeat)
Still protect sweet France, our dear country
From heaven's heights lend us all now thine aid
Let us all feel here in these places
The effects of all of thy graces.
We, thine own, await thy power;
Submit, obey thee in this hour.
We'll die as did Jesus our God,
And our believing King!

Behold O divine Mary
The holy zeal of us, thine own.
Since it's God who us life has given
We accept this death as our own. (repeat)
Reveal thyself as our tender mother,
And present us all to Jesus Christ
That, given life by His Spirit
We may, in taking leave of life:
With the fire of his great love
Join with all the saints above,
And sing, and sing, on heaven's shore,
All his goodness evermore!

A final fragment by Madame Crétien de Neuville, written as she tried to parry the pleas of her mother and sister, has also come down to us. It movingly confirms Madame Louise of France's judgment 17 years earlier about the religious vocation of this young, disconsolate, and childless widow who had asked to be received at Saint-Denis.

> We are victims of our century and we must sacrifice ourselves that it be reconciled to God. An eternity of happiness awaits me. Let us hasten then, let us run toward that end and suffer willingly during the brief moments of this life. The storm rages today, but tomorrow we shall reach the harbor.

We see therefore that the influence of a princess of the House of France who had offered herself as a living oblation was joined by strong ties to the events leading to the martyrdom at the Place de la Nation on July 17, 1794. We shall also see that it was that princess's protégé and namesake who would be solely responsible for the idea of a community oblation, as well as the act of holocaust.

For, within the divine economy, it was given Madame Louise of France to direct Marie Madeleine Claudine Lidoine to the Carmel of Compiègne. There, inspired by what she discerned as a prophecy discovered in a very strange text dating from a century before, the protégé of the Carmelite daughter of the King of France was to become the true mother of the martyrdom of the 16 Carmelites of Compiègne. The mystery of their vocation was, indeed, to be made incarnate in her.

3

Madame Lidoine and the Apostolic Call to Follow the Lamb

(i) Madame Lidoine discovers the text of the "mystic dream." (ii) The apostolic call "to follow the Lamb"; its symbolism. (iii) Madame Lidoine's attraction to the call; what is revealed by her transcriptions in Compiègne's *Foundations.* (iv) Madame Philippe and the mystic dream; improbability of an oral tradition of martyrdom; Madame Lidoine its true mother. (v) The mystic dream shared with the community; reflections on its significance; inauguration of the guillotine; Madame Philippe and Madame Lidoine's transcriptions. (vi) Vocation, mystic dream, and death of Sister Elisabeth Baptiste; her mother's role; her devotion to the *Te Deum* and the singing of the *Te Deum* at the guillotine. (vii) How Madame Lidoine's Teresian formation influenced her response to the apostolic call.

IT WAS APPARENTLY some time after she was elected prioress in 1786 at age 34 that Mother Teresa of Saint Augustine became aware of a document in her monastery's archives dating from the previous century. In a tiny phrase found in this document, she thought she sensed a sort of prophetic call addressed to her community. Her response to that call lies at the heart of the mystery of the vocation of the Carmelites of Compiègne.

The little phrase is found in the narration of a strange "mystic dream" experienced in 1693 by a partially paralyzed young woman of 29 who, for the previous 15 years, had been a paying guest, or "benefactress," of the Compiègne Carmel. Immediately after experiencing this dream the disabled sister was clothed as a novice. The following year, 1694, exactly a century before the martyrdom, she was admitted to final vows.

This unusual Carmelite was Sister Marie Elisabeth Baptiste (Framery de Turpignant) who followed the example of her widowed mother, already a professed nun in that monastery. Given the rigors of the Carmelite Rule, the young woman's physical infirmities would normally have excluded her from final vows. During her 15 years as a paying guest, however, the nuns had come to esteem her unfailing accuracy in discerning, from the moment a postulant arrived, whether she would become a nun or leave. In any case, the prioress took Sister Elisabeth Baptiste's "mystic dream" as the confirmation of a sign she believed she had herself received concerning the admissibility of the partially paralyzed "benefactress" to life vows.

In the mystic dream Sister Elisabeth Baptiste had seen her bloody, scourged Divine Bridegroom enter her cell, accompanied by four women, each a direct historic link between him and the Compiègne monastery. First there was his Virgin Mother who, as Our Lady of Mount Carmel, was patroness of their order. Next came St. Teresa of Avila, its foundress. In third place was the great French prioress of the first monastery, Mother Madeleine of Saint Joseph. Finally there came Mother Madeleine of the Annunciation, late of their own monastery. These four women thus formed a specifically Carmelite escort for the suffering Christ.

The infirm young woman, however, fearing a demonic illusion, repeatedly sprinkled holy water and signed the cross. Though this had no effect on the apparition, she still hesitated to speak until the Divine Bridegroom spoke to her. He said he was happy she was cautious about illusions but that she must not fear. It was truly he who had come to give her a kiss and claim her as his chaste spouse. Moreover, since all things are shared between spouses, he wished that she share with him the incessant sufferings of his life on earth.

> You are now my true spouse: my interests are yours; yours are mine. Be zealous for the increase of my honor and glory. Delight in them as in something belonging to you. By everything you are able to do, strive to increase this honor and glory. I know that you cannot do much, but never miss an opportunity to do all you can.

Sister Elisabeth Baptiste then made her vows of chastity and obedience directly to him. Next, he exacted from her the promise never to leave that monastery: His will was that she become a professed nun there in a year's time. To that end, she was to instruct the nuns that he wished her to be clothed immediately in the novice's habit. Before the end of the coming year she was to dispose of all possessions she had received at her mother's entry into Carmel 15 years before. Thereby would she be ready a year later, in 1694, to make the final vow of poverty and become his chaste bride.

The fateful little phrase that so resounded in Madame Lidoine's heart, however, came only in the second part of the dream in which Sister Elisabeth Baptiste found herself transported out of her cell and into the corridor with her companions. They too had been roused from their cells and were "completely encircled with glory as though they were suns." She next perceived that they had all been "transported into a great place that seemed to me to be paradise, but was not, however."

> There I saw the glory that the nuns of this convent would have and which appeared very great and exalted to me. I saw an angel placing the members of the whole community. What surprised me was to see that many of the young ones were more elevated in glory than many of the older ones. I saw there several sisters I did not know, but whom I recognized afterward. It seemed to me that there was a Lamb at a higher level, who looked

> at us all very lovingly. I immediately felt I was his and, after a long time, he looked at me with eyes brimming with love. He seemed to be giving me little caresses, and I saw him do as much for all the community. As the angel was placing us I noted that he had had two or three sisters, one of whom I recognized, pass over to the other side, and I greatly feared being of their number, since I understood perfectly that they were not to follow the Lamb, and I so wanted to follow him. These two or three sisters he directed to another place, in another part of heaven. As I'd not yet been placed I strongly feared being one of them. And in that very same instant I felt myself transported with the community clothed in a white mantle and a great black veil that I did not have before and that delighted me.

Following this, Sister Elisabeth-Baptiste found herself back in her cell discussing her vocation with her Bridegroom.

ii

Although martyrdom is not even hinted at in this dream, Madame Lidoine was nonetheless struck that the infirm nun had seen the whole community called "to follow the Lamb"—with only two or three exceptions. Caught in the upheaval of the end of the eighteenth century, Madame Lidoine wondered if it might conceivably be their own community the angel had so mysteriously designated. An apostolic call to share more intimately, through their own martyrdom, in the immolation of the supreme "Lamb of God," Jesus Christ, their Divine Bridegroom, could certainly be discerned in such an invitation.

Had the last great prophet of Israel, John the Baptist, of whom no prophet born of woman was greater (Lk 7:28), not proclaimed Jesus Christ as the "Lamb of God who takes away the sin of the world" (Jn 1:29) immediately after baptizing him? Subsequently crucified by Roman executioners and lifted up on the cross that the whole world might be drawn to him (Jn 12:32), the Creator of heaven and earth (Col 1:6) had thereby been publicly manifested as the immolated Lamb of God.

Afire for her Divine Lover, Madame Lidoine's great heart could not remain indifferent to such thoughts. Nor could she be indifferent to the fact that John the Baptist's reference to the Lamb of God had been retained by yet another John, the fourth evangelist, that beloved disciple who had leaned on Jesus' breast at the Last Supper, he to whom the Virgin Mother had been confided. He alone among the 12 apostles had stood by to the very end of the public immolation of the Lamb of God. He alone had borne witness that the heart of incarnate God had been pierced by a Roman spear. Taking up that same symbolism of the Lamb in later life in his Book of Revelation, the beloved disciple, in mystic language, announced Jesus Christ as "the Lamb slain from the foundation of the world" (Rev 13:8) and worthy to reign forever as "King of kings" and "Lord of lords" (Rev 19:16).

The century-old dream would seem therefore to have fascinated Madame Lidoine particularly because of its mention of Judaism's most sacred mystic symbol inherited by Christianity: the Passover Lamb. Just as the Hebrews associated their escape from the angel of death in Egypt with the sprinkled blood of the slain Passover lamb, so did Christians associate the resurrection of Jesus Christ with his blood poured out on Calvary. The Christian faith indeed professes that the resurrection of Jesus Christ from the dead had manifested the power of his blood to destroy the hold of death over the human race, for the blood of Jesus Christ gives life to those destined for death, just as the blood of the Passover lamb had done for the Hebrews in Egypt. Indeed, Jesus Christ is not only each Christian's own personal Passover Lamb—"Christ our passover is sacrificed for us" (1 Cor 5:7), St. Paul affirms—but also the true and universal Passover lamb that "takes away the sin of the world" (Jn 1:29), as first articulated by St. John the Baptist.

The mystery of what was implied by the immolation and resurrection of Jesus Christ thus seems to have enflamed the ardent soul of Madame Lidoine with a fire of mystic love. Recalling that according to the beloved John's Gospel, her Divine Bridegroom had actually been immolated at an hour when the Passover lambs were being ritually slaughtered at the temple in Jerusalem and that his innocent blood simultaneously poured out before God with theirs, she grasped that the ancient symbolism of the immolated Passover lamb had thus once and for all been forever fulfilled for the cosmos. Her own beloved Divine Bridegroom, the Lamb of God that "takes away the sin of the world" had forever annulled the sting of death for all who believe in him.

iii

IN THE MIDST OF THE CHAOS into which France had been plunged—and announced in 1787 by her own patroness, Madame Louise, so shortly before her death—Mother Teresa of Saint Augustine found her generous heart drawn to the mystic symbolism of the Lamb as by a magnet. We cannot date her fascination with the mystic dream, however, earlier than April 8, 1792, the date of Easter that year. Madame Philippe specifies that it was as they celebrated the high feast of the Lamb's victory over death, just five months before their expulsion from their monastery, that Mother Lidoine first mentioned to her community the dream with its apostolic call "to follow the Lamb."

This would tend to prove that the idea of a community martyrdom came to Mother Lidoine only gradually and well after 1786 when she was first elected prioress. What we still read in her own hand in Volume 8 of the nine-volume set entitled *Foundations,* coming from the former monastery, further confirms this. Compiègne's set of *Foundations* groups, in nine leather-bound volumes, various handwritten manuscripts recounting, in strict chronological order, the foundation of every Discalced Carmelite monastery in France.

At the end of the eighteenth century the first Carmel of France had set an example in compiling the first set of *Foundations,* thanks to a sister in that monastery endowed with a gift for quick transcription. She, beginning with the foundation of her own community in Paris in 1604 with Mother Anne of Jesus as prioress, had transcribed, single-handed, the chronicle of the foundation of every discalced Carmelite monastery in France.

This admirable mid-eighteenth-century contribution to French Carmelite history was thereafter much imitated. Other Carmels were eager to possess their own set of *Foundations,* even though lacking such a gifted scribe to carry out the work. As pointed out at the beginning of the twentieth century by Abbé Eugène Griselle,[1] various members of the Compiègne community shared the tedious task. Abbé Griselle's identification of the handwriting of a number of the martyrs throughout the nine volumes of Compiègne's *Foundations* indicates in fact that their transcriptions were made fairly late at Compiègne, and certainly not prior to the decade immediately preceding the 1792 expulsion. In recovering these nine volumes upon her return to Compiègne in

---

[1] Regarding Abbé Griselle, see Bruno de Jésus-Marie, *Le Sang du Carmel ou la véritable passion des seize carmélites de Compiègne* (Paris: Editions du Cerf, 1992; Paris: Plon, 1954), p. vii. His papers, consulted by the author, are in the archives of the Carmel of Sens.

the spring of 1795, Madame Philippe had therefore had more than a mere historical interest in them: they were a tangible relic prepared by her martyred sisters during her own days in the now-extinct community.

That these transcriptions were actually carried out only after Madame Lidoine succeeded Madame de Croissy as prioress in 1786 is further confirmed by what we read in Volume 8 of Compiègne's set of *Foundations.* Indeed, it is Madame Lidoine herself and not Madame de Croissy, we discover, who transcribed the chronicle of Compiègne, France's fifty-third foundation. Madame Lidoine, moreover, displays the free hand of a prioress in extending Compiègne's chronicle well beyond the account of its foundation in 1641. Added material follows, largely in the form of necrological notices of certain outstanding sisters. Such notices, called "circular letters," describe a deceased sister's virtues and are dispatched to other monasteries to request that the order's customary prayers be offered for her. Madame Lidoine chose, edited, and transcribed these circular letters in strict chronological sequence according to death dates.

Chronology was broken, however, in the last 44 pages Madame Lidoine copied out. They consist of two circular letters, plus a text giving the mystic dream. All, however, are older than the date of the 1723 circular letter preceding them. The circular letter for Sister Elisabeth Baptiste's mother, Sister Marie-Elisabeth of the Passion (de Turpignant), who, after 33 years of profession, died at 74 years of age in 1711, is 12 years older than that preceding 1723 letter. The circular letter for Sister Elisabeth Baptiste herself, who died in 1720 at age 56 after 26 years of profession, is three years older. The text giving the mystic dream, written down sometime after the 1693 dream, but prior to her death in 1720, is older still.

These 44 pages all indicate therefore that the definitive association Madame Lidoine made between Sister Elisabeth

Baptiste's mystic dream and her own community's martyrdom came about not only fairly late, but also after she had already finished all her other transcriptions in the Compiègne chronicle.

iv

MADAME PHILIPPE'S ONE REFERENCE to the mystic dream states merely that community martyrdom was discussed at Easter of 1792, inspired by the dream of an unnamed person she erroneously terms a "lay sister." Madame Lidoine's inner life had thus, we know, already begun to reverberate in response to the phrase, "follow the Lamb," at some date prior to April 8, 1792.

Father Bruno de Jésus-Marie suggests in *Le Sang du Carmel*[2] that the 1693 mystic dream had, over the past century, established the idea of a community martyrdom as part of a living, oral tradition within the Compiègne monastery. The discussion of it at Easter of 1792, he believed, only reaffirmed the existence of this oral tradition. A careful reading of Marie of the Incarnation's manuscripts excludes any such possibility. The chief guardians of such a tradition would have been the two most senior nuns, Mesdames Piedcourt and Thouret, both of whom had celebrated their "jubilee" of 50 years of profession. Yet they were the first to be shocked and scandalized by Madame Lidoine's suggestion of a community act of consecration for holocaust. Such instantaneous negative reaction not just from one, but from both jubilarians in the community substantially confirms the absence of any familiar, century-old oral tradition preparing the Carmelites for collective martyrdom.

---

[2] See note 1 of this chapter. We cannot overstate what we owe to the work of this great Carmelite scholar.

We must therefore conclude that the idea of a group oblation, associated with the apostolic call to "follow the Lamb," was born from Madame Lidoine's very personal reaction alone. From the depths of an intense inner life, steeped in the writings of St. Teresa of Avila, this association must have surged up, involuntarily, either at her initial discovery of the text of the dream or during some subsequent reading of it. Whatever the case, at some point prior to April 8, 1792, Mother Teresa of Saint-Augustine had not only read that text, but had been sufficiently inspired by its prophetic potential to make a conscious decision to abandon the chronological order of Compiègne's chronicle in order to append her final 44 pages. Thereafter, she wrote no more. If community martyrdom were indeed to crown their vocation, those three appended texts, dating from the century before, would bear witness to the origins of her own premonitions regarding the call to "follow the Lamb." It would be for her divine Bridegroom alone to confirm or reject her intuition.

V

WHETHER THE TEXT of Sister Elisabeth Baptiste's dream was read by Madame Lidoine herself to her community, or whether she had it read in chapter or in the refectory, we cannot say. We do know, however, that certain sisters at Easter of 1792 immediately took the reference to "two or three" nuns being set aside as referring to widows since, in the Book of Revelation, virgins only are called "to follow the Lamb wherever he goes" (Rev 14:4).

If that reference had in fact been to the community's widows—which, in the end, it proved not to be—Sister Elisabeth Baptiste's dream would have proven remarkably accurate. At Easter of 1792 only three widows had ever been professed as Carmelites of Compiègne. First, from the previous century, was Madame Hamel, Duchess of Lincourt, lady-in-waiting to Anne of Austria and known for her great beauty. She had become a white-veiled lay sister at 43 years of age, following the death of her husband, much to the edification of the queen and court of Louis XIV.

Next there came Sister Elisabeth Baptiste's own mother. Finally, the community's third and last widow was the senior protégé of Madame Louise of France, Madame Crétien de Neuville, martyr. As she was not yet born in 1693, this might even be said to account for Sister Elisabeth Baptiste's hesitancy between "two" and "three" as the number excluded. In any case, Madame Crétien de Neuville not only inspired her sisters through her parody of *La Marseillaise* to "climb the scaffold high," and "give God the victory," but herself also climbed the scaffold.

Thus, in retrospect, we can say that the "two or three" designated as "not to follow the Lamb" had nothing whatsoever to do with their being widows. Rather would this detail be fulfilled by our historian, Madame Philippe, along with Mesdames Legros and Jourdain, all three of whom were absent when the community was arrested in June of 1794. This, of course, was something that remained unforeseeable by Madame Lidoine at Easter in 1792 when she first suggested that "follow the Lamb" perhaps implied a community martyrdom.

Madame Philippe's reference to the mystic dream gives us very few details about the Easter discussion. She does, however, state that Madame Pelras, her contemporary in the novice class, was aware of Madame Hamel de Lincourt's vocation the previous century. Her contemporary thus remarked to Madame Philippe that she could not possibly see how "two or three" widows could be excluded since their community had only had one widow in its entire history.

This remark makes clear that what Madame Lidoine shared with her community was strictly limited to the text of Sister Elisabeth-Baptiste's dream, since both her circular letter and that of her mother speak plainly of the mother's widowed status. Madame Philippe further confirms her own ignorance of the mother's vocation when she, not realizing that Madame Pelras was referring to Madame de Lincourt, pointedly asked her if she were referring to Madame Crétien de Neuville. Madame Pelras was so startled by the idea that Sister Julie Louise of Jesus had been married that she refused to believe it until the prioress confirmed it.

These details from Easter of 1792 were due to Carmelite "licenses" which, at Easter and Christmas, liberate the nuns from their usual obligatory silence, allowing them free interchanges between sisters. In this instance they obviously dwelt on mass martyrdom and widows in the community.

Could such free exchanges that Easter also have led any of the sisters to speculate about the new and much-touted "humanitarian" machine for execution inaugurated that very month in Paris at the Place de Grève, and known as "the guillotine"? Given the prioress's idea that collective martyrdom might have been prophesied for them, certain of the more imaginative nuns may well have reflected upon what the nature of instantaneous death by the new machine's triangular blade might be. In any case, more than three decades later Madame Philippe still recalled that certain of them had actually expressed delight in the idea of community martyrdom, confirming once again that, far from being the century-old tradition suggested by Father Bruno, mass martyrdom proved something of a novelty at Easter of 1792.

Madame Philippe never once refers to Madame Lidoine's violation of chronology in appending her final 44 pages. She does speak, however, of Madame Lidoine's foresight in making it possible for her to complete Compiègne's Chronicle in Volume 8 of the *Foundations* by her own "Relation of the Martyrdom...." For Madame Lidoine, having transcribed the dream and death of Sister Elisabeth-Baptiste, did set aside the 51 blank pages following. At the top of each of those pages she carefully inscribed the title, "Compiègne," thereby reserving them for the continuation of the Compiègne chronicle by her own, or another hand.

It was the desire to fill up these 51 pages so purposely left by Madame Lidoine that prompted Abbé Villecourt, when he was named superior of the Carmel of Sens in 1832, to suggest to Madame Philippe that she write her own "Relation of the Martyrdom...." Respectfully leaving blank the page separating Madame Lidoine's last page from the first page of her own text, Madame Philippe did fill up the remaining 50 pages. But, as we have observed, she failed to take any note at all of the impact of the story of Sister Elisabeth Baptiste and her mother upon the mystery of the martyrdom envisaged by Mother Teresa of St. Augustine.

vi

IN ORDER TO GRASP why this story so moved Madame Lidoine, a quick résumé of the contents of those 44 appended pages is essential at this point. We learn from these pages that Sister Elisabeth Baptiste's partial paralysis had come upon her as a very young girl, leaving both limbs on one side of her body shortened and the hand completely useless. At age seven she had been placed with local Ursulines where she still was, seven years later, when her father died. Her mother, forced to marry when all she had wanted out of life was to be a Carmelite, now found herself free at last. She thus provided for her son, as also for her daughter, who continued with the Ursulines, before withdrawing to the Carmel of Compiègne, some distance from where she left her children. In severing her ties with the world, she said she wished to make a "total" sacrifice of all natural affections.

The 14-year-old girl, missing her mother, arranged to be transported to Compiègne, where the older nuns insisted she remain as a "benefactress" in their own monastery rather than return to the Ursulines. Only her mother objected, saying that in coming to Compiègne from so far away to make her sacrifice, she had no intention of finding there again what she had left behind. She consented only on condition that she not be required to manifest her maternal nature in any way: she would treat her infirm daughter like any other paying guest.

That Madame Lidoine included the account of the mother's vocation is particularly revealing of her own great heart. Herself an only child, born to a 41-year-old mother, she had basked in maternal affection, evident to the end in her mother's letters to her. She was therefore all the more keenly attuned to the truly supernatural solitude in which Sister Elisabeth Baptiste was obliged to live and die within the cloister. Deprived of even the smallest expression of maternal affection, bereft of any natural tenderness or human solicitude, the handicapped Sister Elisabeth Baptiste had had only Jesus Christ to love.

Madame Lidoine's transcription reveals that Sister Elisabeth Baptiste had a particular devotion to the *Te Deum.* Though in Western Christendom this hymn is often associated with solemn thanksgivings or military victories, its text—by tradition first sung by St. Ambrose, Bishop of Milan, as he baptized St. Augustine of Hippo—is not at all centered on earthly things. Rather it is an unequivocal and uncompromisingly orthodox proclamation of Christianity's most basic dogmas of the Trinity and of the Incarnation of God in Jesus Christ. Only such essential truths as these, it seems, were great enough to gladden the deprived heart of Sister Elisabeth Baptiste in her austere situation. Madame Lidoine also records, as one of the last details she transcribed, that Sister Elisabeth Baptiste, as she was dying, actually requested that her sisters sing the *Te Deum* for her.

On the evening of July 17, 1794, as the tumbrels bearing the 40 condemned emerged from the rue du Faubourg Saint-Antoine to enter the Place of the Throne (today, Place de la Nation), is it possible that this detail of Sister Elisabeth Baptiste's last hour passed through Madame Lidoine's mind as she herself intoned the first line of the *Te Deum?*

vii

WHATEVER MAY HAVE BEEN Sister Elisabeth Baptiste's personal devotion to the *Te Deum,* or whatever may have been Madame Lidoine's recollection of that fact, the defiant, public affirmation of those lines was in perfect accord with that hymn's frequent use in Carmel to mark great moments in the life of the community. Nor should we forget that, prior to discovering the text of Sister Elisabeth Baptiste's mystic dream, Madame Lidoine was already profoundly imbued with Carmel's deep missionary tradition and, through her meditations on the writings of Saint Teresa of Avila, had long prepared herself for an apostolic call such as that touching one to "follow the Lamb."

Their holy Mother Foundress had revealed her goal in the very first chapters of *The Way of Perfection.* Her desire was to gather around herself a few sisters united in prayer, solitude, and mutual love whose one purpose in life would be to support Christ and his church. And, very particularly, the saint had in mind the Church of France, rent asunder by religious wars and the Protestant Reformation.

In documents going back to 1780 we learn that it was particularly these Teresian intentions that were the frequent subject of Mother Teresa of Saint Augustine's meditations. Finding herself within the historical and ecclesiastical context of France at the end of the eighteenth century, she therefore grasped the necessity not only of holding her community together, but also of nurturing within it the flame of love for the Divine Bridegroom as the immolated Lamb of God.

Guided by the Spirit of God, Madame Lidoine had thus long prepared herself for her final role as mother of the martyrdom. In all that was happening around her she discovered a burning, intimate significance that might well have escaped another. The apostolic call in the mystic dream therefore insistently reverberated in her Carmelite soul. Moreover, in the light of the Holy Spirit, all those signs seemed to converge. Whether her grasp of St. Teresa's purpose in founding her reform in the sixteenth century, or her assessment of the religious and social chaos of eighteenth-century French society in which she found herself, or the clear and truly apostolic call from the century before to "follow the Lamb," all seemed to point toward a concerted effort by her and her community to respond to that call.

As we shall see, it would be in those unprecedented weeks following the fall of the Christian monarchy and the butchery of the massacres of September 1792 that Mother Teresa of Saint Augustine, illumined by the Spirit of God, would finally be led to propose an act of holocaust to her community.

4

The Last Prioress and the Last Novice Class

(i) Madame Lidoine and MADAME DE CROISSY (Mother Henriette of Jesus), novice mistress; MADAME BRIDEAU (Sister Saint Louis), subprioress. (ii) The "free" election of January 11, 1791; MADAME BRARD (Sister Euphrasia of the Immaculate Conception); her ties with Marie Leszczynska; her cousin, Mulot de la Ménardière. (iii) Madame Brard against Madame Lidoine; her conversion; her relic left to the foundress of the convent of "Les Oiseaux." (iv) Madame de Croissy's novice class; MADAME PELRAS (Sister Henriette of the Divine Providence); her unusual family's strength of character. (v) The enigma of Madame Philippe's profession; the post-expulsion enigma. (vi) Madame Lidoine's concern for MADAME VEROLOT (Sister St. Francis Xavier); the other two lay sisters: MADAME ROUSSEL (Sister Marie of the Holy Spirit) and MADAME DUFOUR (Sister St. Martha); Madame Verolot's faith. (vii) SISTER CONSTANCE (Marie Geneviève Meunier); impossibility of her profession. (viii) Struggle with her family; her fear of the guillotine.

According to Carmelite *Constitutions,* a prioress's initial three-year term may be renewed for one additional three-year term only. After six years the incumbent ordinarily steps down. Nonetheless, in 1786 Madame de Croissy had served not six, but seven and a half years before being replaced by Madame Lidoine. In turn, Madame Lidoine then served an uninterrupted total of eight years. Both of these exceptions were the result of unusual external factors.

In 1779, exactly ten years before the outbreak of the Revolution, Marie-Françoise de Croissy had been elected prioress of Compiègne's Carmel at only 34 years of age. Reelected unanimously in 1782, her second term was unavoidably prolonged. For 18 months the bishop of Sées, whose presence was essential for an election, delayed his visitation.

Since the community had proven united in re-electing its young Prioress at its 1782 election, the bishop's apparent confidence in Madame de Croissy's gifts seemed well placed. Great-niece of Louis XIV's minister, "the great" Colbert, Madame de Croissy had already spent more than half her life as a Carmelite, outranking in seniority certain Sisters older than herself. Madame Philippe attests, moreover, that as Mother Henriette of Jesus she won all hearts by her natural gentleness and affection, as might a real mother.

Disposed from birth for the affairs of God, Mother Henriette of Jesus had been escorted to the Compiègne Carmel at age 16 by the Bishop of Amiens, Monseigneur de la Mothe d'Orléans, renowned for his sanctity. Because of her age and delicate appearance, however, she was refused immediate entry by Madame Descajeuls, Marie Leszczynska's prioress-friend. The venerable bishop's argument that this unusual and pious girl was not only "the friend of God" but "an angel in human form" availed nothing. Madame Descajeuls sent the 16-year-old home to her mother in Amiens to await the passing of another year. Clothed in the novice's habit in 1763, the young Sister Henriette of Jesus made her profession in 1764. On that occasion the queen herself was invited by Madame Descajeuls to place the veil on her head. Marie Leszczynska praised the young nun's wisdom in opting for the rough mantle of the prophet Elijah over the rich trappings of the court, for the sanctity of the cloister over the vanity of the world.

When Madame de Croissy was finally replaced by Madame Lidoine in 1786, the community had again elected a 34-year-old. The new prioress's wisdom and prudence were immediately demonstrated in naming Mother de Croissy as her novice mistress. Indeed, in spite of the eight years separating them, the two women had much in common. Both wrote verses and both displayed considerable artistic talent in works found today at the Carmels of Compiègne and Sens. As the younger prioress strove over the next eight years to hold the community together and pilot it toward its apostolic vocation across the uncharted, troubled waters of revolutionary upheavals, the steadying support of the popular and experienced past prioress could only have proven a positive contribution.

The community elected as subprioress in 1782 a nun a year older than Madame Lidoine, Marie Anne Françoise Brideau, in religion Sister Saint-Louis, born near the Swiss border in Belfort. Her father, a professional soldier, had probably been stationed in Compiègne at some point in his career since we know that Madame Brideau's godfather, a king's barracks' quartermaster, financed his goddaughter's schooling in Compiègne at the Convent of the Visitation. This convent became a prison during the Terror. Prior to being dispatched to Paris for trial, Madame Brideau and her 15 sisters would all be incarcerated there from June 22 until July 12, 1794.

Madame Philippe mentions Madame Brideau's attachment to the rubrics to assure proper liturgical order, the particular responsibility of a subprioress. We also know that on their last afternoon, during the long wait at the Conciergerie for the 40 condemned to be transferred to the executioner, it was Madame Brideau who produced a fur wrap which, after consultation with Madame Lidoine, was bartered for a cup of chocolate for each of the 16 martyrs. Nonetheless, the role of this discreet right hand of Madame Lidoine remains fairly obscure.

ii

COMPLETING HER FIRST TERM as prioress in the tumultuous year of 1789, Madame Lidoine was immediately reelected. The July 14 storming of the Bastille that year led almost immediately to the "provisional suspension" of all religious vows on October 28, swiftly followed by the confiscation of all church property on November 2.

It was a little over a year later, however, on January 11, 1791, that local government officials, wishing to assure that those continuing in the religious life had chosen their superior and bursar in a "free" vote, forced their way into the cloister of the Compiègne Carmel. Madame Philippe has preserved certain details of this government-imposed election in which Madame Lidoine was unanimously confirmed by the community in her position as prioress.

In spite of this unanimous vote, there is evidence that one of the older choir sisters strongly resented Madame Lidoine. Madame Brard, in religion Sister Euphrasia of the Immaculate Conception, then 50 years of age, seems to have felt her gifts had been ignored for too long by her community. With the election of the young Mother Lidoine, yet another who had worn the veil far fewer years than herself had been installed as superior.

Whatever Sister Euphrasia's inner struggle may have been, all we read of her indicates she possessed an undeniable exterior charm. Her quick and ready conversation enlivened community recreations, fulfilling St. Teresa's admonition that nuns should use what talents God gives them to make life pleasant for those living around them. She had entered the Compiègne Carmel in 1756 at age 20. Her wit and easy humor attracted the favor of Marie Leszczynska, who referred to Sister Euphrasia as "my so lovable philosopher nun." As Madame Philippe tells us, however, there was one occasion when the queen's affability was sharply tested by this quick-witted Carmelite.

One evening after the royal visitor had danced a round with the community at recreation, Sister Euphrasia, hoping to amuse the queen, risked an innocent play on words. Indicating Sister Isabelle, to whom a royal hand had been given in the round, she whispered to Marie Leszczynska that that sister was a "rope dancer" (*danseuse sur la corde*). The queen, taking the play on words very seriously, was deeply offended. That a circus acrobat might become a Carmelite shocked her. She might herself even have placed the veil on such a head, she observed, horror-struck. Marie Leszczynska said she had rather not be told such things, since all she wanted to see there were her "good friends, the Carmelites."

A chagrined Sister Euphrasia hastened to explain that Sister Isabelle was a "rope dancer" not because of her past, but only by virtue of dancing while wearing rope-soled sandals—the Carmelite *alpargatas.* Regal calm was restored as recreation ended. The queen forgave her "so lovable philosopher nun" with a kiss, but charged her in the future not to be found wanting in her philosophy.

Such lack of prudence in Madame Brard's character did not always have such a happy ending. Her too-free exchange of correspondence with a cousin in Compiègne had tragic consequences. Named Mulot, but grandly calling himself "Mulot de la Ménardière," her cousin's own lack of prudence unfortunately equalled her own. Twice he spoke unfavorably of the Revolution in letters to her. Just prior to the nuns' arrest, Compiègne's Revolutionary Surveillance Committee seized the monastery's correspondence, and noted Mulot's anti-revolutionary sentiments in the two letters. He was arrested and imprisoned at the Convent of the Visitation with the nuns. Even though married, he was accused of being a non-juring priest who, with the Carmelites, had organized anti-revolutionary assemblies in his home. Transferred to Paris and tried with them, he was found guilty of political crimes against the French people and executed with them as the Carmelites' refractory priest.

As absurd as it was to condemn Mulot as a priest associated with the Carmelites, Compiègne's long-time residents discerned a curious and bitter irony in this event. They still recalled a scandalous incident of Mulot's youth when a group of his drinking friends had dressed up as Carmelite nuns as a public prank. On that occasion Mulot had masqueraded as their priest, farcically hearing their preposterous confessions.

iii

Madame Philippe, who after the expulsion was grouped with Madame Brard in Madame Lidoine's "association," felt sympathy for the older Sister. She reports that she even once spoke of this to their superior, Monseigneur Rigaud. He dismissed her concern, stating that Madame Brard was one of those souls who need endless humiliations in order to be saved.

Whatever the interior drama of Madame Brard, her more than 30 years in the community left a voluminous correspondence. For the most part it concerns priests and religious from whom she sought spiritual direction. It also reveals a strong personality plagued by a certain restlessness, something always potentially problematic in a cloistered community. Madame Philippe, however, has left us details about Madame Brard's remarkable transformation shortly before the community sacrifice.

Three and a half months before the martyrdom, when the young Sister Marie of the Incarnation left Compiègne for Paris at the end of March, 1794, she tells us she actually wept when bidding farewell to Sister Euphrasia. All her attempts at reconciling the older sister with Madame Lidoine had failed. Her sorrow was keen.

Just two weeks later, however, a very intimate letter from Madame Brard was found slipped into the folds of a garment the older nun sent her in Paris. The letter announced nothing less than a complete conversion of heart, saying that it was as if "great scales" had suddenly fallen from her eyes, scales that for so many years had kept her from seeing the terrible precipice toward which her jealousy and pride were leading her. In one of the most moving passages found in Madame Philippe's manuscripts, Madame Brard thus concludes her letter:

> I hope that the Lord, touched by my repentance, will forgive my faults. Now that I am trying to restore myself to a state of grace with him, it seems that far from fearing being harvested by the scythe of the Revolution, I actually desire it. I shall count myself happy to cease living so that I may no more offend my God.

On the way to the scaffold Madame Brard's witness was confirmed by an encounter that ensured the honored memory of her religious name. An awe-struck girl with a religious vocation devoutly followed the tumbrels that day, her gaze fixed on the singing nuns. Touched by her devotion, Sister Euphrasia passed the girl her office book prior to reaching the place of sacrifice.

This girl was Thérèse Binard, who later assumed the martyr's name and became Mother Euphrasia, foundress of the convent of "Les Oiseaux" in Paris. The relic received from the martyr's hands was piously preserved by her spiritual daughters as a memento of the Carmelite martyrdom until it was lost during the return of the community's archives to France from England following World War II. At the beginning of the twentieth century the nuns of her congregation had been forced into exile in England by the antireligious Combes laws. Persecution of Christians by the government was nothing new in France, as the relic of the martyred Sister Euphrasia attested.

iv

FOR THE FIRST FEW YEARS following her final vows a newly professed Carmelite's well-being is overseen by the novice mistress. Thus, when the community of 20 was grouped into four "associations" at expulsion, Mother de Croissy's group was to be composed largely of her "novice class." These were the four youngest nuns of the community, three of them already professed.

The eldest of these three was the infirmarian, Madame Pelras, professed in 1786, the year Madame de Croissy stepped down as prioress. It was actually her second profession as a nun. Before becoming a Carmelite as Sister Marie Henriette of the Divine Providence, she had been Sister Rosalie Gertrud in the Congregation of Nevers, an order devoted to nursing and works of charity. Madame Philippe, her contemporary in the novice class, reports that Madame Pelras feared her natural beauty might prove a danger in a congregation where she was constantly exposed to the outside world. She therefore had sought a more cloistered existence.

Madame Pelras' determination in obtaining her release from final vows in the Nevers community indicates something of her strength of character. Her break with that congregation is all the more striking when we learn that five of her sisters were also nuns in that order.

Strong character, however, appears a common trait in Madame Pelras' large, pious family, in which 18 children were born. Of the ten who survived, two became priests, and six became nuns. At the height of the Great Terror we are told one of these nun-sisters at Nevers displayed a strength of character equal to her Carmelite sister's. While shrouding a man's corpse upstairs in her order's hospice, she was suddenly confronted by a breathless outlawed priest pursued by the police. The frightened fugitive gasped, "Save me or I'm lost!" Without flinching, Madame Pelras's sister told him to lie down, then calmly shrouded him as if he were himself a cadaver. Next, just as she had been prepared to do with the real corpse she had shrouded, she heaved the shrouded priest over her shoulder and started downstairs to the morgue. Before she reached the bottom of the stairs the police arrived, asking if she had seen a runaway priest. She calmly replied that they could go upstairs and look for themselves. She feared, though, that all they would find there would be a shrouded corpse waiting to be carried to the morgue, just like the one she had over her shoulder. Or perhaps they preferred the one she was carrying? They declined the invitation and went upstairs for a vain search.

Certainly Madame Pelras herself showed a great deal of character in the courtroom of the Revolutionary Tribunal on the day of the martyrdom. In order to force the Revolutionary Tribunal's notorious Public Prosecutor, Fouquier-Tinville, into defining what he meant in applying the word "fanatic" to them, she dared feign ignorance of its meaning. Faced with his initial attempt to brush her question aside, she proved unrelenting. In the name of her rights as a French citizen she demanded that she be given his definition. Thus she obtained, from the lips of the Public Prosecutor of the Revolutionary Tribunal himself, a candid statement that it was because of their "attachment to their religion" that they were regarded as criminals and annihilators of public freedom.

As the tumbrels advanced toward the guillotine, Madame Pelras again demonstrated strong presence of mind. A woman of the people, sympathizing with the nuns sweltering in the stifling heat under their heavy white choir mantles, kindly offered them water to drink. One nun was about to accept when Sister Henriette, aware that community unity would be broken if any one of them accepted a drink on her own, intervened, admonishing her sister to wait just a little longer. "In heaven!" she exclaimed, "In heaven! We'll drink long draughts in heaven!" Finally, as we have seen, it was

Madame Pelras who stood unflinchingly by the prioress to the end, voluntary witness to the beheading of her 14 sisters, assisting each in turn up the steep scaffold steps before climbing them herself.

V

SECOND IN SENIORITY in Mother de Croissy's novitiate was Madame Philippe, our historian. Professed in 1788, four years after her miraculous cure before the relics of Madame Acarie at Pontoise's Carmel in 1784, she assumed, as we have seen, Madame Acarie's religious name, Marie of the Incarnation. Her entry as a postulant on September 23, 1786, followed the monastery-imposed two-year wait to assure that her cure was genuine. Six months later she was clothed in the habit on March 23, 1787. Formed in the novitiate by Madame de Croissy, her profession on July 22, 1788, was the next to the last one that Madame Lidoine received.

This profession, let us note, was a full four months beyond the first anniversary of Sister Marie of the Incarnation's clothing, something exceptional in the Compiègne community's practice at that time. Indeed, apart from the two most senior Sisters, Mesdames Thouret and Piedcourt, there is no instance among any of the 11 remaining professed martyrs where admission to final vows stretched that far beyond the first anniversary of their clothing. Final vows were frequently made even on that first anniversary, something Madame Lidoine writes she had originally intended to do in regard to Sister Constance.

Why then did Marie of the Incarnation pronounce her final vows only a full four months beyond the anniversary of being clothed in the habit? Though dispensations for her illegitimate birth might be involved, one would assume that such delicate questions had been settled long before. Or is it possible that Madame Lidoine was perhaps hesitant regarding the true vocation of this descendant of St. Louis? Or did Madame Philippe herself perhaps have ambiguous feelings about her religious vocation?

These questions are all the more intriguing in the light of another enigma. At the moment of the community's expulsion the young Sister Marie of the Incarnation was not lodged with Mother de Croissy as were the other three members of her "novice class," but with Madame Lidoine. Yet the prioress's "association" was already disproportionately large in size. It accounted for seven of the twenty nuns, leaving only thirteen to be divided between the other three "associations."

Madame Lidoine's seven-member "association" thus included five choir sisters: the prioress, Madame Philippe, and the three most senior members of the community. Two of these, Mesdames Thouret and Piedcourt, were martyred at 78; the third eldest, Madame Brard, Marie Leszczinska's "so lovable philosopher nun," was 58. Though it seems natural enough that the three seniors should arouse the prioress's maternal solicitude, for what reason was the young Madame Philippe also included?

It seems unlikely she was chosen to help care for the two septuagenarians. Nothing we know indicates that she was gifted in such practical matters. Indeed, if such a need existed, would not the young infirmarian, Madame Pelras, have been a better choice from Madame de Croissy's novice class?

That Madame Lidoine welcomed the presence of an energetic younger Sister nearer her own age whom, as we shall see in the next chapter, she could dispatch to accompany other Sisters on missions in Compiègne, is, of course, a possible explanation. This seems all the more possible since we know that in April of 1792 the prioress was suffering from bouts with hemorrhoids that, after the expulsion, seem at times to have made mobility difficult for her. Moreover, since we know that it was Teresa Soiron, the weaker of the two extern Sisters, who was chosen by the prioress to live with her, it seems highly possible that Madame Philippe was also chosen because the prioress was concerned about her weaknesses, not her strengths. Given her exquisite sensitivity, Mother Teresa of Saint Augustine may even have sensed that the true vocation of our historian lay, perhaps, elsewhere than in climbing the scaffold steps with the others.

Twice the prioress allowed the young Carmelite to travel freely to Paris on her own, in 1793 and again in 1794. This last time, moreover, after leaving at the end of March, she not only never returned, but actually fled Paris upon learning of her Sisters' June 22 arrest in Compiègne. However legitimate the excuse, such unaccompanied travel was hardly regular. When Madame Legros also left the monastery at the end of March 1794, it was not alone that she went to help her widowed brother, but in the company of Madame Jourdain.

Thirty years later Madame Philippe herself would state that her own vocation as a nun was one of "calling," not of "attraction," even though, for most of those 22 months between their expulsion and the final martyrdom she had daily pronounced the act of consecration for holocaust with the others. That the great prioress would have been totally insensitive to Madame Philippe's deep-seated feelings seems unlikely, whether or not they were ever expressed openly.

vi

THE THIRD AND LAST PROFESSED in Madame de Croissy's novitiate was Sister Saint Francis Xavier. Madame Lidoine received her vows on January 17, 1789, at the beginning of the year the storm broke. A white-veiled lay sister and virtually illiterate, Elizabeth Julitte Vérolot distinguishes herself as much by her youthful zeal and good humor as by her terse expressions of love for Jesus Christ. Unlike Marie of the Incarnation, she seemed to have a vocation of "attraction."

Nonetheless, prior to admitting her to solemn vows, Madame Lidoine, in her final interview, emphasized the possible fate awaiting this enthusiastic daughter of the people, should she insist on vowing herself to God. In January of 1789 the Revolution was already well on its way to destroying Europe's foremost Christian realm. That Madame Louise's royal cry of anguish, "France is lost!" in 1787 would not have been reported to her protégé and namesake, Mother Teresa of Saint Augustine at Compiègne, seems highly unlikely. Just the previous year, after all, Madame Lidoine had been elected prioress of Compiègne.

In any case, Mother Lidoine tried to convey to the simple, uneducated Sister Saint Francis Xavier the potential dangers for a consecrated nun in the times they were living. Her maternal concern for the young woman's well-being is all the more striking because the community desperately needed a young lay sister to assist the two older ones. Madame Roussel (Sister Marie of the Holy Spirit) was 46 years of age and, according to Madame Philippe, in a state of habitual suffering, leaving her companion, Madame Dufour (Sister Saint Martha), 47 years old, sorely overworked and in need of assistance.

Yet Mother Teresa of Saint Augustine proved far more concerned with the well-being of the soul before her than with the community's temporal interests. Before the prioress's emphasis on the tremendous personal risk the novice would be taking if she made her vows at this time, Sister Saint Francis Xavier proved unshakable, parrying all objections in the savory and totally untranslatable French of her class, as reported by Madame Philippe:

> O my dear good Mother! You can rest easy about me, for as long as I've got the happiness of getting consecrated to my God, that's all I wants! So don't go upsetting yourself about me, my dear good Mother, because—come on now!—the dear Lord himself's going to take care of all that!

Born of a great love, the desire to give all to Jesus Christ was thus as strongly present in this soul from the illiterate classes of eighteenth-century France as in "the great" Colbert's great-niece, Madame de Croissy.

vii

THE LAST NOVICE formed by Mother de Croissy was Marie Geneviève Meunier, Sister Constance, a novice for six years. In her last hour, and quite unofficially, she finally pronounced her vows by joining with the community as they, led by Mother Lidoine, renewed theirs at the foot of the scaffold.

Clothed in the habit on December 15, 1788, Sister Constance, with the accord of Madame Lidoine, should have pronounced her perpetual vows on December 15, 1789. The October 28 decree proclaiming "provisional suspension" of religious vows blocked this, as we have seen.

The annihilation of religious life in France was thus not only a specific goal of the new order, but, from the very beginning of the Revolution, an urgent one. Yet it was not the revolutionary government of France that carried out the first European suppression of religious orders in the eighteenth century. Joseph II of Austria, brother of Marie Antoinette, had earlier closed religious houses in the Austrian Netherlands. Madame Louise, along with other prioresses in France, had received the refugee Belgian Carmelites as they bore back to France the precious relics of Mother Anne of Jesus,

France's first prioress and their common Spanish Mother-foundress.

What was happening so thoroughly in France was in fact but an intensification of an all-pervasive questioning in Europe, not only of the validity of the religious life in modern Western society, but more especially of the validity of the claims of Christianity itself upon Western civilization. Did this religion, rooted in ancient Judaism, still have relevance in modern times? Had new philosophical ideas and scientific progress not opened newer and more beckoning frontiers?

In any case the October 28 provisional suspension of religious vows was the first of a whole series of what were meant to be fatal blows inflicted upon the religious life in France. Such repeated and forceful attacks recalled the powerful wieldings of the bar by the executioner when breaking a victim on the wheel. As agonizing as a single blow might be, it never of itself proved immediately lethal, but only a harbinger of the excruciatingly anguished end awaiting the broken victim.

Indeed, after the initial attack of October 28, one anti-Christian decree followed another. The November 2 decree confiscating all church property for the nation instantly deprived religious communities of financial independence, forcing them to become wards of the government. Thus, any infringement of the law forbidding further professions could definitively cut a community off from whatever the new order's government granted them to survive.

Mother Lidoine had to face this dilemma as she considered the possibility of allowing Sister Constance to make final vows on December 15, 1789. If the community were to continue she must obey the law. Otherwise they would all be put out in the street. By obeying the law, Madame Lidoine was able to preserve her community intact as a Christian unit throughout their 22-month expulsion so that, at the end, they might together still strive to attain the mystic crown awaiting those answering the apostolic call.

viii

WE KNOW FROM A LETTER of Madame Lidoine that Sister Constance's parents, having sympathy neither for her piety nor for her vocation, consented to her entry into Carmel only with reluctance. Their acquisition of the confiscated convent of the Annunciation nuns in Saint-Denis during the Terror further reveals their indifference to church affairs. Thus, when it became obvious that Sister Constance could never pronounce her vows, they dispatched her brother to Compiègne to fetch his sister home, using force if necessary. After vain attempts at persuasion, the brother brought in the police. During this scene of high drama in which she stood facing her brother, supported by the police, Sister Constance pled as follows, according to Madame Philippe's text:

> Gentlemen, it was only with the consent of my parents that I entered here. If they now want me to leave because their tenderness causes them to be alarmed by those dangers I may face in wanting to remain, I am grateful to them. But nothing, absolutely nothing but death can ever separate me from the company of my Mothers and Sisters.
>
> And you, my brother, whom I am happy to see, though probably for the last time, please reassure our dear parents that indifference plays no part in my refusal to yield to their desires. My heart is even sorely grieved to cause them sorrow.
>
> Yet surely they won't find it a bad thing that I am led by my conscience. Plead with them then on my behalf, beg them not to worry about me since nothing whatsoever can happen except as it pleases God to allow it. And, in regard to that, I am completely at peace.

Convinced of her own free will in the matter, the police did not force her to accompany her brother back to Saint-Denis.

Yet the puzzlement of her family is understandable. As so often happens between martyrs and their families, there is resentment when the family senses that the martyr's affections are no longer for them, nor even for the things of this world. Rare is the family member who, even if not hostile, proves capable of grasping that through the prompting of the Holy Spirit even the most basic animal instinct for self-preservation has been transcended by a great love that burns and transfigures the deepest affections and longings of the potential martyr's heart.

Sorrowing that she could not hold to her course without wounding her family, Sister Constance embraced her vocation as a martyr, while unflinchingly uniting herself to her immolated Divine Bridegroom. Moreover, in her confrontation with her brother, her words "nothing but death" indicate, well before the 1792 expulsion, a remarkable lucidity on the part of this youngest martyr, whatever may have been her subsequent moments of panic in facing the guillotine.

We know also that Sister Constance's human weakness attracted the attention of Abbé de Lamarche during his clandestine ministry in Compiègne in 1793 and 1794. It is he who passed on an oral account of how he helped this youngest member of the community overcome her fear of the guillotine, a fear that could only have been aggravated by the community's daily pronouncement of the act of consecration for holocaust. According to Abbé de Lamarche's own story he engaged the novice in the following dialogue:

"My daughter, are wounds inflicted upon your ear when your sisters speak of the guillotine?"

"No, Father...."

"Now I'm going to imagine that they come to take you to prison...."

"Ah! please Father!"

"But come on now—do you really suffer from that?"

"No, Father...."

"Well, next they lead you to the Revolutionary Tribunal where you are condemned to death; do you feel any pain?"

"No...."

"They order you up the steps of the scaffold—does that hurt?"

"No, Father...."

"Well, finally they place you under the blade and tell you to lower your head—is that a torture?"

"Not yet...."

"Then the executioner lets the blade fall and you feel your head separated from your body and you enter paradise—are you happy?"

"Yes, Father ... I'm no longer afraid."

The fact that Sister Constance, as she started up the steps of the scaffold, spontaneously intoned the *Laudate Dominum omnes gentes,* declaring the confirmation of divine mercy on the community, bore remarkable witness to the triumph of the Holy Spirit in her, manifesting that those powers of darkness inspiring fear of total annihilation in the hour of death were, in that moment of grace, completely vanquished by the power of God.

5

The Impact of the New Order (July 14, 1789–September 14, 1792)

(i) Decrees against religious orders; decree of February 13, 1790; reaction of the oldest nun. (ii) MADAME THOURET (Sister Charlotte of the Resurrection); her companion and contemporary, MADAME PIEDCOURT (Sister of Jesus Crucified); difficulties of Madame Thouret's vocation; her witness upon arriving at the Conciergerie. (iii) MADAME HANISSET (Sister Teresa of the Heart of Mary); tie with nuns at Paris' Picpus Cemetery; MADAME TREZEL (Sister Saint Ignatius); birth of her niece on November 26, 1792; historic importance of that date for the act of consecration. (iv) The first Bastille Day; other events of 1790. (v) Violation of cloister on August 4 and 5; nuns' unanimous desire to remain Carmelites; the two extern sisters, CATHERINE and TERESA SOIRON. (vi) Laws governing remaining nuns; Rome's March 10 condemnation of constitutional church; other events of 1791; the flight to Varennes. (vii) 1791 ends and 1792 begins; Easter at Compiègne's Carmel; events leading to June 20; the royal family insulted. (viii) August 10, 1792; the September massacres. (ix) Stripping of Compiègne's Carmel; exodus of civilian-clad nuns.

We have seen that scarcely three months after the fall of the Bastille, on October 28, 1789, the "provisional suspension" of all religious vows was made law and that, five days later, on November 2, all church property was confiscated for the benefit of "the Nation." The definitive blow for religious orders, however, came three months later. On February 13, 1790, the October 28 "provisional suspension" of religious vows was made permanent. Thus, despite later decrees dealing with possessions and pensions, or temporary exceptions for female religious engaged in teaching or running hospitals, the death of the religious life in France, begun only three and a half months after the storming of the Bastille, was definitively confirmed, once and for all, a mere seven months after that event.

Madame Philippe reports that the most notable reaction in her community to this definitive suspension of religious vows did not, however, come from its youngest member, Sister Constance, whose hopes of becoming a professed nun were forever dashed by it. Rather did it come from the oldest sister, the 74-year-old Madame Thouret, in religion Sister Charlotte of the Resurrection. She very keenly sensed that that February decree tolled the end of the world she had known. Seized by a visceral refusal stronger than her powers of reasoning, Madame Thouret's revolt against the reality of their situation was in fact so violent that her very life seemed at stake. Yet, as Madame Philippe wrote, "The Lord who had already worked a miracle in her favor, did not allow her to succumb."

ii

Anne Marie Madeleine Thouret, the oldest martyr by two months, possessed a very lively mind. Even as the Carmelite, Sister Charlotte of the Resurrection, she was still so naturally inclined toward gaiety, Madame Philippe reports, that her sister Carmelites one day jokingly asked her why she had chosen to be a nun.

Sister Charlotte had lost her father early in life. A few years later her mother remarried, but the girl resented her new stepfather, whose presence caused her to feel that she had now also lost her mother. To compensate for this sense of loss she contrived with compliant relatives or friends to escape her stepfather's surveillance whenever a ball was scheduled, for at 16 she had a passion for dancing. It was thus to be at a ball that she would feel God's hand upon her. Madame Philippe reports quite simply what Madame Thouret herself said about this event.

> But God, who wanted me all to himself, once allowed me, while attending one of these balls to witness something so tragic, and something that made such an impression on me, that I immediately fled with the firm resolve not only never to attend another ball, but also to leave the world, which, as you see, by the grace of the Lord, I have succeeded in doing, whatever the cost.

Madame Thouret's entry into religion had not been easy, however. Contrasting herself with her contemporary, Madame Piedcourt, her junior by two months, she observed: "For it is not always with sugar that the dear Lord draws his doves to him—as it pleased him to do in the case of my companion, Sister of Jesus Crucified."

Sister of Jesus Crucified and Sister Charlotte of the Resurrection, both born in 1715, were separated from the third oldest member of the community, Madame Brard, Marie Leszczynka's "so lovable philosopher nun," by more than two decades. In 1736, the year of Madame Brard's birth, both reached 21 years of age. Whereas Madame Thouret was just entering Carmel that year, Madame Piedcourt had already finished a two-year postulancy and was clothed as a novice.

Madame Thouret reveals that while Madame Piedcourt had been drawn to the cloister "with sugar," her own vocation had not been by natural attraction at all, any more than was Madame Philippe's or Madame Chrétien de Neuville's. Madame Thouret's three-year wait before receiving the habit, instead of the more usual six months, allows us to surmise something of what her own inner struggle must have been. If Madame Piedcourt's two-year wait to be clothed in the habit seems excessive according to the customs of the time, Madame Thouret's three-year wait seems even more so. What is more, in Madame Thouret's case, the usual one-year delay between clothing and final profession was also doubled, meaning that she had waited five full years instead of the more usual year and a half before making her profession.

Whatever the lack of "attraction" she felt for this vocation, our historian insists that through her zeal to keep the Rule and the spirit of the Carmelite *Constitutions,* Madame Thouret struggled consciously to become "all His." Her great strength of character is moreover illuminated by an anecdote recounted by Madame Philippe.

As infirmarian, Madame Thouret had begun to stoop under the incessant demands of nursing a sister devoured by cancer and requiring three changes of bandages a day. The prioress, noting her stoop, thought Madame Thouret should immediately quit the infirmary before further damage was done to her posture. Madame Thouret quietly protested, saying that though ready to obey, she humbly begged the prioress to observe that she herself felt quite capable of continuing, more especially since she feared that their poor suffering sister, so near death, would suffer even more from having someone new take over her care. The prioress allowed Madame Thouret to remain for the two days the sister survived, then, wishing to assign her work requiring neither stooping nor lifting, gave her a painting job.

This new job quickly proved a disaster, however. Sister Charlotte was required to work in a tiny room with poor ventilation at the height of the summer's heat. The toxic varnish fumes left her in a completely mindless state for about two years. This experience, however, was the occasion for what Madame Philippe refers to as a "miracle," since the doctors had despaired of her recovery. The undaunted nuns sought the prayers of their patroness, the Virgin Mother of Jesus Christ. They pleaded that if it were indeed the divine will that this sister continue to glorify the name of her Son on earth, then she, his Mother, must obtain the manifestation of his power and restore Sister Charlotte's reason.

In 1790 this first "miracle" was recalled as the community confronted Madame Thouret's violent reaction to the passing of the February 13 decree abolishing religious vows in France. Once again they prayed to Our Lady of Mount Carmel that Sister Charlotte might "continue to glorify the name" of Jesus Christ. A second time prayer prevailed and she fully regained her reason as before.

The unnamed priest whose letters sustained Madame Lidoine during those last two years of the community's existence enigmatically commented on God's designs upon this senior member of the Compiègne community. In one letter we find him speaking of "that part which God had reserved for himself" in this oldest of the martyrs.

On July 13, 1794, four days before the martyrdom, Madame Thouret bore witness before the crowd gathered in the courtyard of the Conciergerie to "that part which God had reserved for himself." The Carmelites, plus Mulot de la Ménardière, traveling in two open carts since the morning of the previous day, had just arrived from Compiègne as prisoners with hands bound.

For Madame Thouret, who at 78 walked with a crutch, the long journey of more than 24 hours had been especially cruel. With her hands bound, she was unable to rise and step out of the cart with her sisters when the tumbrels finally stopped that afternoon in front of the prison. Alone, exhausted and abandoned, she sat amid the disordered, soiled straw while they, helpless, watched her anxiously. Suddenly a guard bounded up into the cart, gathered her up in both arms as though she were a sack of grain, and pitched her out onto the paving stones of the courtyard.

Showing no signs of life, the infirm old nun lay there, face down, completely still. Immediately women in the crowd started upbraiding the guard for his brutality. The volume of reproaches rose until the figure on the ground stirred slightly. Slowly Sister Charlotte lifted her head, revealing a blood-smeared, wrinkled face to the circle gathered around her. Then, spotting the brutal guard, she thanked him with warm frankness for not having killed her, thereby depriving her of her share in her community's glorious witness for Jesus Christ.

iii

ONLY TWO OF THE SIXTEEN MARTYRS remain to be mentioned, both of them choir nuns. The slightly older one, Madame Hanisset, in religion Sister Teresa of the Heart of Mary, was a native of Rheims. Daughter of a saddler and martyred at age 52, she served as "interior turn sister," receiving goods coming into the cloister from the outside world. As a young woman she had been introduced to the Compiègne Carmel by the monastery's visitator, Monseigneur Hachette des Portes, Vicar General of Rheims and Bishop of Glandève.

As propagator in France of devotion to the Sacred Heart of Mary, this prelate's influence on Madame Hanisset's religious name is clear. Public devotion to the heart of Mary, then considered inseparable from that of Christ, had been launched the century before in the year 1648 by the great Norman saint, Jean Eudes (1601–1680), restorer of priestly fervor and a fiery apostle of the consecrated life. This particular mystical devotion to the Sacred Heart of Mary was regarded as completely spiritual and thus differed from the better-known seventeenth-century devotion to the Sacred Heart of Jesus propagated by St. Margaret Mary Alacoque at Paray-le-Monial.

It is curious that this devotion continues to this day to unite the Compiègne martyrs with the nuns who keep vigil in

Paris over their burial site: the Congregation of the Sacred Hearts of Jesus and Mary. Their property at 35, rue Picpus, serves as vestibule to the Picpus Cemetery. Through a grilled gate at the back of that cemetery are visible the two huge gravel-covered quadrangles marking the site of the burial pits for all those guillotined at the Place de la Nation between June 13 and July 27, 1794. Into those common graves, in less than six weeks, were tossed the heads and torsos of 1,306 persons. The names of the 16 Carmelites and of Mulot de la Ménardière are but 17 of those 1,306 names inscribed on marble plaques covering the walls of the Congregation's nearby church where prayer is offered continually.

When entering the gates of the Picpus Cemetery, a trivial but rather curious coincidence has struck more than one Gertrud von Le Fort specialist. Facing that entrance is the imposing tomb of the Mother Foundress of the Congregation of the Sacred Hearts of Jesus and Mary, Mother de la Chevalerie, whose imposing noble name is inscribed in great letters. On seeing this, specialists of the German writer recall that prior to naming the heroine of her novella, *Die Letzte am Schafott*, "Blanche de la Force," she had first called her "Blanche de la Chevalerie." Given the ties between Gertrud von Le Fort's novella and the renaissance in our century of interest in the 16 Carmelite martyrs, the coincidence is all the more curious since Gertrud von Le Fort never visited Picpus Cemetery.

A far more curious coincidence is found, however, in the portrait Madame Philippe traces of the last of our martyrs to be considered, Madame Trézel. In religion Sister Teresa of Saint Ignatius, she was a native of Compiègne and martyred at age 51. When writing *Le Sang du Carmel*, Father Bruno de Jésus-Marie consulted a graphologist who spoke of Madame Trézel's handwriting as revealing a mystic with a sense of the Absolute. She was also, the graphologist sensed, without any gift for logical or rational approaches to situations, or even for communicating with others. Still, this mattered little to her since she cared nothing for others' judgments. Living in her own world, she was capable of unusual and highly original actions. An incident reported by Madame Philippe bears out all these graphological observations.

Like the family of Sister Constance, or the mother and sister of Madame Crétien de Neuville, or even the mother of Madame Lidoine, Madame Trézel's own sister in Compiègne failed to understand why, once expelled, the nuns might not freely visit their families. Pregnant with her first child after years of barrenness, this sister was especially eager to share her joy with Sister Saint Ignatius, more especially as she was no longer cloistered.

Though Madame Trézel's hesitancy may have stemmed from the fact that her sister and brother-in-law were antireligious, she was in fact firmly committed to the religious life, whatever might be the worldly setting for carrying it out. Thus she insisted on maintaining the discipline of the cloister even when outside it, despite the community's concern that consistent refusal of her sister's invitations might only make their situation worse.

On November 26, 1792, her sister gave birth to the long-awaited child. According to the genealogical records of Compiègne it was a daughter, not a son, as so solemnly emphasized by Madame Philippe. Madame Trézel refused, however, even to attend the baptism that same afternoon. Madame Philippe tells us that when the bells of Saint-Jacques announced the ceremony she found herself alone with Madame Trézel who, immediately kneeling down, asked the young Sister Marie of the Incarnation to join in the prayer she was about to offer for the child being baptized.

The prayer's request was singular. Beginning with the most orthodox theological invocation of God, she prayed: "O Lord, you to whom all things are present, whether it be the past or the future, deign, I beseech you, to hear the prayer made by your humble servant, that if the child who is to receive the grace of baptism is not one day going to be a saint, then please Lord, make of it an angel."

The baby girl expired during the night, though seeming to be in the best of health. Madame Philippe could only feel that it was related to Madame Trézel's strange request.

When news of the newborn's death that same night reached Madame Lidoine the following day, she insisted that Madame Trézel pay her sister a visit, accompanied by Madame Philippe. Thus do we have further curious details. The physicians, finding the body of the child still supple, could not believe it was really dead. They ordered a 24-hour delay before the autopsy.

It is, however, yet another detail given by Madame Philippe that proves definitively that the recitation of the act of holocaust was in place and already an established community activity before this child's birth on November 26, 1792. Madame Philippe specifically refers to the community act of consecration in describing how, the next day, when they were left alone in the room with the dead newborn, Sister St. Ignatius took up the tiny body in her arms and, pouring out her affection, lovingly begged the dead infant to join its pure prayers to their own community's act of consecration to save France, their country.

Finally, Madame Philippe concludes that she had never seen a book in Madame Trézel's hand during prayer in the choir. Madame Trézel explained this by saying that the dear Lord, finding such abysmal ignorance in her and thinking no one but himself capable of the task, taught her himself. We further learn that Madame Trézel's "exterior so reflected the inner spirit of the Holy Virgin" that the nuns called her "the hidden treasure."

Madame Lidoine once observed to Madame Philippe that she had never seen Madame Trézel fail to maintain silence according to the Rule.

iv

THE DEFINITIVE SUPPRESSION OF VOWS on February 13, 1790, was followed in April by the passing of two laws dealing with all that mass of ecclesiastical property confiscated for the benefit of the nation the previous November 2. It suffices to recall, when trying to imagine its almost incalculable worth, that this wealth provided the means for financing the Revolution for ten years. A law of April 14 placed this vast treasure at the disposal of the local *départements* and districts. Six days later, on April 20, it was decreed that these *départements* and districts should themselves be responsible for establishing the inventory of these goods. Such inventories necessarily took considerable time to complete and the Compiègne authorities only got around to the inventory of their local Carmel four months later, on August 4.

Just three weeks prior to this first violation of Compiègne's Carmelite cloister, Paris had celebrated its very first Bastille Day. Featured was an open-air Mass staged at the Champ de Mars with Talleyrand, Bishop of Autun, as celebrant, and with the king in a place of honor. All national representatives attended and solemnly swore fidelity before an improvised altar fusing the civic altar of the Fatherland with the Christian eucharistic altar. In spite of government propaganda extolling its success, unbiased eyewitnesses report that it rained throughout this grandiose prorevolutionary ceremony with umbrellas blocking the view. Still, the naive thought it marked an end to the conflict with the inauguration of the much-touted constitutional monarchy.

What this public charade actually did mark was the beginning of a profound schism within the French Church. Just two days before, on July 12, the Assembly had voted for the civil constitution of the clergy. The month following the ceremony, on August 24, the king would sign this new law, thereby manifesting his good will to the Revolution. Rome, instead of acting immediately to condemn the constitutional church, hesitated for eight months. During that long Roman silence serious inroads were made by the new national church throughout France, particularly among the parish clergy. As we have seen, every member of the parish clergy in Compiègne accepted the consitutional church. The pope, after all, was silent and the king himself had signed the law.

Rome's hesitation also served to undermine the king's credibility. Obliged, once Rome had spoken, to remain in communion with the See of St. Peter, as had all his forebears, Louis XVI was forced to oppose the constitutional church, whatever may have been his good will toward the Revolution. More fortunate than his queen, he would, however, be accompanied to the scaffold by a non-juring or "refractory" priest.

V

IT WAS IN THE WAKE of that first Bastille celebration at the Champ de Mars that the District of Compiègne's Revolutionary Directors forced the monastery's cloister for the first time to make the required inventory on August 4, 1790. On August 5 these champions of the "rights" of these "unfortunate" women they genuinely believed to be "sequestered virgins," returned, accompanied by a dozen armed guards. They were intent on ferreting out, through a strictly private interview with each sister, which ones secretly longed to live as "normal" French citizens. With armed guards posted throughout the monastery, no member of the community was to have any chance to eavesdrop while each nun was being interviewed by the Directors.

The nuns' replies, still extant as recorded by the Directors' secretary that day, are all signed, save in the case of the illiterate lay sisters. Not a single response from any of those 18 professed members of the community casts the slightest doubt upon each woman's deep conviction that she was vowed to God until death and wished to remain in the cloister. The three lay sisters (all martyrs) and the fifteen choir sisters (ten of whom would be martyrs) all wished to remain nuns. As for the five choir sisters who escaped martyrdom, three were those destined not to "follow the Lamb" (i.e. Mesdames Philippe, Legros and Jourdain) and the two remaining died too soon: Madame Boitel prior to expulsion, and Madame d'Hangest just six weeks afterward.

In their statements, seven of the eighteen professed, including Madame Lidoine herself, invoked the image of death, stating they wished only "to live and die" in their religious state. In addition to her statement, Madame de Croissy, novice mistress and former prioress, pulled a three-stanza poem out of her pocket. She asked the Revolutionary Directors to read her verses on the vanity of the world's cares, its judgments, and its so-called "freedom." She opted for the sweet chains binding her to God, knowing that all the world could offer was of little worth.

Madame Thouret's contemporary, Madame Piedcourt, answered with the same courageous flourish with which she would confront the executioners on the scaffold. She boldly affirmed that after 56 years as a Carmelite she would give "anything in the world to have as many years again to give to the Lord." As for Madame Brard, Marie Leszczynzka's "so lovable philosopher nun," she said that she would not give up her religious habit even if it meant shedding her blood.

Special mention is due the simple, touching intimacy with Jesus Christ found in the answer of the young and semi-illiterate Madame Vérolot, the last professed. Again this young lay sister displays that same faith and childlike abandonment already seen in her answer to Madame Lidoine's concerns prior to her profession. Just as on that occasion she had confidently stated that the dear Lord would take care of any danger she might be in, so now is her reply, as recorded by the Committee's secretary, equally impressive. "Sister St. François-Xavier declared that a well-born wife sticks to her husband, and that nothing in the world could cause her to abandon her divine spouse, our Lord Jesus Christ; and said she didn't know how to sign her name."

These declarations made, all 18 professed nuns were legally entitled to a government pension. The novice, Sister Constance, and the two paid externs, Catherine and Teresa Soiron—the community's three nonprofessed—were not provided for, not being legally Carmelites.

Inclusion of the Soiron sisters as part of the community martyrdom was still problematic for Madame Philippe more than 30 years later, when she started her *Relation du martyre.* Speaking of "fourteen" martyrs only, she explicitly excluded Catherine and Teresa Soiron as she began her first manuscript. It was apparently her discovery of Abbé Guillon's four-volume dictionary of revolutionary martyrs, *Les martyrs de la foi,*[1] where the Soiron sisters are included, that caused her to accept the two unprofessed externs as members of the community and thereafter speak of "sixteen" instead of "fourteen" martyrs.

vi

FOLLOWING THE AUGUST 4 AND 5 VIOLATIONS of the Compiègne cloister, there would be two further decrees. While the second of these, issued on October 16, granted a pension to all who still insisted on remaining members of religious orders, the first one, of October 7, ruled that still extant communities must choose a superior and a bursar during January 1791, in a "free" election directed by a municipal officer.

---

[1] Abbé Aimé Guillon. *Les martyrs de la foi pendant la Révolution française*, 4 vols. (Paris: Germain Mathiot, Paris, 1821).

We have seen that this "free election" took place at the Compiègne Carmel on January 11, 1791, and that Mother Lidoine was unanimously reelected prioress. At that same election Mother de Croissy was elected bursar, again confirming the prestige she maintained in the community. Only 17 of the 18 professed nuns voted in that "free election" of January 1791, however. Madame Boitel, already in her last illness, was too weak to cast her vote.

It was only on March 10, 1791, two months later, that Rome, in Pius VI's brief, *Quod aliquantum*, finally condemned the civil constitution of the clergy. The pope issued two further briefs on March 19, both aimed at sustaining the non-juring church in France. The first lauded non-juring priests, while the second conferred upon former bishops, or the vicars left administering their dioceses, the power to absolve cases normally reserved for Rome. Should contact with the Holy See be broken, they might now proceed with dates for ordinations without reference to Rome. Sure of the fidelity of the "most Christian" House of France, Rome, after eight months' silence, had finally thrown down the gauntlet to the revolutionary government.

That same month of March found the Compiègne Carmelites qualifying for the new pensions by providing government officials with a statement of revenues and expenses. Rather slow in materializing, the new pensions were granted finally only on August 6, 1791, payable from the previous January. A full calendar year had thus elapsed between the Carmelites' declarations of August 5, 1790, and their receipt of any compensation whatsoever for the total loss of their income resulting from the confiscation of their property. Wards of the revolutionary government, their survival was henceforth totally subject to bureaucratic whims and vagaries.

The rift between constitutional clergy and non-jurors increased, as did that between monarchists and the government, particularly following the royal family's ill-fated flight to Varennes on June 20, 1791. Arrested and returned to Paris, the king and royal family were virtual prisoners in the Tuileries Palace for the next 14 months. Implacably, circumstances moved towards the final crushing blow that, the following year, would finally fell the besieged monarchy on August 10.

vii

IN THE MEANTIME, a decree was passed on November 27, 1791, requiring all clergy, active or inactive, to swear the civic oath on pain of being deprived of their pensions. This involved an implicit acceptance of the civil constitution of the clergy. Should there be any popular disturbance concerning this oath, the local priest himself would be held accountable and punished for it. Priests refusing the oath must be listed in each *département*.

On December 19 the king used his constitutional right to veto this harsh law, an action causing revolutionary journalists to label him a "tyrant." In any case the royal veto was largely disregarded and the decree executed as though already law. Monastic chapels were broken into, non-juring priests expelled, and either a juring priest installed or the chapel closed.

The conflict intensified during the first months of 1792. Even as Christians prepared to celebrate Easter on April 8, a Good Friday decree on April 6 suppressed both teaching orders and the wearing of religious habits. In cities such as Lyons, Easter of 1792 was marked by the plundering of churches and the interruption of services.

As we have seen, that Easter of 1792 was the last one the Carmelites celebrated in their monastery, as well as the occasion for Mother Lidoine's first presenting the idea of their perhaps being called "to follow the Lamb." It was not really a surprising proposition, given the schism between those adherents faithful to the juring clergy and those faithful to the "refractory" or non-juring priests, plus the fact that the ever-mounting persecution and hostility toward the non-juring church in France threatened it with extinction. At such a moment Madame Lidoine's great soul could not remain indifferent to the need to sustain France and her church by some spiritual action. Was it not in the best apostolic tradition of Carmel?

France's declaration of war against "the king of Hungary and Bohemia" on April 20 followed Easter by scarcely a week. France's borders would now be threatened, since Austria was aligned with Prussia. At such a moment general fear fed the rumor that non-juring priests were secret foreign agents. This culminated in the decree of May 27, stating that any priest denounced to the *département* by 20 "active citizens" should be deported, unless the district officials disagreed. In such a case an inquest must be held immediately to determine his guilt or innocence.

On May 29, just two days following this May 27 decree, the Assembly removed the king's Guard of Honor. Inexorably everything moved toward facilitating the mob's invasion of the Tuileries Palace on the night of June 20, the first anniversary of the flight to Varennes.

On that sinister night the royal family were grossly insulted. The king, constitutional head of the new revolutionary government, was obliged by the mob to don the red Phrygian cap. Heretofore reserved for convicts condemned to the galleys, the conical cap had been introduced to revolutionary Paris by a contingent of former galley convicts from Marseille. In the new order their emblem of shame had become a symbol of political correctness.

viii

Six days prior to the fall of the monarchy, a decree of August 4, 1792, finally ordered all women's monasteries closed. Then, just three days later, on August 7, 1792, the National Assembly ordered municipalities to verify the official inventory made two years previously—on August 4, 1790, in the case of Compiègne's Carmel. The actual seizure and removal of the monastery's entire furnishings would not, however, be carried out until September 12.

The fall of the monarchy on August 10 entailed the incarceration of the king, queen, two royal children, and the king's pious sister, Madame Elisabeth, in "the Temple," as the twelfth-century Parisian fortress-priory of the Knights Templar was called. Immediately a veritable frenzy against religious orders was unchained in the National Assembly. On August 14 a new law required the Liberty-Equality oath ("I swear to be faithful to the Nation and to preserve liberty and equality or die in defending them") for any Frenchman receiving a pension. Religious orders thereby became completely subservient to the new government's will. Three days later, on August 17, all religious houses were ordered evacuated, save those serving as hospitals.

The last restraints against open suppression of the Christian religion seemed to disappear with the August 10 fall of the monarchy. A letter from the *département* of the Var, read out in the National Assembly that same August 17, attests that veto or no veto, legal or illegal, deportation of the clergy had become a *fait accompli.* Such deportations, accompanied by massacres and barbarous ill-treatment, were on the increase everywhere. Slowly but implacably a reign of revolutionary terror was enveloping the "most Christian" kingdom of France.

Though a decree of August 18 formally exempted nuns from taking the new Liberty-Equality oath, it had no effect on our Carmelites who, as we shall see, all took it on September 19, along with their chaplain, Abbé Courouble. In the meantime a decree proposed on August 23 was being debated. It proposed that all clergy who had not taken the Liberty-Equality oath be required to leave the country within two weeks. It was even debated whether all such refractory priests should be deported to Guyana. This debate was overshadowed, however, by the extraordinary events taking place in Paris on the second, third, and fourth days of September.

More than once it has been suggested that the staggering human butchery of the September massacres in 1792 was no more than a highly regrettable but totally unavoidable popular reaction of "the good people of Paris" to the news that the Prussians were approaching their city. Such a simplistic whitewash of these events overlooks copious documentation showing to what extent the massacres were orchestrated and the assassins organized. Often a butcher was included in the teams going from prison to prison to set up "tribunals" and administer "revolutionary justice." Paid teams were provided with drink as they labored to clear out hundreds of nonjuring priests, as well as others arrested in the aftermath of August 10.

Eyewitness accounts of these massacres match in horror almost anything to be found in the history of Europe. The slaughter, carried out in the name of "the people's justice," proved to be a sort of blood orgy. Though mutilation of bodies and parading of human heads, as well as the display (and even the roasting and devouring) of human organs had been in evidence in mob scenes from the beginning of the Revolution, a particularly striking image has come down to us from the September massacres. An eyewitness reports seeing a group of those administering "the people's justice" resting from their labors during their lunch break. Sitting atop a pile of freshly massacred corpses, they soaked their bread in the blood of their victims.

Such extraordinary events, reported as daily occurrences in Christian Europe's most brilliant capital scarcely a week before the Carmelites' expulsion, cried out for spiritual action. The act of consecration of the Carmelites, undertaken so shortly thereafter, would be their answer.

ix

THE AUGUST 4, 1790, INVENTORY of the furnishings of the Carmelite monastery of Compiègne was finally verified only two years later on September 12, 1792. At that time all items were finally seized and transported to the former St. Corneille Abbey, general depot for Compiègne's confiscated church goods. Since the Middle Ages this venerable Benedictine abbey had constituted Compiègne's heart and cultural center, for the city had grown up around it. In 1792, however, St. Corneille's desecrated and spoiled cloister served only to shelter the rich booty wrested from the Christian civilization it had once nurtured.

Madame Philippe mentions in particular the disappearance at this time of the large collection of fine, life-size wax figures composing the monastery's celebrated "crèche." Its numerous spectacular tableaux of richly dressed images were set up not only at Christmas, but also at other times by royal request. With an indignation rare for her, Madame Philippe opines that those magnificent wax figures had all been melted down to make the candles illumining the works of darkness fomented by revolutionary committees during their sinister nocturnal meetings.

Required by law to evacuate their stripped monastery, the 20 members of Compiègne's Carmel seem to have used September 13 to prepare for their traumatic exit into the world. Housing in the town had to be found through friends such as a local Doctor de Crouy, whose name has come down to us. Finding civilian clothing for the community of 20 was also an urgent problem, requiring a full day's delay and further appeals to friends. Money was short. It was thus only on September 14, with their housing assured and their civilian clothing acquired, that the community of 20 finally emerged from their stripped monastery. The very ill Madame d'Hangest undoubtedly had to be assisted. Disoriented, the 20 women confronted that world on which they had once turned their backs yet for which they would so shortly be offering themselves in holocaust in an act of daily consecration.

In this confrontation most of them probably felt as exposed as their stripped monastery. For more than half a century the two jubilarians, Mesdames Thouret and Piedcourt, had worn only the habit. The transition to low-cut house dresses and jerkins, with only a large scarf to cover their bare shoulders and bosom, must have seemed an offense to common decency.

Madame Brard, who for 30 years had also worn nothing but the habit, had told the Revolutionary Directors of the District of Compiègne she would shed her blood before giving it up. The transition to street clothes must have been traumatic for her also. Could she perhaps have harbored a feeling that, given the circumstances, Madame Lidoine should have manifested greater strength in defying the decree concerning civilian clothing?

The simple bourgeois costume worn by the expelled nuns seems to have been similar to the one worn by the queen on her way to the guillotine, as shown in David's well-known sketch, save for one detail. For members of this community of 20, bonnets enclosed their heads, framing their faces. But below the back of these bonnets their necks were bare, discreetly readied for oblation.

Near the Church of Saint-Antoine, the four residences of the Carmelites after expulsion from their monastery on September 14, 1792. *Upper left:* 9 rue St-Antoine (formerly rue Dampierre). *Upper right:* 14 rue des Cordeliers (formerly rue de la Liberté). *Lower left:* second residence at same address but with different entry. *Lower right:* 24 rue des Boucheries (formerly 8 rue Neuve).

Above: Church of Saint-Antoine, from lithograph in Compiègne municipal library (photo, J. P. Gilson)
Below: Side door of Church of Saint-Antoine (Photo, J. P. Gilson)

6

Witness Without the Cloister

(i) Expulsion on September 14, 1792; significance of date. (ii) The four "associations"; their proximity to St. Antoine's parish. (iii) Funds sought for civilian clothing; signing of the Liberty-Equality oath. (iv) Madame Philippe's 1795 itinerary; her discovery of Denis Blot and the parody on *La Marseillaise;* exclusion from the sacraments because of her oath. (v) Madame Philippe's retraction; fact and fiction regarding her sisters' oath. (vi) Madame Lidoine proposes an act of consecration; reaction of Mesdames Thouret and Piedcourt; reaction of Catherine Soiron. (vii) Of what the act consisted; what we learn from Mgr Jauffret. (viii) Madame Lidoine's Christmas carol. (ix) The act of consecration as a response to the Terror and the Revolutionary Tribunal; desecration of the dead; material insignificance of the Carmelite's mystical sacrifice.

As they turned their backs on the past to step over the threshold of their stripped monastery on September 14, 1792, the 20 members of Compiègne's Carmelite community were keenly aware that the date was heavy with ancient symbolism. Madame Philippe recalls they even remarked on how their own situation on that day must be intimately connected to the mystery of the cross of Christ.

The origins of this symbolism date from the fourth century of the Christian era. In the twentieth year of his reign, the Roman Emperor, Constantine the Great, dispatched his pious mother, St. Helena, to Jerusalem. She was to venerate the holy places and seek out the site of the Holy Sepulcher. Though buried since the enlargement of the city under Hadrian, the tomb's location had been kept alive by oral tradition. The royal visitor thus succeeded in uncovering Christendom's most holy site as well as in discovering nearby three crosses and the nails used for three crucifixions.

With the aid of Makarios, Bishop of Jerusalem, the cross of Christ and the nails used to pierce the Lamb of God were identified. The March 6 date of the discovery, however, was not the date set aside for the church's annual celebration of the mystery of the cross. Rather it was to be September 14, the day the precious relic, having been properly enshrined, was publicly venerated for the first time in Jerusalem.

This first public veneration of the true cross drew a great multitude of people. In solemn ceremony the cross was raised up, or "elevated," so that the mortal eyes of the faithful might behold that Tree on which the immortal Lamb of God had been suspended. Climbing up into the pulpit to support the arms of the precious relic with both hands, Bishop Makarios raised it to the incessant chanting of "Lord have mercy" while the faithful fell to their knees, faces to the ground in veneration.

The basic paradox of Christianity's supreme symbol was thus proclaimed: through Jesus Christ Imperial Rome's gibbet of shame, "unto the Jews a stumbling block, and unto the Greeks foolishness" (1 Cor 1:23), had become for humanity the sign of "the power of God, and the wisdom of God" (1 Cor 1:24), the true sign of glory and salvation over death and annihilation.

An annual fasting feast was instituted on September 14, still kept to this day in the Orthodox Church as the Elevation of the Holy Cross. One of the 12 great days of the liturgical year, it is still a day of strict fast on which the faithful, in memory of that first public veneration in Jerusalem, again fall prostrate as the cross is raised to the four points of the compass, accompanied by the hundredfold chanting of "Lord have mercy."

So it was that on September 14, 1792, the Feast of the Exaltation of the Holy Cross, Madame Lidoine and her 19 daughters stepped back out into that world for which they would so shortly be offering themselves daily in holocaust, saying to one another that the Lord, in willing their exit on such a day, must be reserving "a very large portion" of his cross for them.

ii

FORBIDDEN TO LIVE TOGETHER, this community of twenty divided itself into four "associations," each lodged in a separate apartment, though two apartments were at the same address. Madame Philippe sometimes refers to "four" groups, sometimes to "three." This is understandable since, prior to their arrest on June 22, 1794, 22 months after expulsion, the number of sisters had dwindled from 20 to 16, and the two groups at the same address merged into one. Nonetheless the original division on September 14, 1792, was indeed into four unequal groups, as indicated by Madame Philippe.

We have already seen that initially Mother Lidoine's group had seven members and included five choir sisters: the prioress plus Mesdames Thouret, Piedcourt, Brard, and Philippe. The two additional members were the lay sister Madame Dufour (Sister Marthe), who cooked the meals for all four associations at the prioress's quarters, and the younger extern sister, Teresa Soiron, who assured communication with the other three groups. This seven-member "association" was housed by the Widow Saiget.

It was the Widow Saiget's brother, Monsieur de la Vallée, who offered lodging with his family to the four-member "association" headed by the subprioress, Madame Brideau. This included the older extern, Catherine Soiron, plus Madame Brideau's two choir sisters, Mesdames Hanisset and Crétien de Neuville.

At the third address were two apartments rented from an innkeeper. In one of these were housed Madame de Croissy, the dying Madame d'Hangest, and three members of Madame de Croissy's "novice class": the infirmarian, Madame Pelras; the young lay sister and last professed, Madame Vérolot; and the perpetual novice, Sister Constance Meunier. In a neighboring apartment were the remaining four nuns for whom Mother de Croissy may also very well have been responsible. These four included two future martyrs: the choir sister, Madame Trézel, and the third lay sister, Madame Roussel (Sister Marie of the Holy Spirit) who, according to a passing remark of Madame Philippe's, was in a constant state of suffering. Completing this last "association" were two not chosen "to follow the Lamb," Mesdames Jordain and Legros, both choir sisters. As we have seen, they, like Madame Philippe, would leave Compiègne in March of 1794. The community's young infirmarian, Sister Pelras, was thus housed with the very ill Sister d'Hangest and next door to the chronically suffering lay sister, Sister Marie of the Holy Spirit (Roussel).

Prior to her death just six weeks after their expulsion, Madame d'Hangest is reported to have expressed regret at dying too soon to participate in a great event she sensed awaited their community. One can but wonder if this remark were not tied to their act of consecration. Certainly nothing precludes the act's already being inaugurated well before the death on October 31, 1792, of Sister Pierre of Jesus.

Whatever the actual date for beginning the act of consecration, Madame d'Hangest's death six weeks after expulsion determined the definitive composition of the community of nineteen. It was as it would remain to the end: thirteen professed choir sisters, three of whom would escape the guillotine; three professed lay sisters; one novice; and two externs, these latter three under no vows.

In late March of 1794 the three not meant "to follow the Lamb" all left Compiègne. Madame Philippe went to Paris to liquidate a legacy from her father; Mesdames Legros and Jourdain went to Rosières in Picardy to assist Madame Legros's brother. Thus, by the time of the June 22 arrest, the two "associations" at the same address had merged into one. Also, at that time, Madame Piedcourt was in Madame Brideau's group in the de la Vallée house rather than in Madame Lidoine's group at the Widow Saiget's. We know that this transfer could only have come about after the inauguration of the act of consecration. Madame Philippe assures us that at that pre-November 26 date Madame Piedcourt was sharing a room at the Widow Saiget's with Madame Thouret. All three addresses were centered on the parish church of Saint Antoine in the heart of Compiègne. St. Antoine's parish priest, Abbé Thibaux, like all Compiègne's parish clergy, was a "juring" cleric, swearing fidelity to the constitutional church. He nonetheless kindly offered the Carmelites' "non-juring" chaplain, Abbé Courouble, an altar for the nuns' daily Mass. This arrangement lasted less than three full months, however. In late November six citizens of Compiègne denounced Abbé Courouble as a non-juring priest. By law he was required to leave France immediately.

iii

FOUR DAYS AFTER THEIR EXPULSION, the Carmelites officially solicited government funds to purchase civilian clothing, the only dress allowed them by law. In a letter to the Administration of the District of Compiègne, dated September 18, 1792, they stated the facts of their case. All their property had been confiscated and funds lacked for buying new clothing. In order to conform to the law they had been reduced to borrowing garments from friends.

Over the next three months their request for government funds passed from one committee to another. No action was apparently ever taken, though all committees agreed that the nun's new pensions were too modest to allow for this considerable expense.

In any case, a soft stance on ex-Carmelite nuns was politically dangerous in France in 1792, whatever might be their human need. In the last known correspondence on this question, dated December 2, 1792, the problem was still unresolved. Since we know that in July of 1794 the nuns still possessed no change of civilian garments, one can only assume that they continued to be clothed by the charity of friends. Certainly it is clear that when washing their civilian outfits in prison 22 months after expulsion, they had nothing to change into but their forbidden habits.

On the morning of September 19, the day following their official petition for clothing funds, Madame Lidoine and her 16 professed sisters all presented themselves before the revolutionary authorities of Compiègne. Clothed in their borrowed civilian garments, the nuns were keenly aware of the precariousness of their impoverished situation. They and their chaplain, Abbé Courouble, had come to qualify for the promised government pensions by taking the new Liberty-Equality oath and signing the register.

Since the Carmelite's superior in Paris had authorized them to take the Liberty-Equality oath, there was no scandal attached to it in September of 1792. Madame Philippe's repeated attempts to avoid facing that simple fact, however, provoked heated controversy prior to the 1906 beatification of the martyrs in Rome. An explanation is therefore necessary.

iv

FOLLOWING THE TERROR, Madame Philippe returned to Compiègne in March of 1795, exactly a year after her departure for Paris. With Mesdames Jourdain and Legros she wished to lay legal claim to one-sixteenth of the belongings left by the annihilated community. Since neither Sister Constance nor either of the two Soiron sisters was a professed nun, the official, legally constituted community did consist of 16 professed religious, only thirteen of whom had in fact been guillotined. The three survivors, unsullied by any government indictment or accusations of criminal activity, claimed that since they each had contributed a dowry upon entering the community, each now had a legal right to one-sixteenth of what was left.

The filing of these three claims in March of 1795 was timely. Estates of condemned persons were normally listed for confiscation before the end of the year following their execution. Though the municipal authorities were prepared to advance 200 pounds to each of the three ex-nuns on that sixteenth part they claimed, departmental authorities stopped this.

A note in Madame Philippe's hand found in the archives of the Carmel of Compiègne apprises us that the final sale of the community's property only took place "15 months" after their arrest, that is, in October, 1795. Since we know that Madame Philippe did not travel to Orleans until October to meet Denis Blot, one surmises that she deliberately tarried in Compiègne to await that October sale of her community's belongings.

Thus, between March and October of 1795, the year immediately following the Terror, the ex-Carmelite had eight months in which to collect relics and information about her annihilated community, whether in Compiègne or in Paris. It was undoubtedly in Paris that she learned of Denis Blot's ties with her sisters in the Conciergerie. There too would she have met that young woman who possessed the precious charcoal-written manuscript of Madame Crétien de Neuville's parody of *La Marseillaise.* The young woman, treasuring it as a martyr's relic, flatly refused to surrender it to Madame Philippe.

Forced therefore to make a copy of the parody for herself, the ex-Carmelite became sensitive to the unpleasant fact that while she was seeking safety outside France on the feast of Our Lady of Mount Carmel, her sisters were heroically greeting their day of trial and execution, as "the day of glory." Her grave infidelity to her vows on the anniversary of her miraculous cure overcame her. The memory of this cure that lay behind her entry into Carmel had been completely forgotten: she had, on that solemn anniversary, thought only of saving her life.

Back in Compiègne Madame Philippe tried to clarify her official status with the church. Her community had disappeared, the church hierarchy was in disarray, and the Revolutionary government had completely reorganized the old dioceses for its new constitutional church. The former diocese of Soissons had been suppressed and Compiègne now attached to the diocese of Beauvais. Beauvais' last non-juring bishop, moreover, the much-revered Monseigneur de La Rochefoucauld, had been slaughtered in 1792 in the September massacres. By 1795, his juring replacement had already abdicated his post to marry.

Madame Philippe thus courageously looked to Soissons for guidance, even though she knew full well that Soissons' exiled non-juring bishop, Monseigneur Bourdeille, had condemned the Liberty-Equality oath. She actually reports referring to this development in her last conversations with Madame Lidoine in Paris on June 21, 1794.

In March of 1795, moreover, the vicars Monseigneur Bourdeille had left in charge in Soissons were still incarcerated.

Madame Philippe thus made her way to the house of detention and asked one of these vicars to hear her confession. He quickly informed her that if she had taken the Liberty-Equality oath she must now formally retract it before the proper authorities. Until she had done that, she could not receive the sacraments.

This brutal pronouncement, coming in the wake of the past year, must have seemed particularly cruel to the 34-year-old former Carmelite. Had her community after all not received proper ecclesiastical authorization for taking the oath two and a half years before? Was her own personal struggle during that time not even to be taken into consideration? After surviving three months of the Terror in Paris, she had, though in mortal fear, accompanied the elderly Madame Lidoine to Franche Comté upon learning of the arrest of her sisters. Repeatedly failing to get across the Swiss border to safety, she had been reduced to eating grass on the mountainside like an animal, something she reported at the end of her life to the future Cardinal Villecourt.

The shock of the vicar's virtual excommunication was undoubtedly also compounded by Madame Philippe's sense of personal guilt regarding her own behavior on the tenth anniversary of her miraculous cure before the relics of Blessed Marie of the Incarnation at Pontoise. She, Sister Josephine Marie of the Incarnation, descendant of St. Louis, the only nun in the community with Bourbon blood, on that very day, the feast of Our Lady of Mount Carmel, had been trying to flee France and escape her part in her community's act of consecration while her sisters were singing of braving the guillotine.

A fleeting allusion to her anguished interior state at this time is found in a note Madame Philippe added to a second copy of the parody of *La Marseillaise* made in her own hand in Compiègne in 1795. Presented to the Carmel of

Compiègne after World War II by a descendant of the de la Vallée family, this precious manuscript copy had apparently been made expressly for that family which had proven so faithful to the martyrs. In her note at the end of the page, Madame Philippe, begging the prayers of all those reading it, invokes the "violence" she had done herself in copying it out. This "violence" undoubtedly refers to her excruciating realization that these lines defying the guillotine were first sung at precisely the time she had been trying to escape into Switzerland.

V

DEVASTATED BY HER VIRTUAL EXCOMMUNICATION in Soissons, Madame Philippe returned to Compiègne. The morning after, imbued with the courageous resolve to make her formal retraction, even if it meant arrest, she made her way to the municipal office. Anticipating cold nights in prison as a result of her retraction, she says she prudently took along her prayerbook and nightcap.

According to her own account she strode into the municipal office rather aggressively, defiantly addressing the municipal officials as though they themselves were that Revolutionary Surveillance Committee responsible for the death of her 16 sisters. She states that she there and then "dictated word by word [her] retraction" to the clerk who wrote it down with tears in his eyes. This touched her, for he had once been a familiar figure to her and her guillotined sisters: he was Abbé Thibaux, former juring priest of Saint Antoine's. In postrevolutionary Compiègne he would in fact again become a priest and die a respected public figure.

Madame Philippe specifies moreover that the Mayor of Compiègne had informed her then that between their arrest and their transfer to Paris, all her sisters had also made their retractions in their Compiègne prison. She claims he then had the clerk show her the register containing their retractions and signatures, all of which she, deeply moved, kissed with tears.

The register in which Madame Philippe's own retraction is found proves her story false. It is not a special register for retractions at all but the register they had all signed when taking the oath on September 19, 1792. There, in the left-hand margin of the page bearing all their signatures for taking the oath, is found Madame Philippe's retraction, not "dictated" at all to someone else, but written out in her own hand. The only fact worthy of credence in her story therefore seems to be that she did probably tearfully kiss the signatures, and that the Abbé Thibaux was kind to her on that occasion.

Over the years, however, those signatures that Madame Philippe had tearfully kissed, and beside which she had written out her own retraction, became, in her mind, those of her sisters' retraction, not those for their taking the oath. Indeed, the more she thought of the facts, the more inadmissible they became. Her subconscious denial thus seems to have created in her mind a phantasm that the retraction was recorded in a second register.

Indeed, Madame Philippe's muddled version cannot but raise questions about the function of this nonexistent "second register." Though she never specifies where the friendly Abbé Thibaux wrote her dictated retraction, she does state that it was only after writing it down that he showed her the register with her sisters' signatures for their retraction. This would indicate that he had "written out" her retraction before producing the "other" register. If then there existed a second register for retractions, why was Madame Philippe's own retraction not recorded it in?

The original document, today found in the Bibliothèque Municipale of Compiègne and reproduced in Father Bruno's *Le Sang du Carmel*,[1] further shows that Madame Philippe's story about their being "tricked" into signing this oath was also the fruit of her own imagination. According to her story, the mayor, "two" or "three" "months" after their expulsion, came "one evening" (and not on the *morning* of September 19, just *five days* after expulsion) when, for some reason, the whole community was gathered together. The mayor showed Madame Lidoine a "blank" page he wanted them all to sign. According to Madame Philippe, the prioress was suspicious, asking the mayor if he weren't trying to get their signatures so that he could afterward affix the Liberty-Equality oath to the top of it. The mayor denied any such intent and they all signed. Only later did they learn that, as Madame Lidoine had foreseen, the text of the oath had indeed been inserted above their signatures.

The page they all actually signed, as can still be seen, could not possibly have been blank on September 19 since the signature of a person taking the oath on September 18 appears at the top of it. This simple fact, revealed by even a superficial glance at the original document, completely undermines Madame Philippe's version.

Though Madame Philippe would hardly deliberately misrepresent the facts, the thought that her sisters had not made the retraction that she herself was *required* to make to be readmitted to the sacraments, does seem to have caused her to harbor a dark, nagging suspicion that they might have

---

[1] P. Bruno de J.-M., *Le sang du Carmel ou la véritable passion des seize carmélites de Compiègne* (Paris: Cerf, 1992). The document in question is on the ninth page of illustrations situated between pp. 250 and 251. One reads at the bottom: "Le serment de liberté-égalité." The original edition (Paris: Plon, 1954) reproduced this document opposite p. 264.

died in a state bordering on excommunication. On the other hand, her conversations with the English Benedictines, imprisoned in Compiègne until May of 1795, convinced her that her sisters' sacrifice had saved the Benedictines' lives. Far from reassuring her, however, the thought that her sisters must be *bona fide* martyrs only compounded her confusion. Given her rather conformist mind, the ex-Carmelite felt that if, as it did appear, they were indeed true martyrs, then she, to the best of her ability, must defend the honor of their status with the church.

Her knowledge that they had all freely signed the register and sworn the oath thus was inwardly denied as inadmissible. Nearly 40 years later and at past 70 years of age, when she found herself obliged to write down for a religious superior what she assumed would be the definitive record of her sisters' sacrifice, her ruminations of more than three and a half decades suddenly took shape as authentic historic "facts." Having for so long painfully tried to resolve the enigma of her martyred sisters dying in a state that, just a year later, and according to the vicar of Soissons, deprived her of the sacraments, she tried to convince her readers of what she apparently had convinced herself: first, that neither she nor her sisters could ever possibly have taken the oath except by trickery; and second, that her sisters, before dying as martyrs, had, like herself, also made their retractions.

vi

VERY SHORTLY AFTER THEIR EXPULSION the 39-year-old Madame Lidoine opened her great heart to her daughters, proposing that they offer themselves in holocaust. A close analysis of Madame Philippe's manuscripts shows that this was not proposed to the community as a whole, however, but only to the four choir sisters of Madame Lidoine's own household:

Mesdames Thouret, Piedcourt, Brard and Philippe. The first three, let us recall, were the three most senior nuns of the community. Neither the lay sister, Madame Dufour, nor the extern, Teresa Soiron, was present.

Madame Lidoine put to her four sisters the basic question troubling her: since St. Teresa of Avila, in launching her reform of Carmel, had had the salvation of the kingdom of France—at that time struggling with the inroads of Protestantism—as one of her intentions, should her desire to save France not now inspire them too as Carmelites? Forced back into the world in civilian clothing, should they, who were French, not respond as had St. Teresa, a Spaniard, by offering all for France and her church?

What she envisaged was a community act of consecration for holocaust. Through it they would offer themselves daily, body and soul, to appease the wrath of God. Might they not thereby help restore his Son's peace to the realm? Both France and her church were being sorely tried by massacres, slaughter, mass drownings, and deportations of priests, expulsions and persecution of religious orders, to say nothing of the split between constitutional and nonconstitutional clergy. Did not an immediate and urgent need exist for Christian action to counter this attempt by the powers of darkness to wipe out the church of Jesus Christ in France?

The similarity between Madame Lidoine's reasoning and that of Teresa of Avila is obvious. Nor was it unlike that of Madame Louise of France in wishing to save the king's soul by becoming a Carmelite. It is in fact basic Christianity. Jesus Christ himself taught that only by prayer and fasting do certain earthly manifestations of demonic powers yield to the will of God (Mt 17:21).

In her manuscript, Madame Philippe repeatedly scratched out every phrase revealing that it was only to the four choir nuns of Madame Lidoine's household that the idea was first presented. She did not, however, suppress the fact that both septuagenarians strongly dissented. Horrified by the thought of that newfangled machine inaugurated the previous April for instant decapitation, Mesdames Thouret and Piedcourt were not at all immediately inclined to tempt heaven by proposing themselves as victims to die on it.

Their reaction startled Madame Lidoine, who apparently repented of having made such a proposal. She said that if she had had any idea that sharing this fruit of her meditation with them was going to upset them, she would not have spoken of it. Still, she reminded them, her conclusions were not at all in disagreement with St. Teresa's holy intentions for her Order. Might this not therefore be an important matter for her daughters to take into consideration, more especially as they were French?

Deeply troubled, the two senior nuns withdrew in silence. For the rest of the day they remained in their shared room at the Widow Saiget's, reappearing only that evening. According to Sister Marie, she and Madame Lidoine alone were preparing to sing Matins when they came in.

Does the absence of Madame Brard from Matins that evening indicate a certain hesitancy on her part also? Though she had so dramatically spoken to the revolutionary commissioners of clinging to her Carmelite habit even if it meant shedding her blood, she may well have resented such a bold proposal coming from one so much younger. In any case, according to Madame Philippe's manuscripts, Madame Brard was missing from Matins that evening.

The scene of the two tearful 76-year-old nuns coming to ask forgiveness of their 39-year-old prioress for their lack of courage is movingly described by Madame Philippe. Falling on their knees, they, good Carmelites, first begged forgiveness for breaking the Grand Silence. Though they were violating the Rule, what could they do? They could not sleep with their bad consciences. Would Mother Teresa of Saint Augustine please forgive them their cowardice? They, the oldest members of the community, already "on the edge of the grave," and both having celebrated fifty-year jubilees of profession, had been the ones who hesitated to offer their lives for such a holy purpose. They were ashamed and sorry.

Whether it was the next day or later that Madame Lidoine proposed the act of holocaust to the other three "associations" we do not know. Nor do we know whether she spoke separately with each group, or with all the groups together. The immediate reaction of the others is also unknown. All we can say for sure is that the community did undertake the daily recitation of the act, drawn up by the prioress. The daily offering of this act was an established practice by November 27, on which date Madame Trézel prayed to her dead newborn niece, the day after the infant's baptism, to join her pure prayers with the community's act of consecration to save France. As we have seen, it is also quite possible that the mortally ill Madame d'Hangest was already referring to the act before her death on October 31, 1792, when she spoke of anticipating some great community deed she regretted missing.

We know further that Catherine Soiron and her younger sister, Teresa, had thought of leaving the nuns, since they, as externs, could no longer be assured their wages after expulsion. The act of holocaust so touched Catherine Soiron, however, that she and her sister henceforth refused to leave them. The Soiron sisters thus also went to take the Liberty-Equality oath on December 17, 1792, three months after the community. They thereby qualified for a government pension, awarded them in March of 1793. Only the young novice, Sister Constance, would remain ineligible.

During those few brief weeks between their expulsion in mid-September and Abbé Courouble's departure at the end of November, the nuns did enjoy a sort of brief respite. Though they found themselves without the cloister, they were still blessed with daily Mass, allowing them to take ever deeper cognizance of their situation. For, as the Abbé Courouble offered the unbloody sacrifice of the Body and Blood of Jesus Christ for them each morning in Saint Antoine's parish church, they not only adored him whom Baudelaire calls "the eternal and voluntary Victim," but gradually came to seek an ever more incarnate union with him. Taught by the example of Madame Lidoine's own burning love, they began to grasp that his flesh, offered in oblation, was to become their own flesh, and his blood, shed for many, was also to become their own blood.

If we imagine the community renewing their daily act of consecration following one of those early morning daily masses in Saint Antoine's in that autumn of 1792, an indelible impression emerges. In a country rent by radical revolution, this small community of 19 outcast nuns, stripped of their habits and clothed in unfashionable, second-hand civilian clothes, daily offered themselves to God in holocaust, body and soul, with such meticulous attention that scoffers would have found it all ridiculous. Their shoulders and bosoms covered by large, cast-off scarves, their heads enclosed by nondescript, cast-off bonnets, they pronounced their daily act of consecration in hushed but distinct and insistently articulated voices, totally indifferent to the scorn of the world. Like incense their voices rose toward heaven from their half-hidden side altar in St. Antoine's Church, gently pervading the semi-darkness of the early morning hour. Far from the eyes of a busy world and, indeed, almost invisible to it, these hidden souls, consumed by their love for Jesus Christ, were participating in a divine drama, the only drama that really matters for Christians. On a chilled, grey autumnal morning in the year 1792, while France was in the midst of its Revolution, these 19 French women, in the shadows of a provincial parish church, inextricably joined things of heaven to things of the earth.

vii

The Carmelites' act of consecration would thus faithfully reflect the symbolism of September 14, for the paradoxical mystery of the cross could not but be reflected and made incarnate in their own tribulations as an ousted community of consecrated women. Moreover, since the annual Carmelite pre-Easter fast also begins on September 14, the symbolism of that date seemed even more highly charged for these daughters of St. Teresa of Avila as they contemplated their witness without the cloister.

Madame Philippe's rather vague statement that the act of consecration was made "to lessen the wrath of God and to restore that peace to France and to its church that his divine Son had come to bring" is rendered more specific for us by Monseigneur Jauffret, Bishop of Metz. Writing in 1803, just nine years after the martyrdom, he pointedly referred to Madame Philippe as one of his sources when he published his curiously titled *Memoirs for the History of Religion and Philosophy at the End of the Eighteenth Century*.[2]

This strange title provided the indispensable camouflage required under Napoleon's regime to avoid the wrath of the censor. Indeed, when publishing a volume on the First Empire's most politically incorrect subject, religious persecution during the Revolution, extreme caution was required. For Napoleon had rightly grasped through his remarkable political instinct that no subject was potentially more divisive in postrevolutionary France. With the wealth of so many of his country's *nouveaux riches* derived from the spoils of France's once-mighty church, it was indelicate to speak of these things.

---

[2] Jean-Joseph Jauffret, évêque de Metz, *Mémoires pour servir à l'histoire de la Religion et de la Philosophie à la fin du XVIIIe siècle* (Paris: Le Clerc, 1803).

Napoleonic censorship was also responsible for the 20-year delay in publishing Abbé Aimé Guillon's indispensable four-volume biographical dictionary, *Martyrs for the Faith.*[3] Seized by Fouché's police, the huge manuscript, dedicated to Pius XI, was not released until after the Restoration and published only in 1821.

Of vital interest for us, however, is the fact that in both Abbé Guillon's vast work and in the smaller work of Monseigneur Jauffret, references are made to the witness of Madame Philippe. Both authors had questioned her shortly after the martyrdom when her memory was far fresher than during that period between 1832 and her death in 1836 when, at Abbé Villecourt's suggestion, she set herself the task of writing up her *Relation du martyre.*

Monseigneur Jauffret's 1803 volume, *Memoirs for the History of Religion and Philosophy at the End of the Eighteenth Century,* therefore stands as the earliest published document we have on the Carmelites' sacrifice. We believe it is also the most reliable in regard to details only Madame Philippe could have provided. In a chapter entitled "Relation of the Glorious End of the Carmelite Nuns of Compiègne, Condemned to Death by the Revolutionary Tribunal of Paris on 17 July 1794,"[4] Monseigneur Jauffret says he believes Madame Philippe, whom he cites as a witness, still to be in Orleans at the time of writing.

Madame Philippe's own manuscripts, begun at the very earliest in 1832 when she was already in her seventy-first year, must therefore be compared with this earlier account, dating from more than three decades before. Highly significant is the fact that Monseigneur Jauffret alone tells us both how and where Madame Philippe learned of the execution of her sisters,

---

[3] See note 1, p. 85.

[4] Vol. 2, pp. 351–373.

something she herself never hints at in any of her five manuscripts. He also gives us, as we shall see, a far more convincing version of her and her prioress's encounter with the condemned in Paris on June 14, just a week before the community's arrest.

Yet for us the most important detail to be found in the Bishop of Metz's work concerns the act of consecration. He mentions a supplementary intention, added only at some point during the last year, for the release of souls from prisons and the lessening of the number passing to the guillotine.

This new, supplementary intention cannot but reflect the reaction of Madame Lidoine and her community to the ever-mounting and staggering number of innocent victims being offered up daily on the guillotine-altar of the Revolution. A spontaneous cry coming from an unidentified nun at the foot of the scaffold on the day of the martyrdom, and reported by Monseigneur Jauffret alone, decisively confirms the existence of such an added intention. He states that immediately after Madame Lidoine had led the community in renewing their monastic vows, one of them cried out that she was only too happy to die if her little sacrifice could reduce the number of victims.

In Madame Philippe's manuscripts we can only find a slight hint regarding such an additional intention when she states that Denis Blot, the Orleans wine-grower, pointedly affirmed that his escape from the guillotine was due to her sisters' sacrifice. She further implies that this added intention had been communicated to the English Benedictines by her sisters when she states that the Benedictines spoke to her in 1795 of their debt to her sisters whose sacrifice had saved them.

The Benedictines had naturally been struck by this particular aspect of the Carmelites' act of consecration: they had already lost four of their twenty-one sisters during their two years of incarceration. Suddenly finding they were fellow-prisoners with 16 French Carmelites daily offering themselves to free prisoners like themselves, the English daughters of St. Benedict could not but form a mystic bond with these 16 French daughters of St. Teresa. That mystic bond was still evident in 1983 when one of the descendants of that community, today situated at Stanbrook Abbey in Worcester, England, told the author with no equivocation: "We're here because of them." Madame Philippe's hesitancy in speaking more directly of this additional intention could perhaps stem from the fact that she was actually unfamiliar with it, never having pronounced it. Historically, there is actually a very good reason to suggest that this additional intention was probably introduced only in those very last months, after Madame Philippe's departure. Indeed, it was immediately after her departure at the end of March 1794 that the sudden purge and execution of the Dantonists, on April 5, unchained the convulsions of that violent, bloody spring of 1794 which, on June 10, gave way to the Great Terror.

viii

A DOCUMENT ATTRIBUTED TO MADAME LIDOINE, discovered by the author in 1985 among the papers of Madame Philippe in the archives of the Carmel of Sens, has considerable bearing on the mystery behind the now-lost act of holocaust. A four-stanza Christmas carol, composed "to be sung at the crèche," it goes far in revealing Madame Lidoine's deep mystical orientation as she contemplated the guillotine. Mother Teresa of Saint Augustine's bold, Christocentric spirituality is there revealed as rooted in a burning, loving intimacy binding her to him whom she addresses as the "Infant God." In it are echoes not only of St. Teresa of Avila, but also of St. John of the Cross's "Living Flame of Love." Like her Spanish forebears, Madame Lidoine longed to be clasped faster still within his heart, aflame with love for humanity.

Let thy blade cut, completing all my offerings,
For nothing but thy will for me is sweet.
My one desire is that thy hand be hovering
O'er me thy bride, the sacrifice complete!

Would a soul less consumed by such a dynamic, burning love for the divine Lover—a love stronger even than the fear of death—have been able to preside over the oblation of her entire community with such maternal grace?

The prioress's carol could have been sung either for their first Christmas outside the cloister in 1792, or for their final Christmas in 1793. In either case it could only have centered on a very poor crèche. Unfailingly some of the community, inwardly at least, would have compared the present crèche's poverty to the grandiose and elaborate display of their old crèche with its various tableaux composed of magnificent, richly clad life-sized wax figures.

For Madame Lidoine, however, the image of the Infant God was the essential one, not only for the feast, but for the whole Christian faith. Almighty God, the Creator of heaven and earth, of all things visible and invisible, had taken on human flesh. God thus lay there on the straw at the mercy of his creation. Come to bestow upon man his divine life which is beyond death and suffering, he was the "Lamb slain from the foundation of the world" (Rev 13:8), destined for sacrifice.

Mother Lidoine had plunged deeply into the mystery encompassing the Incarnation of the Divine Logos of the Father. She had found in him the origin and end of all things (Rev 1:8), the answer to all that the human heart seeks or desires (Rev 21:6). Having put off his glory to become man (Phil 2:6–7) and save the fallen, twisted race of Adam, her divine Bridegroom had consented to be slain and buried by those he had not blushed to call his brothers (Heb 2:11).

Madame Lidoine's commitment to the Divine Logos is revealed in her carol as being both total and unequivocal. She there speaks of making his ineffable and eternal "martyrdom of love" her own so that she, through his Spirit, might also become a participant in his eternal redemption of the human race.

O Infant God, naught else can fill my longing,
Yea, nothing else can satisfy my heart!
It's settled then, henceforth I'm thy belonging,
And of thy love, I've now become a part.
My criminal soul, heal of its sin so shameful,
Wound thou my heart, with pain or love's delight.
Let wounds divine, wounds for my soul most gainful,
Martyr my heart to suffer day and night!

O Love divine, I now with all my being
Here at thy crèche abandon all my soul.
I thus yield up my reasoning and my seeing
From this time forth: my faith in thee is bold!
Thy heart alone! Thy heart shall be my master!
Thoughts and desires I sacrifice as weak.
Within thy heart, I would now be clasped faster,
The martyrdom of love alone I seek.

Oh! fix my hope, oh fix it all on dying!
Truly I die from not dying for thee.
And hasten, Lord, the end of all my sighing
Freed from these chains to thee alone I'll flee!
Let thy blade cut, completing all my offerings,
For nothing but thy will for me is sweet.
My one desire is that thy hand be hovering
O'er me thy bride, the sacrifice complete!

Thy shepherd's crook, let it rule as the master
O'er this thy flock entrusted to my care.
Here at thy crèche, I yield to thee, O Pastor,
Mother and flock, abandoning all I dare!
O loving Queen, Mother of might most holy,
O deign to place us all within thy breast!
For in thy power, thy children all, though lowly,
Do set their hope, trusting in thy behest.

The answer of her Bridegroom to her oblation of love as he claimed her for his own would be the fall of that blade "completing all [her] offerings."

For the peace of France and its church, for the quelling of the Terror with its thousands of victims, and for the salvation of her body and soul, let this witness of love be offered then to the Divine Majesty.

ix

REGARDLESS OF WHEN Madame Lidoine's carol was first sung, it sprang from the same source as their act of consecration. It was Mother Teresa of Saint Augustine's spiritual reaction as a consecrated Christian woman to the chaos into which France had been plunged since the night of August 10, 1792, when the king and royal family had fled to the National Assembly, seeking protection from the mob storming the Tuileries Palace. The National Assembly, instead of receiving them as the endangered First Family of France's much touted constitutional monarchy, locked them up in the Temple.

Three weeks later the September massacres announced the unchaining of those dark, malevolent forces at work in France since the beginning of the Revolution. The definitive expulsion of all religious from convents and monasteries immediately followed.

These dark forces launched by the September massacres were even more blatantly evident by the end of 1792. By the spring of 1793, they had proven powerful enough to reshape official French justice with a heretofore unknown creation: the Revolutionary Tribunal. This Tribunal, under the cloak of legality provided by its creation, gave the revolutionary government complete freedom to perpetrate a reign of terror through indiscriminate mass executions.

The Revolutionary Tribunal was in fact the brainchild of Danton, the 34-year-old Minister of Justice. Though he had sanctioned the September massacres, he was sensitive to the political damage done to revolutionary France by foreign criticism of such freelance slaughter. An official, legal structure must therefore be created to allow for continuing the terrorism of mass executions, thus ensuring the Revolution's success through ever-greater audacity. What Danton did not foresee, however, was that he himself would be ensnared by his own audacious creation. A scarce year later, on April 5, 1794, he became the Revolutionary Tribunal's most notable nonroyal victim.

The terrorism Danton favored proved as insensitive to the dead as to the living. It was as if everything human, dead or alive, had to feel the impact of the new order's fanatical championing of "freedom, equality, and brotherhood." Long before 1793, with its desecration of the tombs in the royal basilica at Saint-Denis, and even prior to the storming of the Bastille, profanation of the dead had become a mark of the revolutionary spirit abroad. The macabre orgy of profanation and pillage at Saint-Denis in October of 1793 did not spare even the chaste remains of Madame Louise of France. Expressly sought out in the cemetery of Saint-Denis's Carmel at the end of that ghoulish operation, they were disinterred and pitched into the common pit with the rest of France's "most Christian" royal house, to be covered with quicklime. Christianity's power to transcend birth and royal station was meaningless to the inflamed patriots.

Profanation of the dead in revolutionary France went beyond the mere parading of human heads. As we have seen, it included the mutilation of bodies and, on occasion, even cannibalism. The bloodbath of the September massacres thus only provided a disordered foretaste of the legalized mass effusions of blood ordered by the Revolutionary Tribunal.

These daily hecatombs reached their highest point with the Great Terror that would harvest the 16 Carmelites.

Numerically the Carmelites' sacrifice was negligible at the height of the Great Terror. Twenty-four others perished with them in that same day's "batch" of forty. What indeed are so few when weighed against the thousands slaughtered by the new order in the name of the French people? These 16 women were, however, consecrated to the ever-virgin Mother of that Jewish God-Man whose execution had also once been deemed insignificant. They believed that his life mysteriously burned brightly in them through the dynamism of the Holy Spirit. As he himself had said, none go to the Father but by him (Jn 14:6), and he was indeed their Way, their Truth, and their Life (Ibid.). Had he not promised those who are his that they will have tribulations in this world (Jn 16:33)? Nonetheless he had also charged them be of good cheer, for he had overcome the world (Ibid.).

They came to grasp that the guillotines and gibbets of this world had already been overcome by him and that their deaths, like all human suffering, had also already been assumed by him, the eternal Lamb, slain before the foundation of the world (Rev 13:8). Their offering of love, accomplished in his name, would thus be for them not only a participation in, but indeed an extension of, his own unfathomable love for the human race.

In this gift of themselves to him, they would therefore become participants in his redemptive energies, ever present in the world through the Holy Spirit. Were they not being summoned to take their places at the celestial banquet table, prepared for all eternity for those invited to the mystic wedding of the Lamb? Each act of love poured out for the Lamb from the beginning of time nourishes those heeding his summons to that feast to taste his life-giving manna. All who take their places there shall be filled. None shall go away empty, nor shall they ever hunger or thirst again. In the kingdom of the Father, Son, and Holy Spirit the Lamb nourishes his own from that endless store of love with which he has ever rewarded those who love him, giving them love for love. For his love is himself, since it is only fitting that he be all in all at his own wedding feast. And those answering his call shall see him as he is.

Relying on the fiery presence of the Spirit of God in their midst, Madame Lidoine strove to keep the eyes of her community fixed on Jesus Christ as the Lamb of God. In the dark night of her own great soul's solitude before God, with what infinite and insatiable longing did she not ceaselessly seek him as she thirsted for the martyrdom of love!

Makarios, Bishop of Jerusalem, had once raised up that Roman gibbet of shame on which the Lord of glory suffered, bled and died, that the forces of darkness might be held at bay. So let it now be with each of them raised up on the scaffold-altar of the new order in an oblation of love. Let mortal eyes again behold his immortal might and power rise before them in the midst of the darkness engulfing France and her church. Strapped to the balance plank and tipped forward in a face-down position, let each of them, just as on the day of her profession, when she had lain prostrate on the monastery church floor, her arms extended in a living cross, once again seek the glory, salvation, and eternal life awaiting brides of the Lamb. Let their immolated Bridegroom, as he drew nigh to claim them for his own, find them thus extended on the scaffold before him, waiting to bid him welcome.

Pastel by the prioress, Teresa of St. Augustine (Photo, Hutin)

7

Mysteries, Martyrs, and Rites of the New Order

(i) Mass for the nuns after expulsion; departure of Abbé Courouble; ministry of Abbé de Lamarche. (ii) September, 1792; the guillotine at the Place du Carrousel. (iii) Execution of the king; Le Peletier de Saint-Fargeau, first "freedom martyr"; the creation of the Pantheon; David and the enshrinement of Voltaire and Le Peletier de Saint-Fargeau. (iv) Marat, second "freedom martyr"; his campaign against the Girondins; Charlotte Corday; Marat's apotheosis on the Feast of Our Lady of Mount Carmel. (v) David's "Festival of Republican Reunion"; Citizen Palloy and the cult of the Bastille; a rite of communion; the cult for the "freedom martyrs." (vi) The purge of the Girondins; the fall of Danton; Robespierre's cult of the Supreme Being. (vii) The Festival of the Supreme Being. (viii) Why the guillotine was moved after 13 months; Robespierre and blood sacrifice. (ix) Robespierre's end; the next day's horror.

DAILY MASS IN ST. ANTOINE'S CHURCH was assured for the expelled nuns only until Abbé Courouble's departure at the end of November 1792. After less than three months their comforting daily union with the sacramental presence of the immolated Beloved came to an end. Yet, as they continued to offer themselves for holocaust through their daily recitation of the act of consecration after their chaplain's departure, the act itself became a powerful manifestation of his presence. Indeed, the only peace available to them came from being utterly reliant on him alone. Never had the verses of their holy mother-foundress seemed more timely:

Thine I am, born for Thee,
What then wouldst Thou do with me?

Beginning in 1793 we know that Abbé de Lamarche, in the course of periodic visits to Compiègne to minister to the faithful, ministered also to the Carmelites. Still his periodic Masses could never replace the reassuring grace of a regular, daily Mass with its sacramental manifestation of the Beloved in their midst, day in and day out. But Abbé de Lamarche sustained and encouraged the community in their newfound vocation of absolute self-offering, and we have already seen how he so gently reconciled the young Sister Constance to death by the guillotine. Like a Christian in the early church, this exceptional priest knew how to venerate the presence of the Holy Spirit in those who were being called to witness with their blood.

ii

EVEN THOUGH THE FACT was not announced by the revolutionary government until October 5, 1793, we have seen that, according to the Republican calendar, "day One, of year One, of the One Indivisible French Republic" had dawned on the first equinox after the fall of the monarchy, September 22, 1792. Yet, in the chronicles of the Revolution, the significance of September 1792 went well beyond its being the month that served, albeit retrospectively, to mark the beginning of a new era in human history. No month in that long stretch of months during which France was being purged of the old order proved more astounding. With the continued, and heretofore unthinkable, incarceration of the royal family, with the appalling blood bath of the massacres as that month began, and with the expulsion of the last religious from all surviving monasteries, September of 1792 proved a startling break with the past.

September of 1792 also saw the end of the Revolution's Legislative Assembly. Before disappearing, its members provided for the conversion of the former machine hall of the now-deserted Tuileries Palace into an assembly hall for the newly elected National Convention. Renovations would not be completed, however, until May of 1793.

In the meantime, workmen constructing the new assembly hall could sometimes watch revolutionary justice being administered on the Place du Carrousel by merely looking out the windows. About once a week Sanson, Paris's executioner, could be seen there setting up the guillotine, assisted by his valets. Since the crime for which most of these prisoners were losing their heads was that of having defended the palace's royal occupants against the "patriots" storming it on August 10, the government deemed a last sight of the ex-royal Tuileries Palace particularly salutary for the condemned. Punishment at the scene of the crime held a strong pedantic appeal for the moralists of the virtuous new order when dealing with political prisoners. Indeed, on August 17, 1792, just seven days after the August 10 upheaval, a distinct category for political criminals had been introduced into French justice and a special court created for dealing with all those "criminals" of August 10.

The new order found reassurance in the fact that, following the guillotine's inauguration on April 25, all prisoners condemned to death, regardless of their social status, would benefit from its egalitarian dispatch. Still, even with the classless guillotine, executions for criminals of common law continued to take place at the age-old execution site of the Place de Grève. Only those falling into the new political category were brought to the ex-royal setting of the Place du Carrousel for their punishment.

At the end of the eighteenth century the Place du Carrousel was almost completely enclosed by the Tuileries Palace, juxtaposed as it was to a wing of the Louvre. Because of its enclosed nature it would be eschewed for the king's execution on January 21, 1793. Rumors of attempts to abduct and free the august prisoner were abroad. The place of the execution must allow for the free movement of troops and the open spaces of the Place of the Revolution (Place de la Concorde) were therefore favored. There both the massing of troops and the presence of thousands of witnesses to the regicide were possible. The new government also savored the prospect of beheading France's "most Christian" king at that ex-Place Louis XV, constructed in honour of his immediate predecessor and grandfather. Its fine marble statue of Louis XV, toppled and smashed, had been replaced by a politically correct statue of "Freedom" in common plaster.

Following the January 21 regicide, however, the guillotine did return to the Place du Carrousel. There, about once a week, it continued to function until May 8. Members of the newly elected National Convention were scheduled to move into their renovated hall on May 10, however, and the more squeamish representatives, it was decided, must be spared. The risk of witnessing the administration of the new order's justice just outside their new assembly hall windows thus prompted them to move the guillotine definitively on May 8 to the Place de la Revolution. There, as the new order gained momentum, it functioned ever more frequently, particularly after October 5, 1793, when the ten-day *décadi* replaced the seven-day week. By the end of the 13 months it remained there, it was dispatching an average of 14 political prisoners per day, nine days out of ten. Only on the eve of June 8, 1794, in preparation for the Festival of the Supreme Being, would it finally be moved elsewhere.

Meanwhile king and beggar alike were beheaded with no distinction, and with egalitarian efficiency, as the new order's goal of supplanting Christianity with a less fanatical religion was ardently pursued. Outdated superstitious nonsense about Jesus Christ, that Jew whom Christians believed to be the virgin-born Son of God, and who rose from the dead, were things to be relegated to France's pre-Enlightenment past. Indeed, what could prove more inimical to progress and the modernity of the new philosophical thought than Judeo-Christian superstitions rooted in seven-day weeks, sacrificial lambs, scapegoats, victims of holocaust, or a God who counts every bird that falls (Mt 10:29)?

iii

As IF TO UNDERLINE the rampant dechristianization following the August 10 fall of the monarchy, no church bell would sound in all of Paris on December 25, 1792, even though the new calendar had not yet been proclaimed. Just two weeks before that historic silent Christmas, on December 11, 1792, the king had been put on trial before the National Convention. The conjunction of this silent Christmas with the king's trial was hardly amiss, given that the new order was aware that it had been on Christmas day, 496, that St. Rémi had baptized Clovis and anointed him as France's first Christian king at Rheims.

Four weeks after that uncelebrated Christmas, on the morning of January 21, 1793, the king, attended by a nonjuring priest and condemned to death by a one vote majority—361 to 360—was guillotined. The close vote reminded the revolutionary government that a cult would undoubtedly spring up around the "martyr-king." It was urgent, therefore, for propaganda purposes, that a countercult for a purely revolutionary martyr be created forthwith.

The needed subject conveniently fell available on January 20, the eve of the king's execution. He was an aristocrat-turned-revolutionary named Le Peletier de Saint-Fargeau, representative to the National Assembly. Having voted for the king's execution that day, he had the misfortune, that same evening, of encountering a saber-wielding member of the former Royal Guard named Pâris. In crazed desperation over the death sentence, Pâris had gone out, sword in hand, determined to slay an acquaintance who, he learned, had voted for the king's death. Happening first upon the unknown Le Peletier de Saint-Fargeau, who readily admitted that he too had voted for execution, Pâris immediately pierced his chest with a single thrust. The aristocrat-turned-republican expired without delay.

Revolutionary propaganda moved quickly to exploit this "martyrdom for freedom," occurring in such a timely fashion. Jacques-Louis David, whom we have encountered, was designated to organize the lying-in-state and the pageant-procession to follow the state funeral on January 24. Hopefully the impact of a public pageant of "canonization" for this newly proclaimed first "freedom martyr" would prove a successful coup of propaganda, bewildering the confused masses and deflecting criticism from the regicide.

David's rare talents for such public funeral rites had been brilliantly demonstrated for the first time just a year and a half before. On July 11, 1791, he had been responsible for the elaborate procession and ceremonies for the state funeral for Voltaire's ashes, finally returned to Paris to receive government honors and be enshrined in the new Republican "Pantheon."

It had been in the spring of 1791 that the revolutionary government commandeered the nearly completed domed ecclesiastical masterpiece of the architect Soufflot. Crowning the Montagne Sainte-Geneviève in Paris's Latin Quarter where Paris's sixth-century patroness, St. Geneviève, had lived, the handsome new domed structure was to replace the ancient and now-demolished church housing her relics.

Louis XV had underlined its importance by his royal presence at the blessing of the new church's first stone.

In 1791, however, the new order secularized Soufflot's monumental masterpiece to create a national mausoleum. Thus, as the church of St. Geneviève became a strictly male preserve, proudly limited to the earthly remains of a "grateful fatherland's great men," the ancient Christian cult to Paris's spiritual mother was disdainfully cast aside. The enlightened men of the new order regarded such cults as superstitious nonsense, totally without relevance for the modern world.

The first body solemnly enshrined in the new national mausoleum was that of Mirabeau, whose sudden death in April of 1791—rumors said by poison—deprived the early Revolution of one of its illustrious leaders. Immediately afterward a clamor arose. In reparation for past neglect, should Voltaire, a great light of the new order and a father of the Enlightenment, not now have his ashes brought back to Paris for burial also in the new Pantheon?

David's all-day pageant-procession for Voltaire's ashes on July 11 featured, in the middle of a very long parade, classically costumed characters from the author's plays walking on either side of the sarcophagus-bearing float. Atop the sarcophagus reclined a life-sized wax figure of Voltaire, draped in a sheet, bare chest exposed, being proffered a crown by a waxen muse. It poured with rain the whole day and, hour after hour, as the funeral float progressed slowly across Paris, the rain gradually washed away the colors applied to the reclining wax figure. Upon finally arriving at the Pantheon that evening it was a cadaverous white.

Voltaire's reclining posture was again favored by David for displaying the crowned cadaver of Le Peletier de Saint-Fargeau on January 24 in 1793. It too was extended on a couch in the open air, but at the Place Vendôme, high up on the central pedestal where the pillar bearing a statue of Louis XIV had previously risen. The cadaver's bared chest allowed the people to contemplate his fateful "martyr's wound."

For the state funeral and procession to the Pantheon members of the National Assembly were massed around the pedestal. Republican hymns were sung prior to escorting this first "freedom martyr" to the Latin Quarter. There Le Peletier de Saint-Fargeau joined Mirabeau and Voltaire as one of the "grateful fatherland's great men."

Neither the enshrined Le Peletier de Saint-Fargeau nor most others entombed with republican pomp in the Pantheon was to prove immune, however, to those many and varying strains of political correctness chronically plaguing the new order's government. Only the literary giant, Voltaire, was left to rest in peace. As for the others, manipulated political enthusiasms kept dictating that the grateful fatherland's great man ceremoniously buried there one day, subsequently be surreptitiously removed with as little afterthought as that of a courtesan carelessly casting off last season's fashions.

iv

On July 13, 1793, a year to the day before the Carmelites of Compiègne arrived as bound prisoners at the Conciergerie, Marat was fatally stabbed in his bath by Charlotte Corday. The violent death of the Swiss-born, Edinburgh-educated doctor and former physician to the troops of the Count of Artois, proved as timely for the government as had the demise of Le Peletier de Saint-Fargeau. Although immediately seen by the new order's government as the most perfect candidate possible for the role of second "freedom martyr," David faced grave problems in the ceremonies accompanying his apotheosis.

Far more widely known than Le Peletier de Saint-Fargeau, Marat was recognized throughout revolutionary

France for his vitriolic Parisian newspaper, *L'ami du peuple.* Fancying himself an important theoretical scientist and humanitarian, as well as "the people's friend," he illustrated this latter virtue by repeatedly calling for thousands of heads to fall in order to guarantee the success of the Revolution. His vociferousness was particularly virulent in regard to the Girondins.

Marat's mid-July demise was thus a double windfall for the government. Caught as it was in its spiraling campaign to purge itself of the powerful Girondin party, the canonization of "the people's friend" as the second freedom martyr would win favor from the people and justify the government's propaganda against the Girondins. Since June the government, not daring to carry out an instantaneous purge of such an influential party, had been obliged to content itself with placing the Girondins under house arrest.

Composed for the large part of representatives from the provinces, and notably from Bordeaux and the region around the Gironde River, the "Girondins," in opposition to the Jacobins or prevailing "Mountain" faction, steadfastly opposed the Revolution's being dominated by Paris. The Jacobins, however, working with the municipal government of Paris through the Committee of Public Salvation, were determined to impose Paris's primacy. Though the June house arrests of the Girondins had temporarily silenced the opposition, the enraged Marat kept calling vehemently for their heads. Sympathetic to the maligned Girondins, Charlotte Corday was determined to silence Marat.

Twenty-five years of age and of a good Caen family, Charlotte Corday was a great-great niece of the classical dramatist, Pierre Corneille. She had made the long trip to Paris from Normandy all alone, intent on her self-imposed mission. Acting with the sublime determination and noble self-composure of a heroine from one of her great-uncle's tragedies, she gained admittance to Marat's apartment, then stabbed him in his hip-bath. As was his wont, Marat had been writing one of his inflammatory articles while soaking in his tub, seeking relief from the chronic itching of his diseased skin. "The people's friend" thus died, pen in hand.

Charlotte Corday went to the guillotine four days later, on July 17, 1793, a year to the day before the Carmelites' martyrdom. Combining youth, beauty, and daring with a rare capacity for coolly dispatching a popular, highly controversial journalist, she must have seemed symbolic of the Girondins themselves. Though personally admirable for her daring, she was guilty of crimes requiring her extermination for the good of the Republic.

The ceremonies for Marat's lying in state as the Revolution's second "freedom martyr" were set for the eve of Charlotte Corday's execution, July 16, feast of Our Lady of Mount Carmel. With this second pierced cadaver David hoped to repeat his success at the Place de Vendôme, even though it was deemed more appropriate to stage Marat's lying-in-state at the Cordelier Club. Located in the former Cordelier Church, the Cordelier Club was the Jacobin Club's most serious rival. It had also claimed Marat as its leading light.

But there were complications. Displaying a body with a gaping wound in the chill of mid-January is not the same thing as displaying it in the heat of mid-July. And the state of Marat's body discouraged it. His skin disease, combined with the July heat, had caused decomposition to set in almost immediately. David was thus obliged to renounce his plan for displaying "the people's friend" sitting up in his bath, his entire torso uncovered, in the position in which he was stabbed. Also reluctantly sacrificed were the propaganda advantages of a three-day lying in state.

Precautions had to be taken in displaying Marat's body. For this purpose a very high stage was constructed above the former church's altar so as to assure a prudent distance between the body and the public. Stretched out on a couch with chest uncovered, the martyr, with his gaping knife wound, would still be visible to all eyes.

To offset the inevitable smell, incense was burned continually in huge braziers, one set at each of the high stage's four corners. Far less mystical but equally effective were the two steaming cauldrons of vinegar, kept boiling on the high platform by two male attendants who, stationed at the head of the dead Marat, were continually sprinkling "the people's friend" by means of sponges soaked in antiputrefactive liquid.

When the doors were opened at noon to an eager public, would-be mourners avidly pushed their way in to gape at the extraordinary spectacle. High above them, at the center of the stage, they beheld Marat's body. It was of greenish tinge and swathed in wet sheets, save for the exposed upper torso with its martyr's wound. Even in death, they noted, "the people's friend" still gripped his "immortal" pen.

In spite of the stench, the masses poured in. They stared, full of wonder, not only at the body high above them up on the incense-clouded stage, but also at the display below: the shoe-shaped hip-bath, the murder weapon, and the journalist's ink stand, but especially Marat's heart. Encased in an urn suspended from a vault in the Cordelier church ceiling, it was inevitably associated by the people with the popular cult to the Sacred Heart of Jesus. Wide-eyed and mouths gaping, they could be seen whispering reverently to their neighbor as they indicated the "Sacred Heart of Marat."

The necessarily quick interment of Marat that same evening in a sealed lead coffin in the Cordelier church came only after a solemn but lugubrious torchlight procession of the body through the streets of Paris. Veiled women mourners accompanied "the people's friend," bearing the hip-bath, the murder weapon, and the ink stand.

This precipitous evening burial, however, proved but the first of a series for Marat. A less hasty one took place in the Luxembourg gardens at the beginning of August. Enshrinement in the Pantheon came more than a year later and was of short duration. Political correctness allowed Marat only four months there. He replaced the unceremoniously removed Mirabeau in November of 1794 but was himself similarly cast out in February of 1795.

At the time of his death, however, "the people's friend" had certainly not lacked adulatory rhetoric. Wounded by the initial refusal of the Pantheon, one devotee compared Marat to Plato, Aristotle, and Socrates. He admitted that he had not known them, but his admiration for Marat whom he had known was just as great and posterity would give him his due.

At the funeral oration in the Luxembourg gardens in early August, the inspired orator went further still. Forgetting about the ancient Greeks, he took up a comparison with the God-Man of the Christians.

> Sacred Heart of Jesus! Sacred Heart of Marat! You have equal rights to our homage! Marat and Jesus, divine men whom heaven gave to earth to direct the people in the way of justice and truth!

Comparing the Jacobins to the Apostles, the shopkeepers to the publicans, and the aristocrats to the Pharisees, he even drew an exaggerated parallel between the Virgin Mary and Marat's concubine. Just as the former had saved the child Jesus from Herod's anger, he observed, so the latter had saved "the people's friend" from the anger of his enemy, Lafayette, former mayor of Paris and legendary hero of the American Revolution. Decisively confirming the superiority of Marat's cult, the speaker concluded: "If Jesus were a prophet, then Marat was a god!"

V

LESS THAN A MONTH after Marat's July 16 apotheosis, a far grander ceremony was entrusted to David's talents. This was the "Festival of Republican Unity," celebrated on August 10, 1793, the first anniversary of the fall of the Christian monarchy. Since the final fate of the detained Girondins was still in abeyance, this August event aimed specifically at shoring up republican unity against the Girondin threat. It was also notable for introducing a rite of communion into republican ceremonies.

The celebration was to take place at the Place de la Bastille, confirming the site's increasing prestige, a prestige that had been carefully nurtured by a certain Citizen Palloy, the stone mason who had acquired the contract for demolishing the old fortress and became a successful Parisian businessman. Aware of holding the monopoly on any profits to be made from the old prison fortress, Citizen Palloy was not at all disinclined to tend the cult growing up around it. Certainly the morbid curiosity of foreigners in search of Parisian thrills was obligingly titillated with horror stories of the old structure. Its fame abroad was thus assured, and the pro-republican idea that "the people's Revolution" finally throwing open its dark doors was long overdue, became a commonplace.

Citizen Palloy even built up a small industry selling the old fortress's stones, whether as plain building stones, or carved into small likenesses of the old Bastille, or busts of famous men such as Voltaire, Franklin, or Washington. Even jewelry was fashioned from them. As revolutionary relics replaced Christian ones, Bastille stones came to be much in demand. No commune in France wished to be without its politically correct relic of the Bastille whenever it staged a patriotic event. Compiègne, rechristened "Marat-sur-Oise" in the wake of Marat's assassination, proudly carried its stone from the Bastille with due pomp and solemnity in all its municipal processions.

Citizen Palloy's Bastille cult, destined to such lasting glory, proved quite successful in glossing over certain disquieting facts. Not only were there but seven persons being held in the old prison-fortress on July 14, 1789, but some of these prisoners actually risked their lives trying to save their kindly prison governor from the blood-thirsty "liberators" who gave all appearances of being no less intent upon beheading the Governor than upon liberating the prisoners. Totally disregarded was the prisoners' informed evaluation of their own situation. The governor's head was triumphantly paraded around as a sign of the "people's victory" over "tyranny."

That it was at the site of the former Bastille that the delegates from each of France's 83 *départements* gathered on August 10, 1793, for the Festival of Republican Unity was therefore hardly surprising. To underline Paris as the center for revolutionary unity, and to strengthen the Jacobin cause against the absent Girondins, David, as pageant-master, had the 83 departmental delegates each take a public oath swearing unity. He thereby offered the people, his program tells us, "the sublime spectacle of a nation of brothers embracing one another under the vault of heaven and swearing in unison to live and die republicans." Each delegate surrendered to the President of the Convention the small tree branch he had carried in procession. At the end the President joined all of them together by means of a tricolored ribbon to form the "fasces" of the Republic.

Rather than feeding on the sacramental body and blood of the old Christian order, however, these representatives of a free people were to partake of the "pure and salutary liquor of regeneration" as the confirmation of their oath-taking. This "salutary liquor" shot forth in two strong streams, one from each of the "fecund breasts" of Nature, embodied by a gigantic statue of a seated female nude, of heavy, graceless proportions, raised on the site for this occasion. Flanked by Egyptian lions and high urns burning incense, Nature dominated the large elongated water-filled basin below her into which gushed her two jets of "pure and salutary liquor." Splendid in tricolor sash and tricolored plumes crowning his David-designed hat, each of the 83 delegates proceeded to this act of republican communion. Catching some of the streaming regenerative "liquor" from one of Nature's jets in a chalice, he drank of it, then passed the common cup on to the next delegate.

David's talent for propaganda ceremonies took on a more personal tone, however, on October 16, the day of Marie Antoinette's execution. While the royal basilica at St. Denis was being sacked, we find him not only making his cruel sketch of the humiliated queen on her way to the guillotine, but also staging a ceremony honoring Marat and Le Peletier de Saint-Fargeau at the Louvre, where he resided. His portrait of each of the Republic's two "freedom martyrs" was solemnly displayed at the national museum that day in a quasireligious setting. Like miraculous icons set out for veneration and attendant graces, each canvas rested on its own sarcophagus, in its own improvised chapel, set off by tricolor bunting. A choir from David's own revolutionary section in Paris came that day to sing funeral hymns before the two images. Before departing, they all swore an oath to die for the nation.

Nor was the government's deification of Marat and Le Peletier de Saint-Fargeau as "freedom martyrs" limited to the efforts of David alone. We find them referred to in a play of Radet's entitled *Le noble routier.*

> Where Freedom's friend is dwelling,
> Where patriotism's sincere,
> We find Freedom's two martyrs,
> Both gods that one reveres.

Busts of the two "martyrs" graced the Revolutionary Tribunal's deliberations.

vi

After five months of Jacobin vilification, 22 Girondin leaders were finally executed on October 31, 1793. Those who had managed to slip away from Paris were later captured and executed; others took their own lives. Sympathizers and associates such as Madame Roland were also ruthlessly eliminated.

It was in the wake of that October 31 execution that Madame Roland's celebrated words, "O Freedom! How many crimes are committed in thy name!" were uttered on the scaffold on November 8. Clad in white with hands bound, the beautiful young Girondin hostess raised her eyes to address Freedom's plaster statue presiding over the guillotine in that fateful moment, before being strapped to the vertical balance plank.

The Girondin purge was only the first of several, however. Each one bound France more tightly in the embrace of a faceless terror. As astounding as each purge proved during the terrible, bloody spring of 1794, the fall of Danton and his associates provoked the most profound shock of all. They were executed on April 5, barely three months before the Carmelites of Compiègne.

The destruction of the 34-year-old Danton was indispensable, however, if his rival for political power, the "incorruptible" Robespierre, were to attain undisputed reign. At 35, Robespierre was just a year older than Danton. A lawyer from Arras and a priggish moralist with great personal ambition, he considered the battle against atheism a goal worthy of his fiery sense of personal mission. Robespierre was also particularly eager to fill the social vacuum created by dechristianization.

The attempted cult to "Reason," highlighted by the much publicized ceremony staged in November of 1792 in Notre Dame in Paris, had not really succeeded. Robespierre therefore opted for a cult to the Supreme Being that disciples of the Enlightenment would find compatible with their reading of the philosophers. Certainly it must be a more intellectually sophisticated religion than Judeo-Christian superstitions concerning the existence of a personal, self-revealing God who intervenes in history and is interested in our destiny to the point of numbering the hairs of our heads (Mt 10:30). Such ideas were esteemed childish fanaticism for any French citizen living in the enlightened age of the philosophers.

Robespierre's Supreme Being, on the other hand, was a vaguely benevolent, largely indifferent creator deity. A free people could, with all of "Nature," address hymns of praise to him with no fear of his irrupting into their private or public affairs. In the moralistic sentimentality of the eighteenth century's euphoria as it deified "Nature," the implacable cruelty of the natural order was forgotten. Indeed, as that century continued to seek rational concepts to replace the "primitive" God of Abraham, Isaac, and Jacob, the unmitigated goodness of "Nature" and of "a free people" seemed to attain ethereal heights of beatitude in a sort of rosy, sublime ascension.

Scarcely a month after Danton's April 5 execution, the 35-year-old Robespierre persuaded the National Assembly on May 7, 1794, to pass a bill decreeing that all citizens of "the One Indivisible French Republic" believed in this nebulous Supreme Being. This astounding bill also included a second statement, equally fictional, proclaiming that all French citizens also believed in the immortality of the soul.

Sorely vexed by this May 7 bill, atheists in the Assembly were even more vexed when Robespierre, implacably pursuing his course, had a nationwide holiday voted to celebrate this fusion of religion and political correctness. The Festival of the Supreme Being was set for 20 Prairial, Year II—June 8, 1794, on the Gregorian calendar. For Christians it was the feast of Pentecost, birthday of the church of Jesus Christ and a Christian feast ranked only after Easter and Christmas.

vii

To ensure that the Pentecostal celebration in 1794 be the most elaborate display of republican propaganda yet staged in Paris, the National Assembly voted a budget of 1.2 million francs for David's Committee of Public Education. A procession was to be featured in which, according to David's program, the whole of Paris would take part.

Roused at an early hour by martial music, the city's citizens, the program specified, were to "embrace one another with joy" and adorn their doorways with green branches. Mothers were to braid their daughters' hair with flowers. Sensing the joy of the day, even nursing infants would suckle more eagerly, the program stated, as old men's eyes filled with tears and the sun beamed down. Save for the weather, it is impossible to state just how much of David's all-inclusive program was realized that June 8. Records show, however, that the sun did shine brightly all day.

Stretching outward from the Tuileries Gardens toward the Place of the Revolution that morning, the mass of people impatiently awaited the beginning of the day's ceremonies at noon. An amphitheatre backing onto the old machine hall of the Tuileries Palace had been especially constructed. At its base were grouped some 800 singers and instrumentalists, commandeered for the day by the government from the Paris Opera, the Conservatory of Music, and the Feydeau Theatre. Required to perform the music commissioned for the festival, both here and at the closing ceremonies at the Champ de Mars, the musicians were, for the most part, a disgruntled lot, totally lacking in any desire to join with the people of Paris in escorting the graven image of "Freedom," the new order's goddess, to the other side of the Seine.

By its special construction the day's great amphitheatre allowed the representatives to enter directly on stage from their new Assembly Hall. Some 200 of them had disappeared in the spring purges, but a good 500 survivors still emerged, four by four, led by their president, Robespierre. His new and very elegant powder-blue suit contrasted sharply with their own regulation dark blue suits with red collars, but they all wore David's regulation off-face black hats with tricolored plumes.

David's program called upon each of Paris's 48 municipal sections to provide 50 official representatives for the day. This horde of 2,400 he divided into five categories, each to include 10 representatives from each one of the 48 sections. The three male divisions consisted therefore of 480 boys under eight years of age, 480 adolescents between the ages of 15 and 18, and 480 old men. With the fatherland surrounded by enemies, most men of fighting age were at the front. The adolescents were therefore dressed in uniforms and armed with sabers.

There were but two divisions of women: 480 mothers of child-bearing age and 480 nubile young women between 15 and 20 years of age. Set apart by their white dresses strikingly accented by a tricolor ribbon stretching from shoulder to waist, they differed only in what they carried: the mothers, bouquets of red roses; the maidens, baskets of flowers.

The first part of Robespierre's opening speech concluded with his descent from the amphitheatre to approach the great pool of the Tuileries Gardens, covered over for the occasion with a platform. An imposing, purposely ugly *papier mâché* statue labelled "Atheism" dominated the middle of the platform. It was surrounded by five equally repulsive satellites: "Ambition," "Selfishness," "Discord," "False Simplicity" and "Madness." On the identifying label affixed to each satellite was also inscribed the chauvinist phrase: "The foreigner's only hope." According to the program, a flaming torch applied by Robespierre to the central *papier mâché* statue would precipitate Atheism's immediate demise in a burst of smoke and flame. A beautiful, pristine white statue of "Wisdom," concealed within Atheism, was to emerge from the burst of flames and receive the president's homage in the second part of his speech.

To ensure the people's joy in this miraculous metamorphosis, fireworks had been planted inside Atheism's interior so as to make her fiery demise and the triumphant emergence of Wisdom as sensational and memorable as possible. Once Atheism was ignited, however, the discharging fireworks generated such excessive heat that, to the dismay of all, save Robespierre's gloating enemies, Wisdom herself, plus four of Atheism's five satellites, disappeared in what proved a general conflagration. Nor did the spared satellite fail to rouse appreciative sniggers from the enemy party. While a thwarted Robespierre delivered the second half of his discourse to Wisdom's ashes, Madness looked on.

Though Wisdom's birth from the destruction of Atheism proved a fiasco, that was only the beginning of a very full day's ceremonies. The 500-odd Convention members, each carrying David's prescribed bouquet of wheat, flowers, and fruit, were to form an honor guard around the central float bearing the great, oversized image of Freedom. The new order's goddess reigned majestically, seated under a full-sized Liberty Tree, her right hand resting on the small end of a huge club for crushing tyrants. From the four corners of her float, adorned with various implements of agriculture, artificial fruit and vegetables spilled forth from horns of plenty. David's program also called for "eight vigorous bulls" to pull the great device. Breaking bulls to such a servile task had proven an insuperable problem, however, and eight gilded-horned oxen had to be substituted. Whatever the oxen may have lacked in the virility David admired in "vigorous bulls," the gold of their horns shone splendidly in the bright sunshine.

The Guard of Honor for "Freedom" in turn had its own single-file honor guard enclosing them by means of a seemingly endless tricolored ribbon stretched on either side. According to the program, the two ribbon-bearing single files were to consist of violet-crowned children, laurel-crowned adolescents, oak leaf-crowned adults, plus the elderly, the most gloriously crowned of all with headgear fashioned of olive branches and grape vines, the fruit hanging down to signify "venerable fecundity." An eyewitness, however, insists that, David's program notwithstanding, street girls were actually hired at the last minute and dressed up in white to fulfill this ribbon-bearing function.

David's program also called for a detachment of cavalry, preceded by its own trumpeters, as well as three military bands, a hundred drummers, students from the National Institute of Music, firemen, gunners, the 2,400 section representatives in their five categories, plus formations of men and women in companies placed before and after Freedom's float. Even students from the National Institute of the Blind were to sing a hymn to the Supreme Being, riding on their own float.

Whatever may have been David's success in realizing all these details, a vast sea of people in official and unofficial attire did escort the graven image of the new order's goddess across the Seine that day. Just prior to crossing the river, however, there was a stop for a ceremony at the Place of the Revolution before that plaster image of Freedom to which Madame Roland had addressed her final exclamation the previous November. It was in fact the first time in 13 months that one could comfortably stop there since, overnight, all signs of the guillotine had disappeared. Robespierre thus solemnly offered incense to the goddess, conveniently separated from her guillotine, then made another speech. Finally, once across the Seine, there was another stop at the Place des Invalides. There Robespierre spoke at yet another ceremony before yet another plaster statue, this time that of "The French People."

But the grand climax of the day transpired at the Champs-de-Mars. There, rising to 100 feet at its crest, a vast, 500-foot-wide mountain-shaped stage had been constructed to honor the triumphant "Mountain" party. Crowned with a Liberty Tree and a tall pillar, its *papier mâché* shell included romantic grottos, stairways, and tombs, with tripods and other geometric ornaments reflecting the republican mystique. A witness reports that due to the stage's numerous esthetic features it actually could not accommodate more than some 200 of the representatives nearest Robespierre. They followed him as he climbed up to the top of the "mountain" to deliver his final presidential address of the day from the balcony under the Liberty Tree. The remaining 300-odd representatives were left below to fume over the president's demagoguery. It was, however, with the clenched teeth and unhappy countenances of the commandeered musicians down at the mountain's base that the smiles of Robespierre's companions atop the summit contrasted the most sharply, their hats' tricolored plumes billowing away in celebratory splendor. Impatient to get on with the music ending the long, hot day's proceedings, the musicians below irritably awaited the grand finale.

This was to be a gestured rendition of the stanza closing the day's final hymn to the Supreme Being. The words were by Marie-Joseph Chénier, brother of the ill-fated poet André, guillotined on July 25, just two days before Robespierre's fall. Groups chosen from the 2,400 Parisian section representatives were placed on the mountain between the members of the Convention at the top and the musicians at the base. With mothers, young boys, and maidens situated on one side, and with adolescent youths and old men on the other, each group was to make grand theatrical gestures during the singing of the last stanza of Chénier's text where specific little phrases were to trigger each grand gesture. Thus one saw adolescent "warriors" draw their sabers while, perched above them, the old men raised an arm in blessing. Mothers, discarding their rose bouquets, suddenly seized one of the little boys and hoisted him aloft, offering him to the "Author of Nature" while the contents of the maidens' flower baskets showered down on them from above.

Whatever synchronization may have lacked on the mountain between the gestures and the text, compensation was found in the very enthusiastic singing of the hymn's refrain by the people massed below them. Practiced for days in institutions and by civic groups throughout Paris, the refrain's two alexandrine verses were zealously sung again and again.

> Before we all lay down our conqu'ring swords sublime,
> Let's now all swear the end of tyranny and crime!

Trumpet blares unfailingly signaled the return of the familiar refrain after each stanza while the conscripted singers strained wearily to lead yet another, still louder, rendition of its militant lines. Suddenly, as all sang one last time of ending tyranny and crime, the boom of cannon fire resounded throughout Paris, crowning Robespierre's finest day.

viii

AS SURPRISING AS IT MAY SEEM, the guillotine had not been removed from the Place of the Revolution the night before from any human scruples. Rather was it from fear that the gilded-horned oxen drawing Freedom's float might, like horses, prove recalcitrant at the smell of blood. The organizers were haunted by a nagging fear that these dumb beasts, triumphantly parading the new order's great goddess, might balk at the Place of the Revolution.

David and his committee knew full well that many of those 500 survivors of the purges in the National Convention were totally against the whole idea of a Supreme Being to begin with. Thus, even the slightest possibility that Robespierre's enemies, framed in by tricolored ribbons, might be stranded in the midst of the Place of the Revolution while snorting oxen pawed the earth, wild-eyed, and Freedom's progress came to a halt, was completely inadmissible. To guarantee the tranquil passage of the oxen, therefore, David and his committee not only had the guillotine removed, but also had workmen carefully cover over the blood-impregnated soil with thick layers of sand during the night.

As June 8 dawned, no hint remained at the Place of the Revolution of the strange but harsh daily reality of the times: blood sacrifice, human religion's immemorial rite, was thriving in revolutionary Paris and proved itself the mystical keystone for constructing the new order with its idealism and childlike faith in human nature.

Nor was the veritable cult growing up around the guillotine the only manifestation of this strange truth. Its admissibility was publicly confirmed at the Place of the Revolution by Robespierre when he offered incense to the new order's goddess, Freedom, there where she actually presided over the Revolution's mechanized altar. In repeated, almost desperate daily oblations, effusions of human blood were spilled before her, nine days out of ten, to guarantee her triumph if not actually to placate her. Madame Roland, Girondin partisan and revolutionary hostess, had not at all been misled in addressing her final, despairing cry to the new order's goddess.

The revolting work of the guillotine had become generally accepted as one of the features of the new order over the past 13 months. For those so inclined it provided an assured patriotic spectacle nine days out of ten. Sanson and his valets, faced each day with the necessity of coping with a fresh and ever-swelling "batch" of victims from Fouquier-Tinville's Revolutionary Tribunal, had long since given up dismantling the scaffold each evening. The day's work finished, the executioners simply washed down the machine with water, removed its great triangular blade, and reported to Fouquier-Tinville to learn the number of tumbrels needed for the morrow's "batch."

For the residents of the fashionable neighborhood bordering the elegant ex-Place Louis XV, there was grave concern about the quantity of blood accumulating there. Hastily a grill had been erected under the machine to prevent dogs from licking each day's effusion. But, as the months passed, the soil around the scaffold had become so saturated that those walking over it left brownish footprints on adjoining sidewalks.

Inevitably, the whole of the chic rue Saint-Honoré was affected. Shopkeepers took to closing down in the afternoon to avoid exposure to the daily procession of the condemned. Several tumbrels were now needed to transport the daily "batch." Soldiers, both mounted and on foot, plus a mass of unsavory rabble accompanied them, far outnumbering odd friends or rare relatives in the procession where degenerate women known as the "furies of the guillotine" figured prominently. Gloating over gore, mutilations, and massacres, and, during mob disorders, occasionally even given to cannibalism, these "furies" invariably aimed gallows humor and obscenities at the hapless condemned.

Equally offensive to the inhabitants of that elegant district of Paris was the reddish trail left each evening by the red-painted cart transporting the decapitated bodies to the common burial pit in a cemetery near the Church of the Madeleine. But the worst offense was the indescribable putrefying smell emanating at all hours of the day and night from the scaffold site. Before the guillotine's June 8 removal the intense heat of early June had already begun to accentuate it. The state of what so shortly before had been western Europe's most luminous Christian city now shocked the outside world. In the heart of the capital city of St. Louis, saved and protected by the holy prayers of St. Geneviève, there reigned the stench of putrefying human blood. It spoke far more eloquently of the profound disorder unleashed by the new order than did rites of communion at the Place de la Bastille or cults to freedom martyrs interred in the Pantheon and then removed.

Having hoped his Supreme Being would instigate a new national cult controlled by human reason, the unfortunate Robespierre inexplicably found himself ensnared in the workings of totally irrational forces. These forces revealed that human beings are, in one form or another, not only inevitably religious, but also generally prone to shedding the blood of the individual to assure the well-being of the whole. Indeed, the implacability of these perennial and mysteriously irrational forces was manifested by Marat's cry for thousands of heads, as also by Danton's solid conviction that still "more audacious" means were necessary to assure the Revolution's success. Thus, as new, post-Christian France valiantly strove to banish the superstition and fanaticism of the old order, its mentors, faithful to a basic human instinct demanding religious sacrifice to assure success, publicly cried out for an ever-increasing ritual shedding of blood.

Against such forces neither Robespierre nor anyone else could do anything. The irony of fate had determined that the crude and primitive rite of human sacrifice surreptitiously creep back into French daily life with the government's blessing. The refined, stylized, and mystical bloodless sacrifice of the Body and Blood of Jesus Christ in the now-forbidden Christian Eucharist, even though offered daily for 13 centuries in France's thousands of churches, had now been spectacularly replaced by a more direct and less stylized sacrifice. The guillotine's red-splattered wood and steel supplanted the immaculate white linen of the Christian altar; the stench of the place of sacrifice, the sweetness of the smoking censer. The paltry, totally irrational Christian offering to God of small tokens of bread and wine, which "fanatics" of the Crucified actually claimed became his flesh and blood and the immortal food of human souls, had finally been eclipsed. The new order, on the other hand, offered tangible proof of the progress being made by the Enlightenment, thanks to a more philosophically enlightened daily rite wherein even the mechanism for sacrifice had been devised to achieve human equality.

ix

ON JUNE 8, 1794, Christian Pentecost was thus replaced in France by Robespierre's Festival of the Supreme Being. As its pagan procession, so proudly owing nothing whatsoever to France's 13 centuries of Judeo-Christian heritage, triumphantly escorted its new goddess out of the Place of the Revolution and across the Seine, neither the president nor his intimates could possibly have entertained the idea that their own personal and ill-fated Pentecost had begun that very day. As if a subtle reminder of the abiding power of that God of Abraham, Isaac, and Jacob whose seven-day week they had scorned, they would all be brought back to this site as condemned prisoners 50 days hence and executed in the most appalling circumstances.

More dead than alive, the humiliated Robespierre would be mocked and railed at by a vengeful mob, drunk with blood lust. His elegant powder-blue suit would be worn, dirty and bloodstained from a suicide attempt the night before, when a pistol shot had nearly detached one side of his jaw. The soiled bloodstained bandage that secured it to his face would be ripped off by Sanson as he fixed the Incorruptible's mangled head in the neck-stall for decapitation. The resulting animal howl of pain was quelled only by the crashing blade.

Also executed in a mangled state was Robespierre's 31-year-old younger brother. He too had attempted suicide the evening before with a leap from the Hotel de Ville, crushing his leg. But more grotesque still was the dispatch of the crippled 39-year-old Couthon. His body was so twisted by rheumatism that his lower half was totally immobile. All of Sanson's professional ingenuity was required to twist his head into the neck-stall.

This macabre and bloody Robespierrian Pentecost marked not only 50 days after the Festival of the Supreme Being, but 100 days after the most persecuted celebration of Easter in French history. Faced with open persecution, routed and cowed French Christians had tried to celebrate, clandestinely or otherwise, the resurrection of their Lord and God, Jesus Christ (Jn 20:17), from the dead. The grotesque events on that July 28, 1794, seemed to some, therefore, a sort of ironic reply to Robespierre's flaunting his Supreme Being on the venerable feast celebrating the birth of the church of Jesus Christ.

In any case, those final 50 days of Robespierre's reign were characterized by great darkness throughout France. By allowing accusations to suffice as proof of guilt, the law of 22 Prairial, passed just two days after the great festival, unleashed the full fury of the Great Terror. It would rage, unchecked, until the Incorruptible's fall on July 27. The Carmelites' oblation marked the thirty-ninth day of that Robespierrian Pentecost, Robespierre's own fall the forty-ninth.

Given the new calendar's ten-day *décade*, the fiftieth day after the Festival of the Supreme Being was, of necessity, also a décadi holiday. As an exception, the guillotine functioned that *décadi* and, as we have just seen, in the most appalling manner, being expressly returned from the Place of the Throne to the Place of the Revolution for the execution of Robespierre and his associates. That sorry spectacle was hailed as the greatest event taking place in Paris on that republican day of rest.

But an even sorrier spectacle took place at the same site the following day. Within the space of one hour and forty-five minutes, the Mayor of Paris and all 87 members of his city council were guillotined in a blood orgy of hallucinatory horror. Though labeled "Robespierre's accomplices," the only crime for most of them was their election to the municipal government by their local sections. This staggering official execution of July 29, 1794, where for almost two hours, we are told, there was an effusion of blood every minute and a quarter, is seldom referred to by historians. An eyewitness account is still chilling to read. One recalls that human blood crept outward from the scaffold until a pool stretched 50 feet in all directions. In spite of countless bushels of bran put down by the executioner's valets to stop its flow, before the end the condemned were slipping as they tried to climb the scaffold steps.

For almost two years, the 16 Carmelites of Compiègne, wishing to save France and her church according to the rites of France's old order, had daily consecrated themselves for holocaust that such works of darkness might be held at bay. And as though it were a last gasp following Robespierre's dispatch on July 28, this final, massive hemorrhage on July 29 did in fact mark a definitive turning of the tide of official revolutionary blood-letting. Believers might well say that the nuns' July 17 oblation had begun to quell the Terror.

W 430

affaire audebert Roubeau et 29 autres

Procès-verbal d'exécution de mort.

L'AN Second de la République Française, une et indivisible, le Vingt neuf messidor à la requête du citoyen Accusateur public près le Tribunal révolutionnaire, établi au Palais à Paris, par la loi du dix mars mil sept cent quatre-vingt-treize, sans aucun recours au Tribunal de cassation, lequel fait élection au Greffe dudit Tribunal séant au Palais; je me suis ——— huissier-audiencier audit Tribunal, soussigné, transporté en la maison de justice dudit Tribunal, pour l'exécution du jugement rendu par le Tribunal le 29 messidor contre Jean Laurent audebert Roubeau et condamné à la peine de mort, pour les causes énoncées audit jugement, et de suite je l ai remis à l'exécuteur des jugemens criminels, et à la gendarmerie, qui les ont conduit sur la place dite de Vincennes où, sur un échafaud dressé sur la dite place, lesdits sus nommés, en notre présence, subi la peine de mort; et de tous ce que dessus, ai fait et rédigé le présent procès-verbal, pour servir et valoir ce que de raison, dont acte.

Louise Reynel fe Blaiseau, antoine Louis Calme, Louis Joseph Pyron, ferdinand, françoise Crosy, marie Gabrielle Trezette, marie anne hanisset, marie claudine Lidoine, anne Pelleras, magdeleine Thouret, marie anne Piedcourt, marie anne Brideau, marie Claude cyprienne Brard, rose chretien Ve chretien, marie du four, angelique Roussel, Elizabeth Jule Verolat, marie genevieve Meunier, catherine soiron Touriere, claude Louis Denis Mulot, Théophile Kepple Pere, charles honoré Tellier, clemens Borel, Jean Jung, frederic Edelmann, Louis Edelmann, Jean andré Delamet Bonnet, therese soiron Touriere, Pierre françois Monet,

Enregistré gratis, à Paris, le ... de l'an second de la République, une et indivisible.

Enregistré à Paris ce 4 Thermidor l'an 2e de la Republique française

Death sentence passed on the Compiègne martyrs
(Document from the National Archives of Paris)

8

Coincidences

(i) Madame Lidoine's trip to Paris; her mother's situation. (ii) The prioress's conflict. (iii) The guillotine at the Place du Trône; the procession of the condemned; a prophetic vision; Madame Lidoine's paradoxical position. (iv) Her return to Compiègne; requisition of the nuns' apartments; divine reassurance. (v) Arrest of the nuns; the imprisoned English Benedictines. (vi) What the Carmelites wore at the scaffold. (vii) Grounds for the Carmelites' condemnation; letter to the Committees of Public Salvation and Public Security regarding them; Paris's reply. (viii) How the Carmelites' civilian clothing passed to the English Benedictines on the Feast of Our Lady of Mount Carmel. (ix) The Carmelites' departure for Paris; their arrival on the eve of the fifth celebration of Bastille Day.

On June 13, five days after the Festival of the Supreme Being, Madame Lidoine arrived in Paris to see her mother. Never would she have abandoned her sisters in Compiègne except under obedience to the Carmelites' superior, Abbé Rigaud. Just as a spouse's duties to husband and children override filial ones, so had her responsibilities to her 15 daughters always taken precedence. Yet these responsibilities before God sorely tested her loyalties. She was keenly sensitive to her 78-year-old mother's painful crisis.

Alone and without support, the older Madame Lidoine was about to leave Paris for good. Prior to her husband's sudden death the year before, they had been preparing to go end their days together with his relatives near Ornans, in Franche Comté. That departure the previous year had been brutally canceled, however, by her cruel loss.

For reasons the elder Madame Lidoine found unfathomable, her Carmelite daughter and only child had proven unshakable in her resolution as prioress in Compiègne. She wished to maintain the existence of her community even though, for almost two years now, the community, expelled from their monastery, no longer existed officially. Her daughter's inflexibility the previous year despite her mother's need for her to come to Paris could only be a painful memory for the elderly mother. At 77 years of age she had had to bury her husband alone, then settle his succession single-handedly, her daughter having refused to abandon her flock. Papers had had to be sent to Compiègne to be signed. Now, once again, final decisions had to be made in Paris and papers signed before she could leave.

Apart from legal concerns, however, were the concerns of her maternal heart. She accepted that she would never see Paris again. But must she also accept that she would not be allowed to embrace her only child one last time?

Madame Philippe was destined to play a crucial role in the resolution of this family drama. On business in Paris the previous year, she had been able to visit her prioress's mother and meet other members of her family. The cousins' severe criticism of Mother Teresa of St. Augustine for not having come at the time of her father's death troubled the conscience of the young Sister Marie of the Incarnation. These cousins thought their Carmelite relative a self-centered egotist, and a completely unnatural daughter who cared nothing for parents who had lavished their resources and love on her. Even now was she not bitterly repaying her mother's lifetime of devotion with a cold, unloving heart? How could she refuse to come to Paris in such circumstances, more especially as her community had not officially existed for almost two years?

Sister Marie herself wrote her prioress, begging her to consider that it was, after all, a question of her own mother.

Nothing, however, other than an order from Abbé Rigaud, would make Mother Teresa of Saint Augustine relinquish her charge before God. Alerted to the situation by Sister Marie of the Incarnation, Abbé Rigaud immediately ordered Mother Teresa of St. Augustine to go to her mother. Acting under holy obedience, the great prioress at last felt free before God to lay aside her cares for her dispersed little flock and assume her filial responsibilities that, invisible to her accusers, always tore at her heart.

ii

In his Gospel, Jesus Christ announced that those who love father or mother more than him are not worthy of him (Mt 10:37). It is inevitable, then, that throughout Christian history conflicts have frequently arisen whenever believers find themselves forced to set allegiance to Christ above family ties. Like the elderly Madame Lidoine, the family may feel betrayed. Thinking in the terms of this world and not of the next, they find it hard to understand why they find themselves excluded because of allegiance to God.

Madame Lidoine's case, however, was even more complicated. She was responsible before God for those 15 daughters, most of them older than she, whom they had repeatedly elected as prioress. She had, moreover, for almost two years now led them in their daily act of consecration as victims of holocaust. The dynamic center of her own hidden life in Christ had thus become identified with the responsibility of sustaining her community's focus on this oblation, should it be according to God's mercy to them. Cast out of her monastery, she had found herself in a hostile world, as she secretly awaited his pleasure, always half expecting an unequivocally clear refusal from him. Even so, there continued to burn within her a strong intuition that community martyrdom had been prophesied for them in Sister Elisabeth Baptiste's mystic dream a century before.

Mother Teresa of Saint Augustine was no slave to details, however, such as that widowhood excluded anyone from the oblation. What she did have qualms about was leaving her post. Might she not thereby become one of those "two or three" not to follow the Lamb? Indeed, could she possibly be destined to resemble one of those foolish virgins in the parable who had gone into the city to buy oil for her empty lamp and found herself shut out of the wedding feast (Mt 25:10)? That possibility could not but torture her self-confidence, causing her at times even to doubt her own lucidity about the intimacy of the love that drew her to her Bridegroom.

While containing within herself this painful conflict, Madame Lidoine must at the same time show only her courage and her resolution to her daughters. Their oblation for the peace of France and her church, and for the release of captives, must be perceived by them as the one preoccupation claiming their prioress's great heart.

Should her trip to Paris now cause her to miss the Bridegroom's coming, it would clearly be by his will. As a good Carmelite, she was obeying Abbé Rigaud's order. Nor could she really doubt *him*, her Beloved. Certainly she never questioned *his* power to bring the miracle of the martyrdom to pass without her. Her love for him would be no less were that to be his pleasure. Yet when she allowed herself to consider that possibility, the cost seemed more than she could bear, except by his merciful grace. Though she had always maintained that her love for him was absolute, her lucidity allowed her to grasp that such an unconditional, absolute love could indeed cost her everything—even her deepest personal conviction concerning her own vocation within her little community.

Yet Mother Teresa of Saint Augustine, in her Christmas carol, had asked him to blind her own reasoning, that he alone might be all in all for her. Nonetheless, whenever she tried to conceive of surviving her community's martyrdom, a painful inner stab was felt. Afire for the martyrdom of love, her burning heart gave battle to such an absolute surrender of her own reasoning to the unfathomable will of God.

iii

On June 13, after an exhausting seven-hour coach trip from Compiègne, Madame Lidoine arrived in Paris. It was one month to the day before her more fateful and final return to the city of her birth on July 13, just four days before the martyrdom. She would then be bound as a prisoner, as would her 15 spiritual daughters and Mulot de la Ménardière, arrested with them.

In the chronicles of the Revolution, June 13, 1794, also marked the last of the five days the guillotine stood at the Place de la Bastille during the Great Terror. It had been installed there when cleared away from the Place of the Revolution for the Festival of the Supreme Being on June 8. Mothers of families in that working-class neighborhood, however, had immediately raised strenuous objections. The loathsome spectacle left them as indifferent to the new order in France as to Citizen Palloy's propaganda in exploiting their neighborhood's revolutionary image. Preoccupied with the well-being of their husbands and children, these respectable wives and mothers were revolted that such a horror should be situated in their neighborhood. None of them harbored any desire whatsoever to form a local chapter of the "furies of the guillotine." On June 11, the third day the machine operated there, their objections became particularly strident, and with reason. The passing of the law of 22 Prairial the previous day had immediately doubled both the number of victims and the quantity of blood disgustingly left to putrefy in their midst each evening.

After two more days of protests the Bastille housewives prevailed. Following the executions of June 13, the guillotine was dismantled and moved all the way out to the edge of the city at the Vincennes gates. There, at the very end of the Rue du Faubourg St. Antoine, just inside the municipal customs barrier, stretched a large, open space known today as the "Place de la Nation." In prerevolutionary France the sprawling site had been named "The Place of the Throne" (*La Place du Trône*), but in the immediate wake of August 10, 1792, it had been rechristened "The Place of the Toppled Throne" (*La Place du Trône Renversé*).

The site's association with the throne had begun the previous century, when, following the 17-year-old Louis XIV's marriage to his 22-year-old Spanish queen on August 26, 1660, a throne had been set up there for the sovereigns to receive the homage of their Parisian subjects. Now, 134 years later, at the same site, 1,306 severed heads would fall into Sanson's leather bag in just over six weeks. The two soaring pillars silently towering above the customs houses and witnessing those 40 days of horrific slaughter—account taken for the four *décadi* holidays—still pierce the sky at today's tree-studded Place de la Nation.

Thanks to Madame Philippe, we do have a few anecdotes concerning Madame Lidoine's week with her mother. We know that she met Sister Marie of the Incarnation the day after her arrival, and that on that June 14 they saw pass by them in the rue Saint Antoine, the first "batch" to be executed at the Place du Trône. Madame Lidoine's spiritual sensitivity did not leave her indifferent to what she saw. Madame Philippe states that the horrors of revolutionary Paris produced a strong reaction in her prioress who, Parisian though she was, referred to Paris by the end of her week there as a "place of horrors and abominations."

Such sensitivity, attested by Madame Philippe herself, causes us to favor Monseigneur Jauffret's 1803 account of the two nuns' June 14 encounter with the procession of the condemned over Madame Philippe's own version, written down almost 40 years later. Basing his text on information he could only have received from Madame Philippe herself shortly after the event, the Bishop of Metz states that Madame Lidoine involuntarily shivered upon encountering the procession, and regretted having come that way. Then she noticed how two of the condemned men seemed to be staring at her and Sister Marie. Turning to the younger sister she remarked: "Do you see the way the victims stare at us? You'd say they're calling us to follow them." Sister Marie's laconic reply might be said to echo a certain lack of enthusiasm for any such an eventuality: "Well, Mother, you could say that that's the fate awaiting us." In enthusiastic disbelief, Madame Lidoine exclaimed: "What! You'd flatter me with that hope? Let me embrace you! How happy I'd be if your words were confirmed by what happens to us...."

Such an unusual and spontaneous outburst of emotion from Madame Lidoine, just 33 days before the actual martyrdom, underlines the extent to which her burning ardor for martyrdom was normally reined in and kept in check. At all times she was aware it must be strictly submitted to the divine will.

Thirty-eight years later, however, as Madame Philippe herself was struggling to write up that incident in her *Relation du martyre,* she would fail to mention the prioress's instantaneous revulsion upon encountering the procession. She would also state that it was she who tried to steer Mother Lidoine away from the spectacle, but that the prioress, all-eager to stay, pleaded with her that she was eager to "see how saints go to their death." Given that the majority of the condemned could hardly be termed "saints," this latter statement alone seems bizarre, coming from a woman of Madame Lidoine's intelligence and spiritual finesse. Yet another contradiction with the earlier version is evident when Madame Philippe states that it was she, rather than Mother Lidoine, who remarked on how the victims stared at them as if to say, "One day you'll follow us," thus rendering it impossible for her to make her own laconic reply, "Well, Mother, you could say that that's the fate awaiting us."

Madame Philippe's account in this instance is not only rather one-dimensional and less rich in psychological subtleties than Monseigneur Jauffret's, but also presents Madame Lidoine as a sort of superheroine and a bit overeager to climb the scaffold steps. Neither her natural reticence nor her deep spiritual prudence is detectable. This is all the more striking in that Madame Philippe herself elsewhere always confirms both this reticence and this prudence.

Whatever the case, we are indebted to Madame Philippe for retaining another curious—even prophetic—incident dating from that week. A friend of the two nuns came to them one evening very deeply moved. He had just come from the death bed of a young Christian virgin where he had been assisting Monseigneur de Maillé-la-Tour-Landry in giving the last rites. Even at the height of the Great Terror, this non-juring bishop of the suppressed diocese of Saint-Papoul camouflaged his true identity by an ostentatious charade of fervent patriotism and generous support of all republican causes, even taking his turn at civic guard duty. Thus was he able to continue secret ministrations to the non-juring faithful throughout the relentless persecution.

On the evening in question, the Carmelites' pensive friend, after repeated questioning by the two nuns, finally described what he had witnessed. While the bishop was reciting the prayers commending the departing soul to God, the dying girl had suddenly sat up and exclaimed: "What do I see?

Oh! my God.... What? The blood of your confessors isn't enough then?... You also desire the virgin blood of your spouses!"

When the bishop asked her what she saw, she replied: "I see a great number of nuns, and especially a community, harvested by the scythe of the Revolution. I see them dressed in white cloaks, a palm in their hands, and heaven opening up to receive them...."

On this occasion the prioress's reaction again confirms her effort to contain her ardor for that martyrdom of love that she believed gave supreme meaning to her existence. Indeed, on this occasion Madame Philippe reports that the prioress blurted out, "Oh! my God!... do we dare flatter ourselves in hoping that it might be our community for which such a great favor is predestined by heaven?" Then she added, according to Madame Philippe, and as if for herself alone, "But God keep me from allowing my ardent desire to die for his love to cause the slightest imprudence that might inflict pain on my sisters."

The paradox of so ardently longing for martyrdom, yet being ever prudent in not pressing for it, is a striking dimension of Madame Lidoine's rich and complex character. It is consistently attested to in all the extant documents, save in Madame Philippe's own late version of their encounter with the condemned in the rue St. Antoine on June 14, 1794.

iv

HER MOTHER'S AFFAIRS SETTLED, Mother Teresa of St. Augustine took the coach back to Compiègne on the morning of June 21. Sister Marie, who had come to see her off, mentioned to her that having learned that their exiled Bishop of Soissons, Monseigneur Bordeilles, had condemned the Liberty-Equality oath they had all taken in September of

1792, she was thinking of retracting it. Although at this farewell, destined to be their final one, the prioress approved Sister Marie's sentiments, it was in vain that she tried to persuade the younger nun to accompany her back to Compiègne. Though the young sister's business affairs admittedly did not require her attention in Paris during the coming week, she declined. She feared a trip to Compiègne and back in such a short span might arouse suspicions. While waiting she asked permission to spend a week with some of her family at Vernon. This last-minute decision alone was to determine Madame Philippe's survival as historian and guardian of her martyred sisters' relics.

At the end of the seven-hour return trip Madame Lidoine was met at the coach stop in Compiègne by some of her daughters, all in an excited state. At that very moment a search of all their apartments was under way. Armed guards had been deployed everywhere and the soldiers had even eaten the food the nuns had prepared for themselves, leaving them nothing.

Though outwardly concerned by this announcement, inwardly Madame Lidoine could not but find in it a sweet, sure sign of the presence of her divine Lover. Blindly, out of love for him, she had abandoned all, embracing holy obedience to go to her mother. She had asked for nothing. No bargaining with him about the possible consequences had been attempted, even though she knew that submission to Abbé Rigaud's order meant that she might be one of those "not to follow the Lamb." Blinded as she was by her love for him, all had been accepted in faith, all embraced in total, absolute abandonment. Now, the very minute she set foot back in Compiègne, her daughters' extraordinary announcement could only seem to her as if his loving hand were stetching out to her. He had awaited her return.

In this sign of loving reassurance she found gentle certitude, something she could grasp, something she could cling to as proof of his love for her. Was he not thereby designating her to continue leading them in their daily consecration, even as the revolutionary net ensnaring them now began to tighten?

Sensing his loving presence in this turn of events, all else now seemed as nothing, whether life or death. Her daughters' announcement gave her proof that her deep but so imperfect human love for him had been returned as a manifestation of himself and of his love—a love past imagining, past all understanding. She concealed her joy humbly, but within her heart she pondered its mystery.

Outwardly, however, Mother Teresa of Saint Augustine showed herself uncompromising, checking herself rigidly, "mortifying herself outrageously," according to Madame Philippe. Reassured by this sign, she at last felt freed from doubts about her role. She now felt completely free to concentrate all her energy and strength in confronting the immediate realities of their precarious situation.

V

THE NEXT DAY, JUNE 22, after the requisition of the four apartments had been completed, all 16 members of the community, plus Mulot de la Ménardière, were arrested. All 17 were locked up in the former convent of the Visitation, an improvised house of detention for political prisoners located in the town center.

In this makeshift prison the 16 future martyrs were startled to discover those 17 English Benedictines we have previously encountered. Arrested as foreigners in their monastery in Cambrai, they had been brought to Compiègne for detention in September of 1792, just at the time the Carmelites had been expelled. Founded in France by a granddaughter of Sir Thomas More when Catholic religious orders were forbidden in England, the English community of Cambrai had numbered 21 nuns at the time of their arrest. By June of 1794, however, four sisters had already perished from 21 months of harsh incarceration in Compiègne.

Sister Marie states that partitions were constructed to keep the English and French nuns from communicating with each other. The English account speaks merely of the language barrier and the strictness of the revolutionary guards. Whatever the case, a French-speaking English sister, on at least two occasions, got around whatever barriers there were and spoke with the French community. Thus was she able to relay to her English sisters that the Carmelites' were making a daily act of consecration to restore peace and to free captives such as themselves from passing to the guillotine.

Such a selfless gesture could not but spark a response in the Christian souls of the English nuns. How not be profoundly impressed by the great—even startling—Christian vision motivating such an extraordinary generosity from this eccentric and rather ridiculous-looking group of 16 French women? Though mostly in their fifties, the French nuns ranged from 29 to 78 years of age. They were clothed in the most eclectic collection imaginable of second-hand, slightly seedy clothing, and in no way outwardly resembled nuns of any kind, much less a community of Carmelites. Yet there they were, their neighbors in this insalubrious place that had already claimed the lives of four of their English sisters, doggedly offering themselves daily, in the best tradition of St. Teresa of Avila, with a "determined determination."

Compared to the long incarceration of the English Benedictines, released only in the spring of 1795, the Carmelites' imprisonment would be very brief. Between their June 22 arrest and their transfer to the Conciergerie in Paris on July 12, the Carmelites spent only 21 nights in Compiègne's improvised house of detention. If we add the night of July 12 spent in open carts on the way to Paris, plus the four additional nights in the Conciergerie before trial and execution on July 17, we count only 26 nights between their arrest and execution.

vi

IN THE OFFICIAL VATICAN RECORDS of the proceedings for beatification in 1906, numerous testimonies reveal a firm Carmelite tradition, based on eyewitness accounts, concerning the nuns' dress at their martyrdom. This tradition is worthy of respect. It dates from Carmelite contemporaries, including such highly reliable figures as Mother Camille de Soyecourt, the remarkable restorer of Carmelite life in France after the Revolution and the first to attempt to revive Compiègne's Carmel. She herself had not seen her Compiègne sisters' witness, but she had spoken with those who had, and whom she deemed fully qualified to judge what they saw.

Unanimously all attest to the fact that the Carmelites were indeed clad in white choir mantles covering a brown robe resembling their normal habits. Also mentioned, in agreement with what Sister Marie recalls, is the fact that as they had to give up their habits and veils, Madame Lidoine, prior to their leaving Compiègne, had had them reduce their monastic headcovering to nothing but a vestigial little white cap.

Such a transformation of headcovering would necessarily have been radical. If it were fashioned from the wimple, all that covered the neck and shoulders would have had to be clipped away up to the ears so that the neck was completely exposed as required for the guillotine. Mother Teresa of Saint Augustine wished at all costs to spare her consecrated daughters from being touched by the executioner until the very end.

We can only speculate as to when this indispensable pre-execution operation took place. It would not be unreasonable to suggest that it dated from the very beginning of the 22-month expulsion. As a tiny vestige of their habits, this trimmed-away little cap, covering the crown of their heads, would have been totally invisible under their street bonnets. It would also have served to remind each of them daily, and particularly as the act of consecration was repeated, that the executioner's "last toilette" had already been carried out. Each of them had been readied for blood witness.

In any case, the details we have of their surprise departure from Compiègne on the morning of July 12 make it clear that the headcoverings could certainly not have been fashioned by a few last-minute snips of the scissors as they were being so precipitously herded into the carts. One must therefore conclude that, with her usual foresight, Madame Lidoine had indeed directed this operation well in advance, as Madame Philippe states. Whether it was as they stripped off their old habits to don civilian clothing for the Feast of the Exaltation of the Holy Cross in 1792, or at some later time—possibly even when they inaugurated their act of consecration as victims of holocaust—we cannot say.

vii

IN THEIR TWO-DAY SEARCH of the apartments, Compiègne's Revolutionary Surveillance Committee turned up letters revealing the Carmelites' "crimes" against the Revolution. It was all too clear that the nuns were still stubbornly trying to maintain their forbidden life as a community of consecrated Christian women. Clear also were their strong monarchist sympathies and hostility to the Revolution. Such lapses from political correctness in a post-Christian France had to be dealt with severely.

Wishing therefore to send the nuns to the Revolutionary Tribunal in Paris for trial, the Revolutionary Surveillance Committee of Compiègne was obliged by law first to petition both the Committee of Public Salvation and the Committee of General Security for permission to do this. Indeed, Article 11 of the Law of 22 Prairial specifically forbade "constituted authorities" from expediting prisoners to Paris for trial by the all-powerful Revolutionary Tribunal without previous authorization from these two Parisian Committees. In a deferential letter dated June 25 and addressed only three days after the nuns' arrest to those two right arms of the National Convention, the Compiègne Committee reveals the "crimes" for which the 17 prisoners had been arrested.

7 Messidor, Year II
of the One Indivisible French Republic

The Revolutionary Surveillance
Committee of Compiègne

To the People's Representatives of the National
Convention Constituting the Committees of Public
Salvation and of Public Security:

Citizen Representatives:

Always in pursuit of traitors, we constantly focus our attention on those perfidious persons who dare plot against the Republic or who express wishes for freedom's destruction.

For a long time now we have suspected that the former Carmelite nuns of this city, though lodged in different houses, were still living as a community and following the rules of their former convent. Our suspicions were not in vain. Several thorough searches carried out in their houses produced a highly incriminating correspondence: not only would they put a stop to the progress of the public spirit by receiving persons whom they admitted to a so-called "scapular" fraternity, but they also expressed wishes for the counter-revolution, for the destruction of the Republic, and for the re-establishment of tyranny, as you may judge by the 31 items we join herewith.

We had no hesitation in having the former nuns arrested upon reading these items.

Here are their names:

Marie Claudine Lidoine
Anne Marie Madeleine Thouret
Marie Claude Cyprienne Brard
Marie Dufour
Thérèse Soiron
Marie Gabriel Trézel
Marie Françoise Crozy [sic]
Anne Pellerasse [sic]
Angélique Roussel
Elisabeth Julie Verolot [sic]
Marie Geneviève Meunier
Marie Anne Bridoux [sic]
Rose Chrétien
Marie Anne Banisset [sic]
Marie Anne Piecourt [sic]
and Catherine Soiron.

We point out to you that the nun named Lidoine had in her pocket a portrait of the Tyrant [i.e., Louis XVI] and had just brought back from Paris a relic with a Certificate of Authenticity.

Since the prisoner named Mulot, alias Laménardière, has also been identified through a letter and a poem written in his hand, we have had him arrested as their accomplice.

> The crimes of which these individuals are accused being those falling within the jurisdiction of the Revolutionary Tribunal, we shall await your authorization for their transfer to Paris, in conformity with Article 11 of the Law of the last 22 Prairial. But should there be another way to deal with this, kindly give us your orders regarding it.
>
> Citizen Representatives, you can count on our zeal and our vigilance. We shall know how to unmask villains, regardless of the costume they are wearing.
>
> Greetings and Fraternity.

In its July 10 reply, Paris's powerful Committee of Public Salvation ordered the transfer of the 16 Carmelites and Mulot de la Ménardière to Paris's Conciergerie to await trial. The dossiers proving their guilt were to be forwarded to the Revolutionary Tribunal's notorious Public Prosecutor, Fouquier-Tinville.

This July 10 reply reached Compiègne the morning of July 12. The mayor, eager that Compiègne's revolutionary zeal not be questioned in Paris, acted immediately. He ordered assembled, for immediate departure, two carts with horses, sufficient straw to cover the bottom of the carts, plus a gendarme and ten mounted armed guards for escort. He also gave orders that identical provisions be made at Senlis for the arrival of the prisoners there at midnight. There they were to be transferred into carts with fresh straw and provided with fresh guards and horses.

As soon as the mayor was assured that the two straw-covered carts were ready and the guards assembled, he and his committee, escorted by the soldiers, burst in on the 16 female prisoners. Madame Philippe's manuscripts specify that it was about 10:15 A.M.

viii

AS WE HAVE SEEN, the Carmelites' petition to the revolutionary government for money for civilian clothing in September of 1792 never seems to have brought any verifiable results. The last reference we find to it is December 1792, with no resolution in sight. It seems probable therefore that either their original civilian garments, or others offered them out of charity, were still being worn on July 12, 1794. Indeed, the simple fact that the nuns received permission from their captors to wash their single outfit of civilian clothing on the twenty-first day of their imprisonment seems to confirm that they never did acquire a change of civilian clothing.

The former convent's laundry facilities were thus put to use on the morning of July 12. The nuns took off their civilian outfits to wash them and, lacking a change of civilian clothing, had no alternative but to put on their habits, piously preserved and brought with them into prison.

The twentieth century's totalitarian mentality in requiring that prisoners be stripped not only of valuables, but also of their own clothing and all personal identity, was foreign to eighteenth-century practice. Prisoners had considerable latitude. If they had money they could even arrange for special meals through the jailer. Let us recall, for example, that at the very last hour subprioress Brideau still had with her in the Conciergerie a fur wrap that was bartered for the community's last cup of chocolate.

Whatever the eighteenth-century latitude in prisons, a quite extraordinary conjunction of coincidences was still required for the Carmelites to die in their white mantles as prophesied. Ironically, it would be the revolutionary zeal of those most intent on destroying their memory that not only assured this memory, but also brought about the uncanny fulfillment of the prophecies.

Documents found today in the archives of Stanbrook Abbey, in conjunction with Madame Philippe's own manuscripts, allow us to piece together the events of that fateful July 12 washday. When the nuns donned their habits that morning and put their civilian clothes to soak, no law was being broken: they were not on public view. At ten o'clock, the hour for their normal meal, they left their clothes soaking and sat down to eat. The two septuagenarians, Mesdames Thouret and Piedcourt, had apparently already got splashed and wet.

A quarter of an hour later the mayor and his party of committee members burst in, accompanied by soldiers. The Carmelites' startled surprise could hardly have been greater than the mayor's own upon seeing his 16 prisoners clad in religious habits. He had forgotten his permission for the washday. It was impossible, however, without a day's delay, to require them to put back on their civilian clothing, soaking in the tubs by his express authorization. Any delay in their departure for Paris's redoubtable Revolutionary Tribunal as ordered by the Committee of Public Salvation was not even to be considered at this point, for he himself had had everything prepared for their immediate departure, as well as for their midnight transfer at Senlis.

Madame de Croissy is reported by Madame Philippe to have asked the mayor if he had no shame, telling them to leave immediately, seeing how the older sisters were already soaked. But, as so accurately described by Psalmist, the abashed mayor was caught in his own self-constructed trap: "the wicked is snared in the work of his own hands" (Ps 9:16). His inner peace was also shattered by thoughts of what questions might be raised in Paris about why he and Compiègne's Revolutionary Surveillance Committee were allowing local nuns still to be wearing their forbidden habits 22 months after expulsion from their monastery.

Frustrated by his inability to prevent the Carmelites' departure in their habits, the mayor, before leaving the prison that day, vented his spleen on the English Benedictines. Possessing no clothing other than those habits in which they had been arrested 22 months before, the English nuns were a ready target for his frustrations. He pointedly told them that in case of a riot, he could not answer for the fury their forbidden habits might inspire in the revolutionary populace. They must immediately get changed into civilian attire.

From the English documents it seems that the mayor actually anticipated that the English Benedictines might well be the next ones ordered before Paris' Revolutionary Tribunal, something the Benedictines themselves profoundly feared. Still, in reply to the mayor's warning, the English nuns could only point out that they had no means whatsoever—neither money, nor friends in Compiègne, nor any other resource—for procuring civilian garments. This, however, did not stop the agitated mayor from returning each day to harangue them about the dangers of wearing religious habits in these revolutionary times.

On the fourth day the mayor and his committee removed the seals from the Carmelites' quarters. Spotting their civilian clothing left soaking, they agreed that they had found an answer to the Benedictines' pressing problem. The English documents specifically indicate that these garments were passed to them "fished out of the tubs" and "dripping wet." The Benedictines were ordered to put them on, which they did as soon as the garments were dry.

The date this transfer took place, however, provides us with a curious coincidence. Official revolutionary documents record it as occurring on 28 Messidor, Year II—that is, July 16, 1794, feast of Our Lady of Mount Carmel. It was hardly a conjunction of dates the mayor and his committee would have thought of or particularly have wanted to emphasize.

A still more startling coincidence involved the actual number of garments discovered. Official records are categorical in specifying that what was found in the Carmelites' quarters and delivered to the English Benedictines were "34 bonnets, 34 scarves and 17 house dresses and jerkins." This was the exact number of garments needed to meet the 17 Benedictines' needs, plus a double of the necessary accessories of bonnets and scarves, the latter a particularly vital article with the low-cut dresses of the time. These garments, the committee esteemed, could not be designated "for a better or more solid use" than that of clothing the 17 English nuns whose appearance in religious habits "could only be offensive to republican eyes."

Since the Carmelites numbered only 16, it seems likely that Madame Philippe's clothing had either been left behind, or brought back from Paris by Madame Lidoine. Sister Marie of the Incarnation had no doubt found more appropriate attire for frequenting government offices in Paris.

The coincidence that the transfer of the Carmelite's clothing took place on the high feast of Our Lady of Mount Carmel is striking. More striking still, however, is the coincidence that these relics constituted the exact number of garments needed to clothe the 17 English Benedictines. Thus did those least disposed to perpetuate the memory of the Carmelites become, in the divine economy of God, those who unwittingly perpetuated that memory by placing their relics in the hands of the most faithful of Christian believers. When news reached Compiègne that the Carmelites' act of holocaust had been received by heaven, the Benedictines viewed their second-hand clothing as martyrs' relics. They had no choice, however, but to continue to wear these relics until their return to England on May 2, 1795. There, clothed at last in their own habits again, they immediately undertook the distribution of pieces of the Carmelites' civilian clothing to pious English Catholics, eager for relics from martyrs of the French Revolution.

A century later the arrival of those civilian garments in England on May 2, 1795, was gently echoed in France. On May 2, 1895, important pieces of this same clothing again crossed the English Channel, enshrined as relics for veneration. They were on the way to the new Carmel of Compiègne, a gift from the English Benedictines. These relics are venerated today at the new monastery of the Carmel of Compiègne, located outside the city on a hill bordering the village of Jonquières. From their country hillside today's sisters guard these vestiges of their martyrs as they keep vigil over Compiègne, lying below, in the gentle valley of the Oise.

ix

According to the witness of Dame Anne Teresa Partington, historian for the imprisoned Benedictines, the departure of the Carmelites from their prison resembled that of "real saints." The English sisters watched them all embrace one another before leaving. The French nuns, she states, also directed many waves of the hand and other gestures of affectionate farewell in their direction. Was the English nuns' release not a part of the purpose behind the anticipated sacrifice?

The two carts bearing the 17 prisoners probably did not leave Compiègne much before noon. As arranged, the transfer took place around midnight at Senlis. The 16 nuns and Mulot de la Ménardière finally arrived at Paris's Conciergerie in mid-afternoon of the following day.

Madame Philippe's remark about the prisoners being paraded around Paris all day as they went from one prison to another, seeking free places, seems pure embroidery. They had specifically been ordered to the Conciergerie by the Paris

Committee of Public Salvation. At the height of the Great Terror, with the exception of the *décadi* holiday, one could always count on at least 30 places being freed each day at the Conciergerie because of the daily death sentences. That most famous of revolutionary prisons did serve largely at that time as a holding facility for those scheduled to "pass upstairs" for trial by the Revolutionary Tribunal.

We have already seen how the arrival of the martyrs and Mulot de la Ménardière at the Conciergerie was marked by the moving witness of the oldest martyr, the 78-year-old Sister Charlotte of the Resurrection. Tossed out on the paving stones, she expressed gratitude to her tormentor for not having killed her, which would have deprived her of the glory of martyrdom with her sisters. The brutal guard's impatience was no doubt encouraged by the anticipatory excitement abroad in Paris on that July 13. It was the eve of the fifth anniversary of the storming of the Bastille, and the people looked forward to dancing in the streets, to clinking glasses, and to the excitement of fireworks. What could seem more contrary to the national mood than this pathetic group of recalcitrant Carmelite nuns, the very embodiment of France's former superstitions and fanaticism?

Fireworks had been ruled out that year, however. On July 14, 1794, the new order was at war with the rest of Europe and saltpeter, indispensable for the manufacture of gunpowder, was in short supply. The shortage had become so acute that in Paris citizens were being conscripted for teams to scrape the precious substance from the walls of the city's tombs and underground structures. Thus, to replace the usual fireworks, an elaborate illumination of the ex-royal Tuileries Palace, seat of the National Convention, had been announced.

The *Journal de Paris*, however, reports a curious meteorological coincidence regarding this July 14 illumination of the palace. According to the prorevolutionary reporter, just as the illumination was set off a great black cloud instantaneously covered the whole Paris sky, providing "a striking contrast" to the flood of man-made light.

Those who, 36 days before, believed that the sun showed republican sympathies by shining so brightly on Robespierre's Festival of the Supreme Being, might have been obliged to conclude on this occasion that heaven was, if not actually anti-enlightenment, at least opposed to the celebration of Bastille Day. Against this burst of man-made light on that July 14, 1794, the sky quite literally veiled its face, as if the celebration of eighteenth-century enlightenment on the fifth anniversary of the storming of the Bastille must not reach the stars.

As for the Carmelites imprisoned in the Conciergerie, quite other coincidences preoccupied them. They were in the midst of the novena leading up to the Feast of Our Lady of Mount Carmel. Their transfer to Paris during these nine days had already seemed a sign. Was it possible that they would be tried on July 16, so that the day of their mystic nuptials coincided with their patronal festival?

In mute, self-contained, and joyous expectancy, Madame Lidoine could feel her heart leap as she thought of the approaching festival. When her daughters spoke to her of these things she realized how closely they were all being drawn together, for they too seemed to echo her own inner preoccupation before God. Still she remained silent, pondering it all in her heart. She was sure only of his great mercy to her and of her heart's burning love for him. Had he not already given her all she could desire or hope for in this life? The clear sign that he intended for her to continue to lead his little flock, wherever he might send them, was all she could ask.

At least she was sure now of being included if he did choose them to follow the Lamb.

9

"Enemies of the People"

(i) The Carmelites' preparation for death; what was sung in the tumbrels; how they learned of their trial on the Feast of Our Lady Mount Carmel. (ii) Madame Lidoine faces the morrow. (iii) Predawn summons of the prisoners; the prioress's anticipation. (iv) The Courtroom of Freedom and the Courtroom of Equality; Fouquier-Tinville in both courtrooms; Madame Pelras' challenge; accusations against Mulot de la Ménardière and the Carmelites. (v) Mother Lidoine answers Scellier's charges. (vi) The death sentence; Teresa Soiron faints. (vii) Pre-execution formalities. (viii) Recollections of Denis Blot; the last cup of chocolate.

MADAME PHILIPPE IS MUCH MORE PRECISE in regard to her sisters' preparation for death in her first manuscript than in her second and third ones. In the latter two she remarks rather vaguely that having already made their preparation for death (she says "in the *night*" then changes it to "in the *morning*"), they were left free to sing nothing but "praises" on the way to the scaffold.

Certainly the idea of their singing nothing but "praises" on the way to the guillotine is noble. But Madame Philippe, as we have seen, was given at times to attempts to render her account as edifying as possible. This lack of precision in her second and third manuscripts causes us to question the seriousness of her remarks, particularly when compared with the specificity found in her first manuscript. There she states that after partaking of their last cup of chocolate, all the community together recited the prayers for the commendation of dying souls. This detail she no doubt learned from Denis Blot, a fellow prisoner who was standing beside the 16 condemned nuns in that particular moment in the Conciergerie. In this case, therefore, as in certain others, her first version seems more reliable.

As for what was sung on the way to the scaffold, Madame Philippe consistently mentions both the *Miserere* and the *Salve Regina.* In her first manuscript, in a note marked "P.S.," she also speaks of their singing the evening monastic offices of Vespers and Compline. To this also should also be added the witness of Monseigneur Jauffret, our earliest historian of the martyrdom, who consulted eyewitnesses as well as Madame Philippe. He affirms that the Office of the Dead was sung in the tumbrels, something as plausible as their singing Vespers and Compline.

Indeed, there was time for a great deal more to be sung than the *Miserere* and the *Salve Regina* between the Palais de Justice and the Place of the Throne. One witness of the Great Terror states that the day he followed the procession along that route it took about two hours. The two-mile trip through revolutionary Paris in the springless tumbrels, surrounded by a hostile, curious, and pressing crowd, was, of necessity, always a very slow one. Yet we are told that the nuns sang throughout this public procession of the condemned. It seems quite plausible therefore that a combination of the Office of the Dead, of Vespers, and of Compline, plus other shorter texts might well have been sung during this time.

Whatever the case, we do know that according to the Republican calendar, nine days out of ten were working days. The Revolutionary Tribunal's Public Prosecutor, Fouquier-Tinville, was therefore obliged on the eve of each of those nine working days to anticipate the next day's affairs. So it was that on the evening before each trial, he listed those he himself selected to appear the next day before the Revolutionary Tribunal. His selection made, the prisoners on his list were notified in their cells down below in the Conciergerie to prepare themselves to "go upstairs" early on the morrow for trial.

It remains a striking coincidence that Fouquier-Tinville's formal act of accusation against the 16 martyrs and Mulot de la Ménardière was drawn up, signed and dated "28 Messidor, Year II," that is, July 16, 1794, Feast of Our Lady of Mount Carmel. This was, we have seen, the same day the transfer of the Carmelites' civilian clothing to the Benedictines took place in Compiègne. The Carmelites thus would actually learn of their impending trial on the evening of their patronal festival. As we have also seen, this was being commemorated by singing Sister Julie's five-stanza, death-defying parody of *La Marseillaise*, with its lines about climbing the scaffold steps and giving the victory to their holy patroness's divine Son. Thus as Fouquier-Tinville's announcement broke in to interrupt this austere celebration, they recognized that their boldness before God had instantaneously been crowned with the possibility of their consecration becoming a reality.

Given the circumstances, it would have been strange not to have sensed in all this the presence of their holy patroness, Our Lady of Mount Carmel. Was she not bending down to touch them and bless their act of holocaust? Was it not her own pure hand now opening that door through which they must all next pass if their oblation were to be accomplished?

Madame Lidoine's sensitivity could not fail to have found immediate reassurance in this striking coincidence that, for her, could only be a sure sign. That the Public Prosecutor himself had actually signed this announcement on their high feast day was as divine an irony as had been the stripping of their monastery on September 12, forcing them out into the world on September 14, feast of the Exaltation of the Holy Cross.

Had Madame Lidoine known that Fouquier-Tinville, even while acting as Public Prosecutor for the Revolutionary

Tribunal, actually wore a medallion of the holy Virgin, passed to his family after his execution, she might well have reasoned that he had thereby left himself open to the impact of their powerful patroness's influence, for the choice of July 17 for their trial was Fouquier-Tinville's alone. His alone was the choice determining that they would learn, on their own high feast day, that the long-awaited answer from heaven was set for the morrow.

ii

AS INWARDLY JOYFUL as she undoubtedly was at this development, Madame Lidoine could never, however, lose sight of the fact that the spiritual well-being of some of her daughters might now be in particular danger. If indeed her own aspirations for the martyrdom of love were to be realized, this fulfillment must not risk one single soul for which her Beloved's blood was shed. He alone, therefore, must determine the next day's outcome. She, for her part, would do everything in her power to save her daughters, thereby testing his will in this ultimate drama on which life or death depended. Inwardly persuaded that martyrdom for the whole community had been announced by prophecies and continuing signs, she had done her utmost to sustain this conviction faithfully within the community for almost two years through their daily act of consecration. Yet their act of consecration was neither an article of faith nor a part of their profession as Carmelites. Nor had it been made to her, but to him alone. He alone it must be, therefore, who either accepted or rejected it.

Paradoxically, Mother Teresa of Saint Augustine's continued offering of herself and her community in holocaust still in no way dimmed her very deep maternal instinct to protect her 15 daughters. As we shall see, it was with a natural mother's ferocious insistence for the simple truth regarding her children's guilt that she would defend them from the false and utterly ridiculous accusations of crime put forward by the Public Prosecutor. Never do we find her ready to exploit just any excuse for justifying their deaths merely because they had freely offered themselves in holocaust. If, by his mercy, she herself should be granted martyrdom, never must she presume to determine which others, if any, should join her. The Beloved alone had that right.

The essential paradox of Mother Lidoine's position would be clearly enunciated the next day before the Revolutionary Tribunal. Her attempts to defend her daughters against the accusations of wrongdoing, even while offering herself as the sole victim, bear adequate witness to this, as do her efforts to spare the two extern sisters from execution. Only by his repeated rejection the next day of each of her sincere efforts to test his will in this matter would her own holy prudence finally be vanquished. Then only would she dare believe that his will could, in fact, coincide with her own deepest longings. Then only could she know that her own spiritual intuitions were indeed of the Holy Spirit.

As the long, sweet, unreal night of vigil stretched implacably toward her last dawn, Mother Lidoine's heart burned within as she awaited his pleasure, the pleasure of him whose love she sought even "as the deer longs for running waters" (Ps 42:1). His answer on the morrow, she knew, would determine life or death for each of them.

iii

OF THE 54 PRISONERS tried by the Revolutionary Tribunal on that 29 Messidor, Year II, of the One Indivisible French Republic, 40 would be guillotined as "enemies of the people" before nightfall. The 16 Carmelites of Compiègne actually composed less than half of the Public Prosecutor's sizeable "batch" for July 17, 1794.

Though the trials began only at 10 A.M., those on Fouquier-Tinville's list were roused at dawn. After a far from restful night, this early call assured a lugubrious beginning to what, for most of them, would be their last day on earth. The loud creak of the Conciergerie's first grille being opened, then banged shut, brutally announced their last sunrise. With the Revolutionary Tribunal sitting above in the Palais de Justice, their musty underground prison had become the nerve center of revolutionary Paris's judicial system. Given that few escaped the death sentence, the Conciergerie was truly, for most of them, death's threshold. Shrouded in anticipatory anguish and the stoic muffling of true feelings, the events that inaugurated each day in the subterranean prison became a sort of anticipatory funeral rite.

Armed with a mass of giant keys, and accompanied by huge mastiffs and lantern-bearing assistants, the jailer escorted the bailiff and his gendarmes through the maze of grilles partitioning off the cold, humid vaults stretching into the bowels of the earth. Creaking grilles echoed piercingly throughout the vast spaces as the procession was formed at the still-dark hour. The bailiff's gendarmes herded the accused together as they came forward in response to his rough, repeated shouts of the names on Fouquier-Tinville's list.

Then the gendarmes herded those summoned and collected past the next grille and yet another gate banged shut behind them. In spite of the attempt to contain anguish during this tense, drawn-out ritual, re-enacted nine days out of ten, a sobbed farewell or a cry of despair did sometimes pierce the early morning stillness. It seems highly unlikely, however, that any audible signs of emotion escaped any of the 16 Carmelites that morning. The night before they had sung joyfully of this "day of glory" and their lamps were now filled and trimmed. They were ready.

As for Madame Lidoine, mother of the martyrdom, her brightly burning lamp was certainly no less boldly held aloft than those of her well-trained daughters. Nor was it less trimmed, less filled, or less aflame with love to bid welcome to him for whom she so longed. Never had she felt more intensely that she was about to realize, in all its magnitude, the true reason for her coming into the world. The possibility that, as she had said in her carol, she might, on this very day, "be clasped faster" within his heart, gave her unspeakable joy. For, as the sequence of events crept forward, Sister Elisabeth Baptiste's witness did not cease to burn within Mother Lidoine, drawing her ever deeper into its ponderous mystery. Might she now at last claim for herself that same sweet and ineffable intimacy discovered in him alone by that bereft and handicapped sister who had had no one else to love? Let him come now and claim her also for his spouse. How gladly would she too kiss the glorious scars of his wounded humanity!

iv

THE REVOLUTIONARY TRIBUNAL'S MAJOR COURTROOM, used in the thirteenth century by Saint Louis himself, had been rechristened the "Courtroom of Freedom" by the Revolution. Its capacity outstripped by the number of accused tried each day, an adjoining courtroom, christened the "Courtroom of Equality," had been inaugurated. Both operated simultaneously to dispatch the ever-swelling influx of provincial prisoners dispatched to Paris for trial since the passing of the law of 22 Prairial.

On that July 17, 35 people were tried in the "Courtroom of Freedom," 19 in the "Courtroom of Equality." As we have seen, 40 of these 54 accused would be guillotined at the Place of the Throne before nightfall.

The show trial of the Queen of France had taken place in the Courtroom of Freedom nine months before. Heavy with memories of St. Louis and symbols of France's Christian monarchy, the courtroom had now been stripped of all vestiges of its royal past and a conscientious effort made to inspire grave awe before the solemnity of the new order's justice. The bust of Rome's republican hero, Brutus, and of the Revolution's own two "freedom martyrs," Le Peletier de Saint-Fargeau and Marat, were mounted on the front wall, beneath posters of the New Constitution and of the Rights of Man. The three busts formed a new-order trinity, presiding over the courtroom's administration of justice.

The somber dress for officials of the Revolutionary Tribunal had been designed by David himself. The three judges, the clerk of the Tribunal, the Public Prosecutor and his deputies he shrouded in black cloaks. Wearing black off-face round hats, surmounted by imposing upright black plumes, the three judges sat at tables with gryphon's feet, directly underneath the two posters proclaiming human rights. The medals suspended from a tri-coloured ribbon around their necks bore the inscription: "The Law" and were distinguishable from those worn by the prosecutors, which read "Public Security." Also, the black plumes on the prosecutors' hats lay flat rather than standing upright.

As Public Prosecutor, Fouquier-Tinville was responsible for what transpired in both courtrooms. His deputies assured his representation at all times in both places, leaving him completely free to pass from one courtroom to the other during the proceedings. He is reported at times even to have planted spies among the prisoners who would also appear for trial. Their acquittals always looked good and swelled the small number found not guilty of being enemies of the people. On such occasions a cynical comedy might even be acted out at the end of the trial as these "innocents" received embraces and congratulations from the judges and jurors.

As we have seen, Fouquier-Tinville was challenged by the Carmelites' young infirmarian, Madame Pelras, to define his use of the word "fanatics" that she heard him use to describe them. His admission that it was because of their attachment to their "religion" that they were classified as "fanatics," was, as far as their martyrdom was concerned, a key statement. Though not found in the official accusation, it did reveal, as Madame Pelras rightly grasped, the truth behind the legal proceedings not only against the Carmelites, but also against thousands of French Christians.

Fouquier-Tinville's long official Act of Accusation against all 35 prisoners tried that day in the Courtroom of Liberty is reproduced by Father Bruno in *Le Sang du Carmel.* We retain here only the accusations against Mulot de la Ménardière and the 16 Carmelites.

MULOT, alias LAMENARDIERE

> Mulot, alias La Ménardière, ex-non-juring priest in the commune of Compiègne, was the leader of a counter-revolutionary assembly, a sort of center for Vendée sympathizers, composed of ex-Carmelite nuns and other enemies of the Revolution. In his correspondence with these women, submitted to his will, one can discern, as he sets down the counter-revolutionary principles and feelings inspiring him, that profound treachery familiar to Tartuffes[1] who are in the habit of mistaking their passions for a rule of the Divine Will. It

[1] Tartuffe is the eponymous hero of one of Molière's greatest classic comedies. His name has become synonymous with gross and exploitative hypocrisy. For the antireligious revolutionaires it is understandable that anything smacking of Christianity and the monastic life was thought to be a blatant manifestation of such exploitative hypocrisy, including the "lifestyle" of the Carmelites of Compiègne.

appears to have been he who joined to his letters a text that reads:

"To the general intentions concerning the needs of the church, you will add intentions that members making up the districts and municipalities may be enlightened to know all the evil they do by lending themselves to the execution of decrees contrary to Religion; and that they may be faithful in refusing evil, even at the cost of their lives; and that they will not accept any employment that cannot be allied with Christianity."

Another manuscript on his refusal to take the Oath, known as the "constitutional oath," establishes that his resistance to legitimate authority was premeditated. His correspondence proves that the most cruel enemies of the Revolution were his friends. In one of his letters, intrepid defenders of the Fatherland are described as dishonest immoral do-nothings, most of them composed of the dregs of the lower class with neither feelings, honor nor heart: "I've always been revolted by the flags and red caps."

Finally Mulot ends a piece of poetry addressed by him to one of the nuns with these four verses:

Insects all get destroyed by the cold.
Oh! might it with the wicked be as bold!
Jacobins—whatever their qualities!
And Representatives—in great quantities!

LIDOINE, TOURET etc...

As for the ex-Carmelite nuns, Lidoine, Touret, Brare [sic], Dufour and the rest, though separated by their dwellings, they nonetheless organized meetings and counter-revolutionary cells amongst themselves and others, whom they gathered together, and where, reviving their *esprit de corps,* they conspired against the Republic. A voluminous correspondence found in their dwellings shows that they did not cease intriguing against the Revolution. The portrait of Capet; his testament; hearts, which are a sign of rebellion in the Vendée[2]; fanatical and childish objects, accompanied with a certificate of either a foreign or immigrated priest—the certificate dated 1793; all prove their correspondence with enemies outside France. Such are the marks of the union formed amongst them. They lived under obedience to a Superior and, as for their principles and vows, their letters and writings make these things clear in writing. In a pretended hymn, said to be about the Heart of Jesus and Mary, one reads:

> Cause the avenging eagle to advance
> Against the devouring vultures!
> And let the olive be reborn
> Upon the ashes of our tyrants!
> Let that Heart, the world's salvation,
> By which Satan was crushed,
> Appear in the midst of thunder
> In the midst of the blazing sky!
> At its sweet and terrible appearance
> I see the factious grow pale.
> France shall then have peace,
> Her king be free, her people happy.

---

[2] The Vendée, famous for its resistance and stubborn guerilla war against the Revolution in 1793, was mercilessly crushed by Turreau's "infernal columns," known for such atrocities as the tanning of human skin and the rendering of human fat for the manufacture of soap. In 1989, behind banners of the Sacred Heart, processions of Vendéens marched on Paris to protest the national celebrations of the Revolution's bicentenary. Emile Gabory's classic work on this subject, *Les guerres de Vendée,* crowned by the French Academy, has recently been reprinted (Paris: Robert Laffont, 1989).

> This counter-revolutionary hymn was no doubt the one used by the priests of the Vendée to lead the blind victims of their rascality to the murder and assassination of their brothers. One sees in their correspondence with what pleasure they spoke of the treason and other maneuvers practiced by the despots united against the French Republic. In one of the letters found in the dwelling of the Lidoine woman one reads:
>
> "They say that the Austrians have forced the French patriots to lift the siege of Maastricht and the six thousand emigrants defending it. God grant success to all this for a still greater good. As for me, I hope that we may serve him more freely and that I, in a cloister, may do reparation for all my infidelities."[3]
>
> Thus, according to this conspirator, men's blood had to be shed to reestablish convents. Finally, all these ex-nuns refused to recognize national sovereignty and the empire of its laws: they refused to make the oath society had the right to demand of them in granting them the means to subsist. They offered only a reunion and gathering of rebels, of seditious persons who nourished in their hearts the desire and criminal hope of seeing the French people put back into the irons of its tyrants and enslaved to priests whose thirst for blood equals their imposture, as also of seeing freedom swallowed up in torrents of blood shed through their infamous intrigues organized in the name of heaven.

The statement in the closing paragraph that "these ex-nuns ... refused to make the oath society had the right to demand of them in granting them the means to subsist," has

---

[3] Though Madame Lidoine's sympathies may well have been for the French refugees in Maastrich, one would be hard put to prove her personal politics here. Her sacrifice as a consecrated Christian woman alone really mattered.

encouraged some to take seriously Madame Philippe's story about the nuns retracting their *Liberté-Egalité* oath in prison. But is the seriousness of this document itself not very much open to question? Its preposterous opening statements identifying Mulot de la Ménardière as an "ex-non-juring priest in the commune of Compiègne," should serve to measure its value. Accusations issued by the Public Prosecutor for the Revolutionary Tribunal were seldom to be counted on for establishing the truth.

V

EACH OF THE TWO COURTROOMS had its three judges, one of whom presided. The presiding judge in the Courtroom of Liberty that day was Scellier, a native of Compiègne, as we have seen. It was his mayor-brother who had so precipitously dispatched the Carmelites to Paris five days before. When the trial finally got under way we find Madame Lidoine alone answering the charges he read out. This would imply, as only seems logical, that the exchange between Madame Pelras and Fouquier-Tinville about the word "fanatics" must have taken place prior to the trial itself. Her query was in fact probably provoked by a remark she overheard him make in instructing one of his deputies. Pretrial instructions to the deputies were necessary with Fouquier-Tinville himself moving from one courtroom to the other as he followed the two simultaneous trials each day.

According to Abbé Guillon's version in *Les martyrs de la foi pendant la Révolution fançaise,* copied out by Madame Philippe in her manuscripts,[4] the trial of the Carmelites began

---

[4] See *Le sang du Carmel,* pp. 464–467, where Father Bruno compares her text, dating from 1832–1836, to Abbé Guillon's, published in 1821.

with a preposterous accusation read out by the presiding judge: "You are accused of hiding weapons in your convent that were intended for immigrants who had left France."

To match the outrageousness of the far-fetched accusation, Madame Lidoine reached into her bosom. She pulled out her crucifix of profession and held it up, brandishing it in defiance: "The only weapon we've ever had in our convent is this. You cannot prove we have ever had any others."

Scellier ignored her bravura and passed to the second item: "You have dared expose the Blessed Sacrament under a canopy shaped like a royal cloak."

The prioress's reply would lead us to think that she had heard of the talk of their being part of a conspiracy, perhaps again from remarks she overheard Fouquier-Tinville make to his deputies. The Committee of Revolutionary Surveillance of Compiègne, in their original accusations against the Carmelites, had actually preposterously tried to link the nuns with Catherine Théot, a deranged Parisian concierge who called herself the "Mother of God" and to whom Robespierre's enemies tried to link him while precipitating his downfall.

In disbelief the prioress retorted: "That canopy is an old altar furnishing. Nothing in its shape distinguishes it from any other such canopy. Certainly it is in no way whatsoever related to this conspiracy in which you want to implicate us because of it. I fail to understand how you can seriously infer that our possessing it can be a crime."

This time Scellier answered her: "That altar furnishing indicates your attachment to the monarchy and, therefore, to Louis XVI and his family."

Sister Marie's account of this exchange, borrowed from the Abbé Guillon's, repeats his observation that the prioress might at this point have held her tongue, even though their monastery had been bound by close ties to the royal family from its foundation. But her great and generous soul exacted unashamed loyalty to France's "most Christian" kings. Even trying to save her daughters was secondary to that. Thoughtfully she answered from her heart and with her whole soul: "Well, Citizen, if that be a crime, then all of us are indeed guilty and you will never be able to take from our hearts our devotion to Louis XVI and to his august family. Your laws can never impinge upon that feeling: they cannot dominate the affections of our souls. God and God alone has the right to judge such things."

Continuing the charade, Scellier read out the third charge: "You have corresponded with those who have emigrated and you have sent them money."

Madame Lidoine recognized the reference to her correspondence with Abbé Courouble in Belgium: "The letters we received were from the chaplain of our convent, condemned to deportation by your laws. Those letters contain nothing but spiritual advice. Moreover, if that correspondence be criminal in your eyes, that crime regards me alone. It is not a crime of the community to all of whose members our Rule forbids all correspondence, even with the closest relatives, without the superior's permission."

With absolute boldness and no desire whatsoever to push for a community martyrdom based on such paltry, ridiculous, and utterly false reasons, Madame Lidoine seems at this point to have reacted with firmness and great conviction. A tinge of defiance would even seem implied in her voice in her next bold affirmation, so poignantly revealing her Christian heart and soul: "If you must have a victim, here I am. Take me. I alone am the one whom you should cut down. My sisters are all innocent. They have done nothing, nor could they do anything, except by my orders."

"They sucked your milk," Scellier immediately retorted. "All of them are your accomplices. Every one of them shall perish!"

As thoughts of Teresa Soiron passed through her mind, Mother Lidoine contemplated her next step. In innocent good faith she was determined to try to save what she could. She had had to shore up the extern's courage during that terrible trip from Compiègne four nights before when both Teresa Soiron and Mulot de la Ménardière were railing against God and their fate. Though on that occasion she had succeeded in getting Teresa to repent and offer her death to God, there was no reason she should now perish if she and her older sister could be spared. Neither of them was under any vow, although, as paid employees they had faithfully served the community for more than two decades. "If you consider them all my accomplices, what do you say about our extern sisters?"

"What do we accuse them of? Weren't they your agents when carrying your letters to the post?"

Virtually illiterate, the extern sisters could have had no idea of the meaning of the writing on the letters. The accusation was thus ridiculous.

"But they had no idea of what was contained in those letters. And they did not even know the places to which I addressed them. Besides, their duty as paid employees was to do what was asked of them."

"Be quiet!" Scellier impatiently snapped, cutting her off. "Their duty was to come advise the Nation about those letters."

At this point, in accordance with the law of 22 Prairial, the jury declared itself satisfied. It thus heard no further evidence, nor a single word in the Carmelites' defense, even though a sympathetic lawyer, Monsieur Sézille de Montarlet, was there to plead their innocence.

vi

THE VERDICT DETERMINING THE FATE of all these 35 prisoners tried in the Courtroom of Freedom that day would not have been announced until mid-afternoon. Thirty were found guilty of having "turned themselves into enemies of the People" and of "conspiring against the People's Sovereignty." The 16 Carmelites, in addition to being "enemies of the people," were also convicted of "organizing counter-revolutionary groups and cells," of "maintaining correspondence with enemies outside France," of "possessing hearts, symbol for rallying the Vendée rebels," and of "collecting writings" that aimed at "annihilating freedom," since they all wanted "to see freedom swallowed up in streams of blood that their infernal activities had caused to be shed in the name of heaven." This latter accusation was based on the fact that images of the Sacred Heart of Jesus, particularly identified with the Vendée uprising, had been found in their possession though having, in fact, nothing to do with the Vendée uprising.

The unfortunate Mulot de la Ménardière, incriminated because of two letters to Sister Euphrasia, was condemned as a non-juring priest and ally of the community. He was said to be guilty of authoring royalist and counter-revolutionary texts as well as of organizing meetings of fanatics "*in his house.*" Mulot's desperate pleas that he was married and that his wife was imprisoned at Chantilly, which fact he could prove by affidavits, availed no more than did his frantic plea that Scellier check his identity with his own mayor-brother of Compiègne who, Mulot assured him, knew him well. In what must have been an inner panic bordering on hysteria, he heard Scellier's laconic, death-sealing retort: "I don't know you!"

Finally the sentence was pronounced on those 30 found guilty.

> The Tribunal, after having heard the Public Prosecutor's conclusions on the application of the law, condemns to death all those named in the declaration of the jury cited heretofore, being 30 in number, in

> conformity with the disposition of Articles IV, V, and VII of which reading has been given and thus presented:
>
> "THE REVOLUTIONARY TRIBUNAL EXISTS TO PUNISH THE ENEMIES OF THE PEOPLE.
>
> THE ENEMIES OF THE PEOPLE ARE THOSE WHO SEEK TO ANNIHILATE PUBLIC FREEDOM, WHETHER BY FORCE OR BY SUBTERFUGE.
>
> FOR ALL THESE CRIMES OF WHICH THE REVOLUTIONARY TRIBUNAL HAS TAKEN COGNIZANCE, THE PENALTY IS DEATH."
>
> At the request and dispatch of the Public Prosecutor we order that the present judgment be carried out within 24 hours on that public square of the city, formerly called the Vincennes Gates, and that it be printed and posted throughout the whole of the indivisible French Republic.

There was a dead thud. Teresa Soiron had fainted. Madame Lidoine asked one of the gendarmes for a glass of water. Madame Philippe's account of the incident insists upon Teresa's sorrow, regret, and repentance because of her weakness. She even adds that the extern remarked that the dear Lord had allowed this in order to humiliate her, though he knew her joy in dying in order to possess him in heaven.

Such details, if accurate, would have had to come from someone present at the trial. The daughter of Sézille de Montarlet, the lawyer from Noyon prepared to defend the nuns before the Tribunal, was a Madame Pain who lived in Compiègne. Contacts with her, or even with her father, would certainly have been possible for Madame Philippe during her eight-month stay in Compiègne in 1795.

vii

THE 30 CONDEMNED from the Courtroom of Freedom were herded back downstairs by way of winding passages to the Conciergerie. There they were joined by the ten who had been condemned in the Courtroom of Equality. All had to be officially transferred by the jailer to the executioner, Sanson. There was, it was often remarked, an uncanny accuracy in Sanson's always having waiting in the stone-paved courtyard of the Conciergerie exactly the right number of carts to transport the condemned to the scaffold. This came from the fact that the executioner, after completing his evening's bloody work, always reported back to Fouquier-Tinville to learn the number to be included in the "batch" of the condemned the next day. Since the number given the evening before the trial always corresponded with the number condemned, this can only imply that the fate of those to be condemned had already been settled by Fouquet-Tinville himself before the trial, give or take one or two exceptions per day. The case of Mulot de la Ménardière serves well to illustrate this arbitrary administration of justice by the Public Prosecutor.

Before being loaded into the carts, each of the condemned had to sit for a "last toilette." Sanson or one of his valets would shear away any hair covering the neck, and remove or slit all collars so as to expose the neck area completely. Mother Lidoine's foresight in having long since prepared her own 15 daughters for the guillotine exempted them now from this humiliating necessity.

Madame Lidoine sensed deeply, in this great hour of victory over so many doubts and fears, to what extent the Holy Spirit had touched her when her heart first leapt upon reading Sister Elisabeth Baptiste's dream. They were indeed now "all together" to "follow the Lamb," however disquieting the more legalistic mind might find this mixture of virgins with a widow, of professed with non-professed, to say nothing of the two hired extern sisters. All were equally dear to her as to him, and all would now receive, with no distinction whatsoever, the same glory, the same martyr's palm, the same victor's crown. How the right glory of God's uncreated light burned away the petty dross of man's too-human categories! For there where the Carmelites' oblation would place them for all eternity, there in the glory of his kingdom, the paradox of the last being first, and of the first being last (Mt 19:30) was so discreetly true, for with God all things are possible (Mt 19:26).

During the long, drawn-out delay between sentencing and departure for the place of execution, women known as *fouilleuses* searched the prisoners for hidden jewelry or money. As we know, Madame Lidoine clasped in her palm a tiny clay statuette of the Virgin and Child that the sisters all kissed at the foot of the scaffold. We know also that Madame Brard retained a service book that she passed from her tumbrel to Thérèse Binard. The work of these *fouilleuses* therefore could not always have been all that thorough. No doubt their interests lay in any case far more in money and jewelry than in valueless service books or poor clay statuettes.

All eyewitness accounts agree on the slowness of the process following sentencing. One mentions that during this long wait to be loaded into the tumbrels, the Carmelites sang once more Sister Julie's death-defying stanzas on *La Marseillaise.* Surely it would have been an appropriate action, graphically emphasizing the divine warfare in which they were engaged. For the old Enemy of the human race, the Beast, was he not intent on destroying these women consecrated to the Virgin Mother of that Lamb slain before the foundation of the world (Rev 13:8), voluntary and cosmic victim for fallen humanity created in the image and likeness of God? Yet this incident seems highly unlikely. For the nuns to sing the politically charged tune of the prorevolutionary *La*

Marseillaise at such a moment could have caused considerable public confusion about the true meaning of their community holocaust.

viii

MADAME PHILIPPE REPORTS that at her initial meeting with Denis Blot in Orleans in 1795, he threw himself upon her neck and kissed her upon learning she had been a Carmelite of Compiègne. He was convinced, he told her, that her sisters' expiatory sacrifice had saved him from death. He thus owed them his life as well as his freedom.

Arrested and imprisoned for assisting an outlawed priest near Orleans, Denis Blot had been transferred to Paris for judgment by the Revolutionary Tribunal and almost certain death. He had hardly arrived at the Conciergerie, however, before he had a chance to make himself useful to the sorely overworked jailer, Lebeau. Inundated by the arrival of the members of the Parliament of Toulouse who had been arrested *en masse* and sent to await trial before the Revolutionary Tribunal, Lebeau sought a prisoner-assistant. Denis Blot thus came henceforth to enjoy free movement within the prison.

A pious man, Blot had recognized the Carmelites by their habits upon their arrival four days before, and he had made a point of trying to be useful to them. He it was who procured bits of charcoal so that Sister Julie could write her verses for their patronal festival. Now, however, it was with tears and a very full heart that he watched them return downstairs from their trial and sentencing. He reported to Sister Marie the next year that their faces were "beaming with joy."

Until that moment Blot had always been reticent about engaging the Carmelites in conversation. Now, however, deeply touched by what had transpired upstairs, and even more by the thought of what these innocent women were about to undergo, his feelings of admiration overcame his reticence. His heart brimming over with love, gratitude, and veneration, he beheld incarnate there before him, in those women, all he held to be holy and noble and true. He summoned his courage, knowing it was a moment unique in his life. Stammeringly, and with great effort, he tried to say what he felt he must say to them before God: "Sisters ... you have now reached ... your last hour. Perhaps I too am not ... very far from ... my own. I ... come to commend myself ... to your prayers."

"What?" they asked, surprised to learn that he was not just a sympathetic jailer. "You're a prisoner here too? But why?"

Their immediate reaction sustained him. Even at death's door they had time and concern for him. His reply came more easily: "As a fanatic ... responsible for the escape of Monsieur Porcher, parish priest of Fadoville."

Confidently they replied. Their courage and certainty were contagious: "Well, our friend, it is you who must pray for us during the rest of this day. We shall certainly need it. But, this evening, we do hope to be praying for you in heaven."

The encounter with Blot in no way distracted Madame Lidoine from thoughts about what she should do as a last motherly gesture. The imminent ordeal would not be easy. Although the young Sister Constance's fear of the guillotine had been sympathetically dealt with by Abbé de Lamarche, she, their mother, could still be sure of nothing except God's mercy. How profoundly she understood the Psalmist's wisdom that it is better to trust in the Lord than in men (Ps 118:8). And how well she understood how rudely the physical can contend with the spiritual, not only throughout all of one's life, but especially in the last hour.

She was mindful, moreover, that Teresa Soiron had already fainted once. She also realized that the whole community had been roused at dawn after a night of little or no sleep, then herded about the Conciergerie, up into the courtroom and back, with endless waits in corridors and on stairways. Reflecting that nothing had been eaten or drunk throughout the whole of that endless, horrendous day, she noted that it was now past five o'clock. The two-mile trip in rough, bumpy carts in the sweltering heat out to the Place of the Throne still had to be made. Having witnessed just such a procession a month before with Sister Marie of the Incarnation, she realized that neither she nor any of her daughters had any idea of the abuse they would be subjected to during that last and so dramatic lap of their earthly pilgrimage. Before they reached the end, nuns other than Teresa Soiron might also feel faint. In this, their supreme witness where he himself now clearly willed that they be "made a spectacle unto the world, and to angels, and to men" (1 Cor 4:9), Mother Lidoine was determined that sheer physical exhaustion not be allowed to suggest a lack of moral or spiritual fiber in the least of them.

After a brief consultation with her subprioress, it was agreed, as we have seen, that a fur-piece of Madame Brideau's be bartered for a cup of chocolate for each of them. This we know from Blot's account, reported by Madame Philippe. All, he said, participated in this modest, final community repast, calmly savoring the sweet sips from tiny cups with grateful appreciation. And, as we have seen, it was, according to Madame Philippe, followed by a joint recitation of the prayers for the commendation of the souls of those who were dying.

Then, just prior to their being ordered into the carts, Blot reported he himself took the liberty of embracing each of them in turn, individually bidding each nun a final, personal farewell. He assured Madame Philippe 15 months later that in those moments his emotion before God had been so great and so deep that he still retained within himself a vivid, burning memory of each martyr's face. He could, moreover, even still affix the correct name to each face. He recalled also that just prior to climbing into the tumbrels, the nuns were busy exchanging exhortations with each other to be brave, to hold firm, to show no sign of wavering or flinching.

Finally, when Fouquier-Tinville's sizeable "batch" was readied for that day's hecatomb to be offered by the new order for the good estate of revolutionary France, the 40 condemned emerged into the stone courtyard where the tumbrels waited. The little group of 16 Carmelites stood out. As foreordained in the mystic dream of 1693 and in spite of the heat, their white mantles topped their brown habits for the regal festival. The bottom of their white cut-away headcoverings and the white border of their mantles conspicuously framed their naked necks.

Clad in this most chaste of bridal array, and ready at last to depart for mystic nuptials with the Lamb, the 16 consecrated women climbed into the tumbrels. Their singing began immediately.

10

The Wedding Feast of the Lamb

(i) Procession to the scaffold; *Miserere; Salve Regina;* comment by a woman of the people. (ii) Arrival at the Place du Trône; *Te Deum.* (iii) The horror of the site; the sympathetic executioner. (iv) *Veni Creator Spiritus;* predeath renewal of vows; spontaneous outcry of one of the nuns; Sister Marie Henriette (Pelras) assists the prioress; Sister Constance is called first. (v) Sanson's working attire; Sister Constance's song; *Laudate Dominum omnes gentes* taken up by other nuns. (vi) Death of Sister Constance; difference of these executions. (vii) The order of the executions; Sister of Jesus Crucified's (Piedcourt's) remarks on the scaffold. (viii) Sister Euphrasia (Brard) sheds her blood; speculations on identity of sister who cried out; impact on two boys watching. (ix) Death of Sister Henriette (Pelras). (x) Mother Teresa of St. Augustine contemplates the fulfillment of the prophecy; her death; the completion of the day's blood sacrifice; disposal and stripping of the bodies at Picpus. (xi) Survivors of the martyrs: Mother Lidoine's mother; Sister Constance's parents; the sister of Sister St. Ignatius (Trézel); the mother and sister of Sister Julie of Jesus (Crétien de Neuville); Madame Philippe; Soeur Henriette (Pelras) manifests herself to her brother. (xii) Martyrdom as theophany; unity of eastern and western Christian traditions in this martyrdom; conflict between the glory of God and the glory of this world.

The journey to the scaffold had begun. Escorted by mounted guards and foot soldiers on that hot late afternoon in July, the tumbrels bearing the 40 condemned bumped slowly over the paving stones of the Conciergerie courtyard before emerging from the gates of the Palace of Justice. As the procession of guards, horses, foot soldiers, and jolting, springless tumbrels advanced along the uneven stone streets, accompanied by a highly eclectic escort of vociferous regulars, curious street rabble, and a few sympathizers, the *Miserere* arose from the tumbrels.

> Have mercy upon me, O God, after thy great goodness.
> According to the multitude of thy mercies, do away mine offenses.
> Wash me thoroughly from my wickedness and cleanse me from my sin.
> For I acknowledge my guilt and my sin is ever before me.

Attributed to a penitent King David after realizing the enormity of his sin in having Uriah the Hittite killed in battle so that he could take for himself Bathsheba, Uriah's wife, these psalm lines pierced the afternoon heat with their monotone. They were used daily by the nuns, proclaiming the true position of humanity before God. Venerable lines, they had long sustained Jews before being taken up as an integral expression of the Christian soul before God.

> Thou shalt sprinkle me with hyssop and I shall be clean.
> Thou shalt wash me and I shall be whiter than snow.
> Thou shalt make me to hear of joy and gladness that the bones which thou hast broken may rejoice.
> Turn thy face from my sins and blot out all mine iniquity.

The universal silence greeting the procession has been attested to by all witnesses. On that evening those passionate voices that daily railed against the condemned were struck dumb, even to the "furies of the guillotine" at the place of execution. All watched silently, waiting in a sort of eerie, hushed expectancy.

> Create in me a clean heart, O God, and renew a right spirit within me.
> Cast me not away from that presence, and take not thy Holy Spirit from me.

Was it the nun's serene expressions, their white cloaks, or their singing that produced the strange, embarrassed silence along the route? At play for certain spectators must have been that intangible psychological factor Dostoevsky calls a "holy memory." The nuns' faces—which, we are told, radiated joyous anticipation—as well as their white cloaks and chanting undoubtedly inspired within some a poignant echo of a lost past, a past when the things of God had been respected. Others may have been impressed by the obvious assent of the nuns to what was happening to them, for something ineffable emanated from the visible firmness of their resolution. They projected no hint of tragedy, no reason for regret. A rare glory of being seemed to demonstrate that death by the guillotine was for them the crowning of their lives. Had they not, just the night before, sung of this as their own "day of glory"?

The combination of Vespers and Compline, mentioned by Madame Philippe, plus the Office of the Dead attested to by Monseigneur Jauffret, would have taken up the major portion of the journey to the scaffold. Again Dostoevsky's "holy memory" would have tugged at the heartstrings of some spectators as they recalled the last time they heard the Office of the Dead sung. Associated with the death of a mother, father, brother, or sister, it represented the old order, a time when the godless upheaval of the past five years would have been unimaginable.

Also sung en route to the guillotine were the words of tender, helpless abandon of the *Salve Regina.* Never for these Christian women consecrated to Our Lady of Mount Carmel had they seemed more appropriate.

> Hail holy Queen! Mother of mercy!
> Our life, our sweetness, and our hope!
> To thee do we cry, poor banished children of Eve.
> To thee do we send up our sighs,

Mourning and weeping in this valley of tears.
Turn then, most gracious advocate,
Thine eyes of mercy towards us.
And after this, our exile,
Show unto us the blessed fruit of thy womb, Jesus!

The 24 other prisoners could not but be engulfed by the strange hush as the procession advanced. Like their fellow-prisoner, Mulot de la Ménardière, they too were ensnared in a senseless, absurd net from which escape was impossible. As the nuns continued text after text, the austere and implacable monotone of their effortless chanting, like a cool current, flowed through the oppressive heat of this unbearable stretch of time. Every street, every shop passed, they knew, brought them nearer annihilation.

The comments of one Parisian working-class woman that evening as she watched the Carmelites pass by have been preserved for us in the manuscripts of Madame Philippe. They could have come only from an eyewitness who heard this simple woman observe to all and sundry, as the people of Paris have ever been wont to do at public events: "What good souls! Just look at them! Tell me if you don't think they look just like angels! I tell you, if those women don't go straight to paradise then we'll just have to believe it doesn't exist!"

We have already encountered the anecdote concerning the kind woman who offered a drink of water to the singing nuns in the tumbrels, and how Madame Pelras intervened to preserve community unity.

That certain sensitive individuals in the crowd could actually enter into a sort of mystic communion with the condemned has also already been illustrated. As we have seen, on June 14 Sister Marie and Mother Lidoine had felt that the eyes of two men on the way to the guillotine were inviting them to follow them. We have also seen how Thérèse Binard's admiring devotion was mysteriously communicated to Madame Brard who passed her office book to the girl before reaching the guillotine. Undoubtedly there were instances where onlookers were moved to tears by the mere sight of these women in banned white mantles over brown habits, their heads covered only by little white cut-away caps, pointedly exposing their necks.

Monseigneur Jauffret, who seems to have been totally unaware of the ties with the Abbé de Lamarche, reassures his readers that throughout the Terror priests in disguise would either escort the prisoners from the Conciergerie or place themselves along the route. Prisoners who were pious Christians could be advised through such contacts as a Denis Blot in the Conciergerie where they might hopefully look along the route to receive a clandestine final absolution. Thus, even at the height of the Great Terror in Paris, a discerning eye might somewhere have detected along the long route to the Place du Trône, if not at the scaffold itself, the slightly raised hand of a priest disguised as a ferocious *sans-culotte,* blessing and absolving.

ii

BETWEEN THE TIME the sentence was passed in the late afternoon and the arrival at the Place du Trône, three hours would probably have elapsed. The hot evening was thus well advanced before the bumping tumbrels finally reached the vast site. Even at an hour nearing eight o'clock, however, the light would still have been intense, as it is at the end of long, clear Parisian midsummer days when an intense twilight's bright, hot light tenaciously holds night at bay.

The emergence each day of the first tumbrels from the rue du Faubourg Saint-Antoine into the Place du Trône was always a moment of high drama. The nauseous stench hit the unprepared condemned in the pit of the stomach while the impatient crowd watched intently, stalking their reaction with the gaze of birds of prey. Restless, intoxicated from anticipation of the day's great spectacle, they were inured to the stinking heat of the site. Staring voraciously, they evaluated the day's "batch." Breaths quickened, hearts beat faster. Tonight, however, there was the austere chanting of the 16 nuns wearing habits and it continued, unabated. The silence that had accompanied their passage had suddenly engulfed the crowd.

Mounted on its high scaffold, stark against the still bright midsummer evening sky, the realism of the naked blade defied the courage of the would-be martyrs. The resourceful prioress allowed no time, however, for inner battles with fear. As we have seen, she was prepared for this fateful moment and greeted the scaffold's uncompromising reality with the equally uncompromising theological affirmations of the *Te Deum.* Paradoxically she seemed to hurl its powerful, dogmatic praises at the violent promise of that mechanism of steel and wood. With firm boldness and clear voice she intoned: "It is Thee whom we praise, O God!" With one heart and one voice the nuns took up the chant: "It is Thee whom we acknowledge to be the Lord!"

For those familiar with the Latin words, attributed to the divine inspiration of St. Ambrose, Bishop of Milan, as he baptized the 40-year-old St. Augustine, it all seemed startlingly incongruous. Heedless of their impending destruction, these white-cloaked women were praising God. The awed surprise inspired by this extraordinary approach to the guillotine may even partly account for the fact that the crowd maintained their respectful silence while the tumbrels progressed, very slowly, across the vast stretch of the stinking open place. Verse followed verse, implacably. They chanted calmly and with serene force even as they drew right up to the scaffold and came face to face with the steel blade. Still the nuns' voices resounded, unshaken by the proximity, affirming boldly the truth for which they were about to die.

"It is thee, the Father everlasting, whom all the earth doth worship!"

In this unique hour and in the long evening shadow cast by the triangular blade, they sang now with a new awareness of that countless army they were about to join: the army of martyrs who, before them, had witnessed by their blood that Jesus Christ is God and one of the Holy Trinity.

It is Thee whom the noble army of martyrs praise!
It is Thee whom the holy Church throughout all the world doth acknowledge to be the Lord:
The Father of an infinite majesty;
Thine adorable true and only Son;
And the Holy Spirit the Comforter.

With greater strength than any of them had expected to muster in such an hour, their voices continued to mount in intensity. Virginal hearts and souls cried out to the divine Bridegroom with a love as strong as death (Sg 8:6) as they invoked, one last time, the great, eternal events of the life of their Beloved.

Thou art the King of Glory, O Christ!
Though art the everlasting Son of the Father!
When thou tookest upon thee to deliver man,
Thou didst not abhor the Virgin's womb.
When thou hadst overcome the sharpness of death,
Thou didst open the Kingdom of Heaven to all believers.
Thou sittest at the right hand of God, in the glory of the Father.
We believe that Thou shalt come to be our judge,
We therefore pray thee, help thy servants,
Whom thou has redeemed with thy precious blood.

Prudently reminiscent of the spiritual dangers lurking to seduce souls in that dread place, they could only chant the great hymn's closing petition with soul-felt pleading.

It is in thee, O Lord, that have I put my trust:
O never let me be confounded!

iii

SUCH A SALUTATION of the guillotine was unprecedented. A visceral revulsion could usually be detected when the condemned arrived at the hideous, repugnant site with its loathsome smell. An unbearable stench emerged from a plank-covered pit of putrefying blood at the head of the scaffold. The pit had been enlarged once, but had long since filled up again. The earth thus seemed to refuse the oblation of the daily effusion. Paris's revolutionary municipal government had then proposed that a deep, lead-lined container be constructed for catching the blood. Mounted on wheels and placed each day over the plank-covered putrefaction, it could be pushed each evening to the Picpus burial pits for emptying, along with the carts bearing the cadavers and severed heads.

But the immediate horror of the stench from the pit seemed minor when the wind caught the more noxious gases wafted toward the Place du Trône from Picpus. There, for more than a month, more than a thousand cadavers and heads had been thrown into two huge burial pits, dug in the garden of the former convent of Canonesses of Saint Augustine. From the beginning the daily layer of quicklime and earth had proven totally ineffectual against the smell. In desperation the pits were both covered with huge wooden platforms, fitted out with trap doors for access. Still the stench reigned. As the Great Terror gathered momentum the revolutionary government awaited the perfection of a four-bladed guillotine, the new order's latest egalitarian refinement. This would allow for more efficient use of Sanson's time as well as a far more expeditious dispatch of still larger "batches" being anticipated for the daily sacrifice. To accommodate the anticipated increase, city authorities had confidently ordered a third pit dug in the walled garden. The site of that third pit is still pointed out to visitors to the Picpus Cemetery.

If the horror of the smell could in no way be alleviated, some effort was made to spare the prisoners the sight of the executions themselves. On benches constructed for that purpose, the condemned, once they were taken from the tumbrels, were made to sit with their backs to the machine. It was esteemed an act of great virtue, and a display of exceptional moral courage, to accept freely to be the last in one's "batch" to die. On May 10 the king's sister, the virtuous and pious 30-year-old Madame Elizabeth of France, had given such a noble witness. Comforting her fellow condemned, she admonished them all to thoughts of God. After receiving a last homage from each of them, she followed the last one up the scaffold steps. Even there she charged the executioner, out of respect for his own mother, not to remove the scarf covering her bosom. Her modesty was respected.

The executioner was also compliant in granting Madame Lidoine time to complete community devotions before beginning his work on that July 17. It was but natural that as the mother of the martyrdom she would wish to preside over this sacrifice and be the last to die.

Such cooperation by the executioner is surprising until we learn that Charles-Henri Sanson, Paris' executioner, was opposed not only to the Terror, but to the guillotine itself. As the horror of the Great Terror increased he would more and more frequently use his arthritis as an excuse for naming one of his sons to replace him as chief executioner on the scaffold.

Whether he or one of his sons presided on that July 17 we do not know. In any case, Christian piety was not foreign to the values transmitted in that extraordinary Sanson family which, over the centuries, formed a veritable dynasty of hereditary executioners in France. Respect for God and the King formed the cornerstone of their profession, passed from father to son, for whom an arranged marriage with another executioner's daughter assured the continuation of the line. A very distraught Madame Sanson, we are told, had been on her knees before holy images with candles burning on the bitterly cold and gloomy morning of January 21, 1793, a year and a half before, when her husband had had the unthinkable duty of dispatching France's "most Christian" king. Tradition has it that Sanson himself sought out a non-juring priest that very same night and paid for a Mass for the King's soul. This story Balzac apparently gleaned from an interview with Charles-Henri's son, then used it in his highly fictionalized story, *Episode sous la Terreur.*

iv

After the singing of the *Te Deum,* the devotions led by Madame Lidoine were those normal for a dying Carmelite. If possible, the dying nun, after the Holy Spirit had been invoked, renews her monastic vows of poverty, chastity, and obedience, her hands between those of the prioress. Thus is explained the hymn next sung before the guillotine: the *Veni Creator Spiritus,* invoking the Holy Spirit to quicken and enflame the nuns with the Holy Spirit as their consecration to him was renewed.

> Inflame our senses with thy light,
> Reclaim our hearts for heavenly love,
> With strength perpetual fructify
> Our bodies' poor infirmity.

Monseigneur Jauffret specifies that with this hymn of invocation completed, the nuns renewed their vows in "loud and intelligible voices," led by the prioress. But Madame Lidoine had certainly not anticipated that one nun, aflame with the Holy Spirit, would at that point cry out: "Only too happy, O my God, if this little sacrifice can calm your wrath and reduce the number of victims!" This spontaneous outburst by an unidentified nun, reported by Monseigneur Jauffret, confirms that other detail we learn from him concerning the Carmelites' offering themselves for those in prison.

Certainly the Carmelites' sacrifice on July 17, followed by Robespierre's fall one republican *décade* later on July 27, has caused many to believe that their sacrifice was efficacious. What is sure is that with the Great Terror ended, a less ominous fate awaited prisoners such as the English Benedictines and Denis Blot. Those not actually liberated would at least be more properly tried before being guillotined.

As far as the Carmelites were concerned, they were confident that the Holy Spirit invoked in the *Veni Creator Spiritus* was indeed the "Lord and Giver of life." That Spirit was the very breath of God which, at the beginning of time, had breathed upon the waters of chaos, bringing forth the earth, the dry land, and all living things. They believed that their invocation of him in that stinking, putrefying site of daily slaughter could indeed transfigure their immolation, allowing it mystically to release powerful spiritual energies of goodness, life, and glory for the life of the world.

The 41-year-old Madame Lidoine moves up to the foot of the scaffold, the worn little clay image of the Virgin and child clutched tightly in her palm, a last, pathetic relic of all that had once been the royally favored Carmel of Compiègne. Her glance passes over, as though it were nothing worth, the freshly washed, oiled and sharpened steel blade, suspended and readied for its first mighty death-giving crash of the day. In this hour, as from the beginning of time, his will for her coming into the world had been to preside over this imminent dispatch of her community before submitting to it herself.

Sister Henriette of the Divine Providence, Madame Pelras, the community's young infirmarian, now offers to stand by Mother Lidoine and assist the others up the steps. She still shows that same calm boldness, the same unflappable presence of mind with which she had challenged Fouquier-Tinville only a few hours before in the Revolutionary Tribunal. It is that young sister's calm possession of herself at this moment that will free Mother Teresa of Saint Augustine to give herself completely to the final acts of spiritual love yet to be offered up by each of her daughters before dying. The logistics of getting each of them up the scaffold steps is thus mercifully spared her.

In this ultimate moment, as all was about to unfold before her eyes, one may well imagine a detail of Sister Elisabeth-Baptiste's prophetic dream coming into sharp focus for the prioress. In that dream she recalled that some of the younger nuns had been perceived as being "greater in glory" than some of the older ones. Sister Constance, the youngest member at age 29, had been the last to join the community. For five long years she had been forbidden by law to make her final vows. Now, just moments before, as the others renewed their vows, she, joining in, had at last also pronounced hers. Let her then, the last, be the first to enter into the bridal chamber. Let her be first among them to take her place at the Lamb's marriage supper. For he himself, the Lamb of God who takes away the sin of the world, had he not said that "The first shall be last, and the last first" (Mt 20:16)? Let his will be hers in this.

Was it at this point, or earlier, that Sister Constance was seized with uncertainty, suddenly accusing herself to the prioress of not yet having finished her office, with Mother Lidoine replying reassuringly, "Come, come my daughter, have faith! You'll finish it in heaven..."? This anecdote, coming from the Abbé de Lamarche, confirms both his own proximity to the nuns at the actual martyrdom, as well as his continued concern for the young novice's courage when brought face to face with the reality of the guillotine.

It seems probable that the other 24 condemned prisoners remained seated with their backs to the machine while the 16 Carmelites were dispatched. No word is found anywhere in regard to this, though all accounts imply that the nuns passed first. As we know that the executioner agreed to allow the prioress freedom concerning the order of their deaths, it is clear that the list of the 40 condemned for July 17, published in the *Moniteur* on July 23, 1794, mixing the misspelled names of the 16 Carmelites with the others, is based on a document provided by the office of the Public Prosecutor. Certainly it had nothing to do with the order of the executions at the Place du Trône.

V

SANSON HAD REPEATEDLY made claims to the Revolutionary government for damages to his clothing by the daily effusion of blood. His claims had been ignored. Allowed no compensation, his solution had been to don, prior to beginning his work, a large, well-worn, and blood-stained wraparound leather apron. All watch while this is done.

Madame Lidoine is ready. Sister Constance, in a panic so shortly before for not having finished her office, is summoned by the prioress and confidently approaches. Reports are that all panic was suddenly gone. Fully conscious that her vows had at last been pronounced and that she was indeed dying as a professed Carmelite, she seems transfigured by the life-giving Spirit just invoked. She kneels at her prioress's feet, her first and last act of submission as a professed Carmelite. A final maternal blessing is given and the tiny clay image of the Virgin and Child, cupped in the prioress's palm, is proffered to this youngest daughter for a last kiss.

Head humbly bowed, Sister Constance, asks in a clear, young voice:

> "Permission to die, Mother?"
> "Go, my daughter!"

It is reported that it was after rising from her knees to face the machine, and as she started up the steps of the scaffold, that Sister Constance intoned the first line of the psalm, *Laudate Dominum omnes gentes.* It was the psalm sung by Saint Teresa of Avila at the foundation of a new Carmel. In 1604 Mother Anne of Jesus, just arrived from Spain under the escort of Cardinal de Bérulle, had introduced this Teresian custom into France when she walked into the church of the first Carmel in Paris. At that historic moment the great Spanish nun is reported to have startled her sisters by this sudden outburst of praise. They, reportedly totally unprepared, took up Mother Anne's chanting "with greater fervor than harmony."

> Praise the Lord, all ye nations!
> Praise Him all ye people!
> For His mercy is confirmed upon us,
> And the truth of the Lord endureth forever!
> Praise the Lord!

Now, 190 years later, in that same city where Christian civilization seemed to be in its death throes as the old order collapsed, the familiar verses, spontaneously begun by Sister Constance at the foot of the guillotine, were again taken up by the surprised nuns "with greater fervor than harmony." They would continue throughout the community's immolation, punctuated by the recurring fatal thud cutting short voice after voice. As the Teresian psalm of foundation paradoxically announced the end of the original, earthly foundation of Compiègne's Carmel, it mystically signaled the inauguration of its eternal foundation in the Kingdom of the Lamb. There, in the constellation of those who shed their blood for the Lamb, it would shine forever. Had he himself not said, "those that thou gavest me I have kept, and none of them is lost" (Jn 17:12)?

vi

SAID TO HAVE BEEN AS RADIANT as "a queen going to receive her diadem" as she mounted the steps singing, Sister Constance is also reported to have waved aside the executioner and his two valets upon reaching the top of the steps. She thus approached the vertical balance plank unaided, chanting that God's mercy was confirmed upon her.

It was not by accident that such details were noted and reported. Normally at the top of the scaffold steps the hesitant, confused victim was seized on the left by the executioner, on the right by the first valet. The second valet quickly bound the prisoner's hands behind him while forcing him forward until he was up against the vertical plank, to which he was attached with straps.

The confident waving aside of the executioners by a radiant young nun was thus impressive, especially to those hardened to this daily ritual. Luminous dignity and sense of purpose marked her approach to the vertical plank. Strapped to it, her feet left the scaffold as the first valet tipped it forward into horizontal position. In seconds the second valet had adjusted it for length so that her neck was properly placed for securing by the neck-stall. Only then could the chief executioner pull the cord, releasing the triangular blade.

Reports from this period of the Great Terror say that a dozen prisoners could thus be guillotined in 20 minutes.

Witnesses recall the ominous pattern of three sounds accompanying each decapitation. First the bump of the balance-plank swinging down into horizontal position; then the click of the neck-stall closing to form a perfect circle around the victim's neck; finally the rushing swish of the falling blade's dead-thudded slice. A muffled fourth sound never spoken of, however, followed this threefold pattern. It was the soft thump as the headless body hit the red-painted cart set by the guillotine. As for the heads, they fell into a blood-stiffened leather bag placed by the executioner at the end of the machine.

The three familiar sounds announced Sister Constance's entry into the Kingdom of the Lamb. The nuns' chant rose in defiance.

For His mercy is confirmed upon us!

Professionals hardened to the most violent of human emotions, ever confident in their professional ability to assure death, whatever might be the resistance of the condemned, Sanson and his valets had guillotined nuns on several occasions. The blood of Madame Lidoine's friend, Madame Chamboran of the Carmel of Saint-Denis, had been poured out on this same scaffold in March. Still the execution of a whole community of 16, determined to offer themselves in what appeared to be a ritual sacrifice, was unprecedented. The women's implacable acceptance of everything happening to them, their simple joy as they sang, awaiting certain death, pointed toward a dimension beyond their expertise. Normally masters on their own scaffold, this evening the executioners found themselves minor players in an unfamiliar drama where death had lost its dread. The crowd of regulars gathered around the scaffold this evening had mysteriously sensed this. All watched in an unprecedented silence.

vii

APART FROM SISTER CONSTANCE'S being the first to die, and Madame Pelras dying just before Madame Lidoine at the end, we know nothing of the order in which the martyrdom proceeded. These three facts come to us through a sister of Madame Pelras, Mother Emilienne, Superior General of the Sisters of Charity at Nevers. We know that she wrote in 1836 to the future Cardinal Villecourt, as he was completing his little volume based on Marie of the Incarnation's manuscripts, that she had received this information from an eyewitness.[1]

After Sister Constance's inauguration of the sacrifice, we can be sure that Madame Lidoine's motherly compassion would not have prolonged the cruel wait for the two externs, the Soiron sisters. Teresa had fainted that afternoon upon hearing the death sentence. At 46 she would undoubtedly have preceded her 52-year-old sister, Catherine, who, let us recall, had refused to be separated from the community once they had started pronouncing the act of consecration. She too now claimed her share in its glory.

It seems highly probably that the three serving sisters, Sister Saint Martha (Dufour), 52, Sister Marie of the Holy Spirit (Roussel), 51, and Sister Francis Xavier (Verolot), 30, last-professed of the community and next youngest after Sister Constance, would have been allowed to pass before the choir sisters. In anticipation of this moment five years before, Sister Francis Xavier as a young novice had said to Madame Lidoine that she was sure that the dear Lord was going to take care of any danger she might be in. Madame Philippe also

---

[1] Abbé Villecourt refers to her on p. 108 of his *Histoire des religieuses carmélites de Compiègne, conduites à l'échafaud le 17 juillet 1794. Ouvrage posthume de la Soeur Marie de l'Incarnation, carmélite du même monastère* (Sens: Thomas-Malvin, 1836).

reports her as saying with great confidence, "The power of men is extended only to what concerns my body, but God alone has jurisdiction over my soul." And had she not also replied to the Revolutionary Commissioners of Compiègne when asked if she wished to leave Carmel, that a well-bred wife sticks to her husband? Now a spectacle unto the world and to angels and men (1 Cor 4:9), the fidelity of this daughter of the people was crowned with bloody nuptials.

> Praise Him all ye peoples!
> *For His mercy is confirmed upon us!*

As for the eight professed choir sisters other than the prioress and the young sister infirmarian, we may well believe that Mother de Croissy, novice mistress and former prioress, stood by to encourage the others, as her prestige demanded. At 49 years of age she may well thus have been the third-to-the-last to die. On her name-day, July 15, 1793, she had tried to reassure Sister Constance who feared pronouncing the word "death" before her. Madame de Croissy had also once observed that she felt she could manage martyrdom by the guillotine, though she dared not speak of a more prolonged form of death.

The 78-year-old Sister Charlotte of the Resurrection, Madame Thouret, undoubtedly had to be helped in this last hour. Brutally tossed from the tumbrel onto the paving stones of the Conciergerie courtyard only four days before and still bruised, the septuagenarian is without her crutch. Tenderly assisted toward the steep, ladder-like scaffold steps by the confident Sister Henriette, she is firmly grabbed, then energetically hoisted up by the executioner's two valets. In the divine economy she was destined thus to crown more than 50 years of consecration to God. No hour in her half-century of compassion, devotion, and even a certain number of miracles, had been finer than this hour of violent death.

The same was true for her friend and contemporary, the 78-year-old Madame Piedcourt, Sister of Jesus Crucified, who had shared her companion's mortal fear of the guillotine. Now, even in her last hour, Madame Piedcourt still proved as irrepressible as when the Revolutionary Commissioners of Compiègne had asked her two years before if she wished to remain a Carmelite. Then she had boldly answered that she only wished she still had an equal number of years to give to Jesus Christ. Today as she watched Sanson and his valets at work, she was heard to say: "The poor wretches! We must feel sorry for them since they are blinded and don't know what they're doing!" Then, as an afterthought she added reflectively, "In any case, how could we bear them ill will since they're the ones who are opening up the gates of heaven for us?" The 78-year-old kneels to receive the 41-year-old prioress's blessing. Piously she kisses the little image. Speaking in a humble, hushed voice, honed by more than half a century of self-effacing obedience, she softly asks:

> "Permission to die, Mother?"
> "Go, my daughter!"

Helped up the steps by the young infirmarian, she remains clear-headed and undaunted, in spite of her 78 years. Up on the scaffold, as the three executioners strap her to the vertical plank, she audibly proclaims in the best Christian tradition: "I forgive you, my friends!" Not content with this, however, she added poignantly, reflecting the depth of her own love of God in this ultimate moment: "I forgive you with all that longing of heart with which I would that God forgive me!"

Sister of Jesus Crucified's feet leave the platform. The balance plank swings forward, coming to rest with a thud. The neck-stall is dropped, the blade slices. The community chants defiantly:

For His mercy is confirmed upon us!

Amid the stench and heat, against the eerie silence of the numbed, silent crowd and the ever-diminishing chanting of the psalm, the professionalism of the three executioners assures the efficacious accomplishment of the new order's bloody effusion. Heads fall into Sanson's large leather bag, reddened by what Christians, with noble euphemism, have always adamantly maintained throughout their history is, in fact, "the seed of the church."

viii

TWO YEARS BEFORE, the Revolutionary Commissioners of Compiègne had received a particularly bold answer from Madame Brard when they carried out their investigation about each nun's desire to continue in the religious life. Sister Euphrasia, the "so lovable philosopher nun" of the Queen of France, had then said that she would shed her blood rather than surrender her habit. Until today these had been vain words. Like all the rest of the community, she too had been obliged for 22 months to survive in civilian dress. But today, even without her veil, and with her white headcovering trimmed above the neck, her brown habit and white cloak once more clothed her body as a Carmelite. She was ready. Humbly she too kneels before that young prioress she had so resented. Her revolt at last transfigured by the Spirit of God through her recent conversion, she is at peace. She knows at last that she is ready, as she wrote Sister Marie of the Incarnation, to be "harvested by the scythe of the Revolution."

"Permission to die, Mother?"
"Go, my daughter!"

Was the 58-year-old Sister Euphrasia also the one who cried out after the renewal of vows that she was only too happy if her little sacrifice could reduce the number of victims? Such a final flourish would not have been out of character with what we know of her nature. Or could that public personal witness have come from Madame Trézel, the 51-year-old Sister Saint Ignatius who, in her single-minded way, had prayed that her niece be made an angel at baptism if the Lord did not foresee that she would be a saint? She relied heavily on her own interior dialogue with him, convinced that she was not clever enough to be taught by human beings, and was totally dependent on his infinite mercy in dealing directly with her great poverty of spirit. Or could that frank explication have come from the irrepressible jubilarian, Madame Piedcourt? It would have been characteristic of what we know of her.

Or, in the emotion of this moment, could this bold outburst have come from the aristocratic Sister Julie Louise of Jesus? Fifty-two years old and the community's lone widow, Madame Crétien de Neuville had foreseen this hour in more than a casual way in composing her parody on *La Marseillaise.* Her vocation to be a nun, as she clearly stated, was one of calling, not of attraction. The intensity of her intimacy with Jesus Christ was great, however. Consciously facing the expiatory death to which she had daily pledged herself through the community's act of consecration, she had consistently refused the solicitations of her aristocratic mother and sister to come to them, even when her sister cruelly lost both her daughter and newborn grandchild in childbirth. Faithfully holding her chosen course toward God against her most natural inclinations, Madame Crétien de Neuville was convinced that her vocation was to brave the storm and redeem the time through her part in the holocaust. Then only would she at last attain that safe harbor for which she so longed.

The discreet 52-year-old Sister Thérèse of the Heart of Mary, Madame Hanisset from Rheims, may well have passed before certain younger sisters, for one may presume that the 42-year-old subprioress, Madame Brideau, Sister Saint Louis, would, as befitted her office, have waited to the end with the former prioress, Madame de Croissy. In any case, though inevitably diminished in volume as the voices were cut off, the psalm chanting continued, transfixing the spectators by unfamiliar emotions. They were as if frozen in the hot stench of the July evening air.

> Praise the Lord, all ye nations!
> Praise Him all ye peoples!

From the wall of a nearby boarding school schoolboys watched, fascinated. In the five weeks since the guillotine had been installed in front of their institution, they had become so familiar with its workings that they had fashioned themselves a tiny working model with which to decapitate birds. One of these school boys was the young Count de Malet.

Sensitive to the great contrast between this evening's spectacle and the usual one, he inquired about the identity of these white-cloaked women who, climbing the steps, sang so effortlessly, stilling the passions of the usual daily crowd. "They are daughters of Saint Teresa," he was told. This enigmatic statement immediately stirred a mysterious sympathy in him for that unknown saint who could inspire such daughters. We are told that afterward, as he pursued a military career, he always carried with him, in memory of that evening's events, the biography of the great Spanish saint. Losing his wife after five years of marriage, he became a priest.

Another boy in the crowd also watched, fascinated. The 11-year-old son of Madame le Féron d'Etrepigny had accompanied his mother to Paris in her quest to learn the fate of imprisoned relatives. Unsuccessful in obtaining any information, and desperately fearing that they might be included in Fouquier-Tinville's "batch" for that day, his distraught mother had made her way to the repugnant Place du Trône, accompanied by her son. An indelible impression was left on the 11-year-old boy who died at age 87, in 1870, probably one of the last, if not actually the last, surviving witness of the Carmelites' immolation. His daughter-in-law reports that even after 76 years, and particularly just prior to his own death, he frequently recalled the martyrdom of the Carmelites, always with the most profound emotion.

ix

FOURTEEN TIMES the implacable three sounds have been heard. Fourteen times a headless body has been tossed into the cart. Now Madame Pelras' turn has come. She kneels before the prioress, is blessed, and gives her last kiss to the little image cupped in the Madame Lidoine's palm.

> "Permission to die, Mother?"
> "Go, my daughter!"

The 34-year-old Sister Marie Henriette of the Divine Providence, reported to have been of great natural beauty, remains unshaken either by the spectacle in the red cart below, or the blood on the scaffold, or even by the splattered executioners as she climbs up to face them. As the chanting fades the appearance, up on the scaffold, of this young nun who had proven of such *sang-froid* in helping all the others, could not but make a profound impact upon the still silent crowd. In these last moments her rare strength of character undoubtedly emanated from her, dominating the silence. Before the Revolutionary Tribunal, she had boldly challenged the redoubtable Public Prosecutor to define his use of the word "fanatic," just as she had also boldly withdrawn from the Sisters of Charity of Nevers to become a Carmelite of Compiègne. For from the beginning of time had his will not been that she participate in this holy sacrifice with all the inner beauty of her great and confident soul?

From the foot of the scaffold, the 41-year-old Mother Teresa of Saint Augustine watches. Her gratitude is great as she beholds this last, so touchingly faithful daughter strapped to the vertical plank, her arms bound behind her. It is now all almost over. By his mercy it had been given her to escort all 15 of them to the threshold of his bridal chamber. Now she must make haste. She too was invited to the feast.

X

In the verses she had written to be sung at the crèche, Madame Lidoine had addressed him, her great love and eternal Bridegroom, as a helpless babe. Acknowledging herself as completely under the empire of his love, she had, in decisive lines, mysteriously foreshadowed the absolute oblation now awaiting her.

> Let thy blade cut, completing all my offering!
> For nothing but thy will for me is sweet!
> My one desire is that thy hand be hov'ring
> O'er me, thy bride, the sacrifice complete!

She bows her head. Raising her palm to her mouth, she kisses the statuette. Thoughtfully she crosses herself. Then, for the first time since taking up her station at the foot of the scaffold, she suddenly seems to hesitate. A pious woman, standing near, has understood. Slipping up to the solitary Mother Teresa of Saint Augustine, she surreptitiously extends her hand and receives the little worn clay image, unobtrusively assuring her that this mystic hour of consummation will be remembered by future believers who, years hence, will kiss this tiny relic, blessing God for what it represents of his mercy to men.

The downward bang of the balance plank, the click of the neck-stall and the fatal, rushing swish of the falling blade is heard once again: the decapitated body of Sister Marie Henriette of the Divine Providence falls into the cart. Headless, the cadavers of all 15 of Mother Teresa of Saint Augustine's daughters now sprawl there, piled one on top of the other, swimming in blood. Their white choir cloaks, no longer anchored at the necks, are now askew, red-splattered, blood-soaked. She must join them.

The author of the Epistle to the Hebrews had written that prior to the Lamb's coming into the world, righteous witnesses for God, "of whom the world was not worthy" (Heb 11:38) had suffered terrible tribulations for their faith. Still they had not received the promise reserved for the Lamb's disciples, for God had provided better things for Christians, so that those who had come before "should not be made perfect" (Heb 11:40) without them. What she was now doing was thus not just for herself, but for that whole vast company of righteous souls who, since the beginning of time, had lived in the world. How many of these, because of their love of God, had already been washed in their own blood!

Mother Lidoine moves toward the steps.

All she had ever wanted was to die out of love for him, her only Love. Her eyes glowed now with ardent longing to be drawn nearer still to that wounded God who, of his own will, had laid down his life. Was he not her Beloved, her Life, her Hope? In an instant she knew that she would, at last, behold him face to face in the glory of his resurrected body, resplendent with uncreated light.

How evident his beloved pierced hand in all this! He had brought it all so perfectly together with tact and discretion, even to allowing that the white mantles of the three not called to follow the Lamb be available in this hour to clothe those last three, professed only at the eleventh hour. And as for the three missing—had that not been foreseen more than a century ago by Sister Elisabeth Baptiste? Having loved her daughters, Mother Teresa of Saint Augustine loved them all to the end, just as her Bridegroom had loved those given to him (Jn 13:1).

Climbing the steps, Mother Lidoine is transfigured. Briefly freed in these fleeting seconds from all worldly responsibilities to others, she savors a bride's joyous assurance of belonging only to the Bridegroom in the hour of her nuptials.

His all-engulfing presence now clothes her as in a raiment of light. The demonic illusions of the utter absurdity of what was happening to her are swallowed up in his splendor. Lost in his glory, she realizes that all she had had to do was to say "yes" to what he offered her. For it is by her consent that he is reliving his death in her. It was that so intimate "yes," murmured heart to heart with him, that had freed her from bondage to the fear of death, for perfect love casts out fear (1 Jn 4:18). "I am the Resurrection and the Life," he had said. "He that believeth in me, though he were dead, yet shall he live" (Jn 11:25). In him, she knew, she could never die.

Below in the crowd all eyes are fixed upon the yet-unsullied white mantle of the 41-year-old prioress. The blood-spattered executioners bind her hands and strap her to the balance plank. Like a sheep before its shearers, like a lamb led to the slaughter, she, like her Master, opens not her mouth (Is 53:7). For a few shining seconds she grasps that it is being given, even to her, to enter into the fullness of the most ineffable divine mystery known to the race, a mystery older than the world itself: the mystery of the Lamb, slain from the foundation of the world (Rev 13:8).

The balance plank swings forward. It is finished.

The unanchored, red-spattered mantle of Madame Lidoine now encloses her headless body sprawled atop the 15 others as the executioner and his valets continue the day's hecatomb. Before the evening's work is done 24 more victims, including the pathetic Mulot de la Ménardière, would be slaughtered to complete that day's offering for the well-being of the new order. Then there would be the onerous task of transfering the 40 bodies and heads to the Picpus burial pits. There, by the light of lanterns and of a huge bonfire built there each night, each body would be totally stripped. In spite of its heat, the bonfire did provide light for the lugubrious work. Thyme, sage, and aromatic branches of juniper were thrown into it periodically to mask the unbearable smell from the two pits.

This ghoulish job, performed nine nights out of ten during the last six weeks of the Great Terror in the City of Lights, was as meticulous as it was gory, as methodical as it was revolting. The executioner's right to the clothing of the condemned had been abolished by the Republic. Now an inventory of every scrap of clothing worn by the 30 to 40 guillotined each day had to be made, down to the last sock and handkerchief. After inventory the clothing was sent to be washed, then distributed to public institutions. A lantern, register, writing equipment, table, and chair for the clerk carrying out this macabre but tedious nightly task were kept in the former convent's garden grotto. Now enclosed against the wind and weather, it was accessible through a door kept locked throughout the day. At night, however, as soon as the carts began arriving from the Place du Trône, the door was opened and the former grotto, with its light and proximity to the bonfire and stinking pits, became the hub of each evening's hideous activity.

Thus, before the cadavers and severed heads of the 16 Carmelites were thrown that evening atop those others decomposing there in the fetid pit since June, their bodies were stripped naked by drunken workers. As the pure body of their Christian God-Man, Jesus Christ, had also been stripped to the jeering of the crowd before being raised up on the cross to suffer in the flesh for his creation, so in death was the created matter of the Carmelites humiliated. The only kiss their corporal relics received from the world for which they died was the corrosive bite of quicklime. Modestly it dusted their nakedness once the evening's work was done.

xi

THAT SAME EVENING, far from the noxious Place du Trône and the fetid miasma of Picpus, the 78-year-old mother of Mother Teresa of Saint Augustine in Franche Comté undoubtedly again wondered what had been the fate of that only child, embraced for the last time less than a month before. She had learned of the nuns' arrest on June 22 before leaving Paris with Sister Marie of the Incarnation. She could not but be anxious. Certainly she accepted that their farewell had been definitive. It was in any case here that she, an outsider amid her husband's family, must prepare for her own end. Such was the adorable will of God.

Just outside Paris in Saint-Denis, rechristened "Franciade" by the Revolution, the family of Sister Constance probably learned that same evening of what had happened. Their bitterness against the fanatical religion that had brought their daughter to such a pointless end could now be no less. Even prior to the nuns' arrest, Sister Constance had not dared visit her parents for fear of being detained, and Madame Philippe's attempts to communicate with them had proven fruitless.

The sister of Sister Saint Ignatius in Compiègne, rechristened Marat-sur-Oise, would, at the latest, have learned of the execution the next day. At best, her feelings could only have been mixed. Their own first cousin, Trézel, was a member of the Compiègne Committee of Revolutionary Surveillance. His signature figures on the documents delivering the Carmelites to the Revolutionary Tribunal in Paris. Though Madame Trézel's sister herself would hardly have gone that far, we know from what was said at the death of her infant daughter on November 27, 1792, that neither she nor her husband were at all religious.

The aristocratic mother and sister of Sister Julie of Jesus, so recently bereaved by the double loss of the sister's daughter and infant grandchild, undoubtedly bore this third loss with the fortitude befitting their state. All their solicitations to get Sister Julie safely away from Compiègne had been refused by the 52-year-old widow turned Carmelite. This did not, however, alleviate the cruelty of their suffering.

As for Sister Marie of the Incarnation, as we have seen, it was in an inn in Besançon that she, traveling as a very frightened and rather desperate "Madame Philippe," learned of the end of her sisters. She passed on to Monseigneur Jauffret the crucial remark made that evening by a man just arriving at the inn from Paris. He had said that they should take hope that their troubles would soon be over, for a number of nuns had been sacrificed in Paris.

Fearing she might be arrested at any moment because she was a daughter of a Prince of the Blood rather than because she was an ex-Carmelite of Compiègne, Madame Philippe, stranded in France, was convinced that she was being constantly pursued and spied upon. Terrified for her life, she felt she had to be constantly on the move during the months immediately following the martyrdom. It is perhaps only natural then that some 40 years later, when told to complete Madame Lidoine's *Chronicle* of the Compiègne community with her own *Relation du martyre* of the martyrdom, she neglected to recall that evening in Besançon, recounted so many years before to Monseigneur Jauffret. Writing up her account had, in any case, cost her dearly, for she had been forced to relive the trauma of once having been told she could not receive the sacraments.

In the south of France on the evening of the execution, the brother of the 34-year-old Madame Pelras, returning home after his wife had gone to bed, noticed a mysterious light that seemed to accompany him home, then follow him up the dark stairs of his house into their bedroom. His wife was awake and also saw the strange illumination. Neither could explain it, for there was no moon outside. Both went to sleep wondering what it all meant. Only when the martyr's brother learned the date of his sister's execution did he reflectively remark to his wife: "Poor Annette! It's you who came to see me!"

The cult of the "Blessed Annette Pelras" survives to this day in the village parish church of Carjac (diocese of Cahors) where Sister Henriette and her many brothers and sisters were baptized. Her statue is honored by the local faithful seeking the protection of 34-year-old Sister Marie Henriette of the Divine Providence. That young Carmelite infirmarian who had learned to care for the sick while still a Sister of Charity of Nevers had the audacity of a saint. This is clearly shown both by her defiance of Fouquier-Tinville before the Revolutionary Tribunal and her heroic stance at the guillotine at the prioress's side to assist her 14 sisters before herself climbing the scaffold steps.

xii

EVEN IF ONE ALLOWS that Robespierre's fall one *décade* later, signaling the end of the Great Terror, may, in fact, be attributed to the Carmelites' sacrifice, is that all that can be said of its significance?

Attempts to propagate the Christian witness of this martyred community have often concentrated on well-intentioned but totally ineffectual accounts of edifying anecdotes concerning the virtues of each participant as an individual, neglecting the martyrdom itself. Emphasis has thus inevitably shifted away from anything actually *divine* in the martyrdom to its more *human* aspects, which one feels free to analyze psychologically. The well-disposed, skeptical nonbeliever can thus discuss, even in an erudite manner, a whole series of edifying anecdotes without ever being challenged to seek in this unusual act of community sacrifice any manifestation *of God himself.*

Indeed, one sometimes forgets that martyrdom is essentially a *theophany*, a manifestation of *God* rather than of man. This fact alone justifies Christianity's unbroken cult for martyrs. Indeed, only in this truth is to be found key to the *mystery of the vocation* of the 16 Carmelites of Compiègne.

As observed at the beginning of these pages, martyrs are looked upon in Greek liturgical texts as "the bearers of God" who are offered by the universe as its "first-fruits" to assure the peace of the church. One might also observe that for a great number of reasons, historic and otherwise, devotion to martyrs is often a more living, active cult in the Eastern Christian Church than in the Latin West. The remarkable thing is that the Greek Christian view is so perfectly applicable not only to what happened on July 17, 1794, at the Place de la Nation in Paris, but more especially to Madame Lidoine's originally stated purpose in offering the act of consecration, that is to restore peace to France and to her church. Thus might the Carmelites' oblation be said to be in perfect accord with the great, unbroken tradition of both Eastern and Western Christian Churches.

Moreover, since the Carmelites' sacrifice was offered in the name of their Lord and God, Jesus Christ, their sacrifice was thereby, spiritually, a mystical participation in his own offering. Through the power of his Spirit working in them to make of them "bearers of God," they did indeed mystically reenact, within the limits of their earthly being, his own *kenosis*, his own emptying out of himself in his divine condescension in becoming incarnate and in offering himself as a victim for the world. Conscious of this, Sister Julie Louise of Jesus explicitly said in her parody of *La Marseillaise* that it was "Under the cross, God's great banner" that they climbed the scaffold as a community to be decapitated, thereby giving their Christian God who died the "victory" in their witness.

Because it thus bears all the marks of Christian martyrdom according to the great unbroken Christian tradition of both Eastern and Western Churches, the execution of the 16 Carmelites should never be dismissed as a mere manifestation of the martyrs themselves, or even of the powerful personality of their prioress. Rather must it be viewed, as martyrdom should always be viewed, as an exceptional but very great mystical manifestation of God at work, making of the martyrs "bearers of God" through their oblation. For through the inexplicable, self-imposed, and unprecedented silence that accompanied their long procession and continued throughout their ceremonial sacrifice, it was *he*, through them, who was revealing something of his presence and power in the world at that hour.

For more than a month, implicitly if not explicitly, nine days out of ten, the one indivisible French Republic had continued, day after day at the Place de la Nation, to confirm quite graphically the basic *religious* necessity for men to offer blood sacrifice to advance their causes. And, as has ever been true of blood sacrifice, it was idealism that guided those behind the Terror as they attempted, through this daily mechanized hecatomb, to bring about what they conceived of as human well-being, just as a primitive religion might offer the blood of bulls and goats to ensure its success.

Far removed from late twentieth-century skepticism where liberty, fraternity, and equality seem goals as nebulous and elusive as the inevitability of universal progress, fervent republican idealism in 1794 rendered its adherents ferocious against all opponents. Convinced that the Revolution was the crowning of a century of philosophy and humanist enlightenment, they believed it held within itself the only hope for the future of humanity. Indeed, its adherents would even have argued that one very clear sign of human progress was their unprecedented success, after almost 1300 years, in uprooting the outdated, antihumanist belief in that Jewish God-Man, Jesus Christ, who, against all human reasoning, was alledged to have been born of a virgin, then crucified, before preposterously rising from the dead.

The new order's categorical position against Christianity, as we have seen at the beginning of these pages, had been definitively manifested on October 5, 1793, by proclaiming that September 22, 1792, had been Day One of Year One of the One Indivisible French Republic. The firm intention to scrap forever not only the Christian "Year of the Lord," but, what is even more radical, the actual Jewish concept of the seven-day week, essential to both Christianity and Islam, meant that the Judeo-Christian roots of European civilization were to be extirpated from France, and the whole Judeo-Christian experience of a self-revelatory God blotted out forever from the memory of the French.

Whether this lost memory was to be replaced by some sort of Supreme Being, as favored by the eighteenth-century deist-philosophers, or by no God at all, as favored by the many atheists, or by some civil religion, as would shortly thereafter be attempted, was really secondary. What prevailed was animosity toward everything pertaining to man's experience of the one, self-revelatory God of Abraham, Isaac, and Jacob, as well as of the incarnation of that God in Jesus Christ. Such tenets were totally unacceptable in modern times.

The idealists had forgotten, however, that some concepts do not die with the majority vote of a progressive government, and that the resistance of these concepts can be amazingly tenacious where the deepest and most glorious identity of a whole people is concerned. Effacing all traces of France's ancient pact with the Christian God was not to prove an easy goal to reach. As long as one Frenchman would still die to witness that his personal identity with his ancestral God was by no means dead, the government was powerless to annihilate the ancient pact, for it survived intact in that Frenchman. Having one's head severed for Christ was, after all, a noble Christian tradition, hallowed from the beginning and consecrated throughout the whole of the church's history. And had not John the Beloved in his Revelation seen the privileges accorded to "the souls of them that were beheaded for the witness of Jesus, and for the word of God, and which had not worshipped the beast" (Rev 20:4)?

Is it therefore really surprising if the spurned Christian God, in the midst of the bloody struggle to impose the new order, should, for the benefit of his own faithful, so reassuringly manifest himself at what today is known in Paris as the Place de la Nation? And what more propitious moment than when 16 French women, offering their consecrated lives to his Virgin Mother for the good estate of the kingdom of France and of his church, were being slaughtered by the new Republic in ritual sacrifice for "crimes against the people which sought to annihilate public freedom"? Could one imagine a more discreet, yet more powerful theophany, than that experienced on the evening of July 17, 1794, by all those present?

Amid the stench of that festering site in the City of Lights, humanity was that evening reduced to an inexplicable silence, respectfully maintained till the end of the immolation, while those being immolated praised God for confirming his mercy upon them through this action. Could there be a better witness that the banished Christian God had not been banished at all, but was even then stooping to touch not only the 16 victims, but also all present at that place of sacrifice with something of his glory, that "glory of the only-begotten of the Father, full of grace and truth" (Jn 1:14)?

The glory of Jesus Christ the world can never contain, for it is not of this world. Yet, even so, in the Father's great mercy to our fallen race through the Holy Spirit, the glory of the only-begotten Son can be seen and experienced in this world. The records show it was indeed seen and experienced by those who, in self-imposed silence, participated in the theophany that constituted the martyrdom of the 16 Carmelites of Compiègne.

Picpus, site where grotto of the Canonesses of Saint-Augustine was located. Transformed in 1794 to an office for the daily inventory of clothing taken from those guillotined.

Picpus, site of the common burial pit into which the bodies of the Carmelite martyrs were thrown

Plaque at entry to Picpus enclosure, with names of the 16 Carmelite martyrs of Compiègne

Index

The Carmelite martyrs of Compiègne are listed alphabetically by family name in boldface